W9-CWN-226

PLACE IN RETURN BOX to remove this checkout from your record.
TO AVOID FINES return on or before date due.
MAY BE RECALLED with earlier due date if requested.

DATE DUE	DATE DUE	DATE DUE
FEB 25 6 2009	JAN 0 5 2010	
	0 8 3 1	
AUG 0 9 2010 06 2 0 1 0		

Cool Conduct

WEIMAR AND NOW: GERMAN CULTURAL CRITICISM
Edward Dimendberg, Martin Jay, and Anton Kaes, General Editors

1. *Heritage of Our Times,* by Ernst Bloch

2. *The Nietzsche Legacy in Germany, 1890–1990,* by Steven E. Aschheim

3. *The Weimar Republic Sourcebook,* edited by Anton Kaes, Martin Jay, and Edward Dimendberg

4. *Batteries of Life: On the History of Things and Their Perception in Modernity,* by Christoph Asendorf

5. *Profane Illumination: Walter Benjamin and the Paris of Surrealist Revolution,* by Margaret Cohen

6. *Hollywood in Berlin: American Cinema and Weimar Germany,* by Thomas J. Saunders

7. *Walter Benjamin: An Aesthetic of Redemption,* by Richard Wolin

8. *The New Typography,* by Jan Tschichold, translated by Ruari McLean

9. *The Rule of Law under Siege: Selected Essays of Franz L. Neumann and Otto Kirchheimer,* edited by William E. Scheuerman

10. *The Dialectical Imagination: A History of the Frankfurt School and the Institute of Social Research, 1923–1950,* by Martin Jay

11. *Women in the Metropolis: Gender and Modernity in Weimar Culture,* edited by Katharina von Ankum

12. *Letters of Heinrich and Thomas Mann, 1900–1949,* edited by Hans Wysling, translated by Don Reneau

13. *Empire of Ecstasy: Nudity and Movement in German Body Culture, 1910–1935,* by Karl Toepfer

14. *In the Shadow of Catastrophe: German Intellectuals between Apocalypse and Enlightenment,* by Anson Rabinbach

15. *Walter Benjamin's Other History: Of Stones, Animals, Human Beings, and Angels,* by Beatrice Hanssen

16. *Exiled in Paradise: German Refugee Artists and Intellectuals in America from the 1930s to the Present,* by Anthony Heilbut

17. *Cool Conduct: The Culture of Distance in Weimar Germany,* by Helmut Lethen, translated by Don Reneau

18. *In a Cold Crater: Cultural and Intellectual Life in Berlin, 1945–1948,* by Wolfgang Schivelbusch, translated by Kelly Barry

19. *A Dubious Past: Ernst Jünger and the Politics of Literature after Nazism,* by Elliot Y. Neaman

20. *Beyond the Conceivable: Studies on Germany, Nazism, and the Holocaust,* by Dan Diner

21. *Prague Territories: National Conflict and Cultural Innovation in Franz Kafka's Fin de Siècle,* by Scott Spector

22. *Munich and Memory: Architecture, Monuments, and the Legacy of the Third Reich,* by Gavriel D. Rosenfeld

23. *The UFA Story: A History of Germany's Greatest Film Company, 1918–1945,* by Klaus Kreimeier, translated by Robert and Rita Kimber

24. *From Monuments to Traces: Artifacts of German Memory, 1870–1990,* by Rudy Koshar

25. *We Weren't Modern Enough: Women Artists and the Limits of German Modernism,* by Marsha Maskimmon

26. *Culture and Inflation in Weimar Germany,* by Bernd Widdig

27. *Weimar Surfaces: Urban Visual Culture in 1920s Germany,* by Janet Ward

Cool Conduct

The Culture of Distance
in Weimar Germany

Helmut Lethen

Translated by Don Reneau

UNIVERSITY OF CALIFORNIA PRESS
Berkeley · Los Angeles · London

The translations of Bertolt Brecht's "Report on a
Tick" (chapter 1) and "On the Infanticide Marie
Farrar" (chapter 6) are from *Bertolt Brecht Poems,
1913–1956*, ed. John Willett and Ralph Manheim
(New York: Methuen, 1976). They are reproduced
by permission of Suhrkamp Verlag, Frankfurt am
Main.

University of California Press
Berkeley and Los Angeles, California

University of California Press, Ltd.
London, England

Lethen, Helmut.
    [Verhaltenslehren der Kälte. English]
    Cool conduct : the culture of distance in
Weimar Germany / Helmut Lethen ; translated
by Don Reneau.
        p.   cm. — (Weimar and now ; 17)
    Includes bibliographical references and index.
    ISBN 0-520-20109-4 (alk. paper)
    1. Conduct of life.   I. Title.   II. Series.
BJ1583.L5713 2002
943.085—dc21   2001027679

Manufactured in the United States of America
11   10   09   08   07   06   05   04   03   02
10   9   8   7   6   5   4   3   2   1

Contents

Preface to the American edition   ix

Acknowledgments   xiii

1. Fending Off Shame: The Habitus of Objectivity   1
2. The Rapture of Circulation and Schematicism   21
3. The Conduct Code of the Cool Persona   33
4. The Cool Persona in New Objectivity Literature   101
5. The Radar Type   187
6. The Creature   195

Afterword   215

Notes   217

Index   239

Preface to the
American Edition

Distance and closeness between people in their social space is a central concern of cultural sciences. Arthur Schopenhauer formulated the necessity of solving this problem in his famous parable of the freezing porcupines. On a cold winter's day an assortment of porcupines needs to set an adequate distance among its members. Being too close, they risk mutual injury from their quills; being too far apart, they are bound to die of exposure. The porcupines, as Schopenhauer writes, are torn between closeness and distance until they settle on a moderate temperature at which they can tolerate their situation.

This book is about "adequate distance," which is a construct of cultural history. The historical setting is Germany from 1914 to 1945, the time of a thirty years' war. The book depicts the traumatic situation after the capitulation of 1918. The familiar horizons of the Wilhelmian empire are gone. After the loss of the authoritative system, people experience the immediate confrontation with modernity as a freezing shock. In counterreaction, the ideal of a glowing community displaces the coldness of industrialized civil society.

In this situation of a cult of community with its fatal political consequences, the philosophical anthropologist Helmuth Plessner intervenes with a manifesto on cool conduct, *Grenzen der Gemeinschaft: Eine Kritik des sozialen Radikalismus* (The boundaries of community: a critique of social radicalism). It is a document of a culture of distance, rare and precious because German cultural history never appreciated it.

Plessner escapes from the intelligentsia's traditional views on civilization to discover the open horizon of possibilities in the anonymity of
public existence. *Grenzen* is also an early manifesto against the "tyranny of intimacy," as Richard Sennett labels it five decades later. In 1924
Plessner states: "As a guiding principle, authenticity is not right for
strangers. . . . After a sudden collision, the coldness of outer space must
sink between them."

Plessner's manifesto interests us today because of its uncanny relevance to the problems that have arisen in the debate on communitarianism. In a harsh polemic against the cult of *Gemeinschaft* (community),
Plessner stresses the dark side of the communitarian ideology. He respects the longing for community, inasmuch as it is a wish to avoid separation from others. However, his critique addresses the shortcomings
of that concept. The German ideology of community obscures violence
and hatred inside a community; it overlooks the necessity of, and the
right for, spheres of mistrust. It forgets that it is only a part of the social
framework, that its critique of liberal society benefits from the latter's
basic principles. And, finally, its fundamentalism strips away the boundaries of the individual's body, destroys his personal space; its cult of authenticity and the reign of terror are kindred spirits.

Plessner contrasts the identikit picture of community as a symbiotic
companionship with an idea of society that lacks idyllic features. It is an
open system of unencumbered strangers. Abstract juridical norms regulate its sphere, in which human beings appear only as persons. In order
to function according to its laws, they must forget their primal embed-
ding in community, distance themselves from those spheres of trust "in
which we still kept ourselves warm." An absence of values, rather than
shared moral ideas, marks its public space. It comprises the spheres of
education, of state and economy. The subspheres' moral values must not
influence the public sphere:

> In every sphere of human interactions, the idea of realizable order must take
> precedence over the law of pure values. That is because what dims and re-
> fracts the pure light of values is the complete disjunction in human existence
> between familiarity and objectivity.

The public sphere consists of equal, disconnected persons, "not because
they are equal *to*, but because they are equal *for* each other." Plessner
knows that individuals must use force to free themselves from their familiar space of trust, and that life in the "coldness of society" involves a
permanent balancing act.

Leading a life in alienation is an art. To do so, people have to develop rules of a social game that will allow them to "get close without violating each other, and to separate without injury." Social rites bring relief to this balancing act: ceremony, diplomacy, and tact. Supplied with these, individuals can achieve elegance and power. In these reflections Plessner touches problems that will resurface fifty years later in the debate on communitarianism. But Plessner believes he solved the problems, in a single stroke, by constructing an anthropology of the social person.

From a communitarian viewpoint, the concept of liberalism as represented in John Rawls's *Theory of Justice* starts at the point where membership in society outranks membership in community. It obliges individuals to let go of familiar moral values in community to prove themselves as juridical persons in society. Communitarians attacked Rawls's "unencumbered self" as a figure of coldness. Ralf Dahrendorf called liberalism itself a "cold project."

Indeed the concept raises broad questions about violent abstraction from community existence, questions that Rawls was unable to answer:

On which passions, hunger, longings, eros is the necessary separation from familiar bondage to be based? Which interest can form the reason for the art of separation?

How violent must the force to abstraction be in order to make a community being a juridical person? How can this force be institutionalized? Can institutionalized power find a mooring in the human psyche?

As he addresses these problems, Plessner does not follow Thomas Hobbes's plan to impel human beings to submit to social norms. Instead, Plessner assumes that individuals develop their inner nature to the full in a violence-based public life. That is because—as his paradox says—"man is artificial by nature." The violence-based artificiality of civilization is the genuine medium of life! The leading principles of this anthropology are succinct: at birth, man is in an "eccentric" relation to his environment. He needs the artificiality of a second nature, a cultural context that he weaves around him in order to survive. Man is naturally a cultural being; he has to conduct his life.

"Artificiality in action, thought, and dreams is the inner means by which man comes to terms with himself as a natural being." All expression of his psyche is subject to the fluctuations of the laws of symbolic order. This stroke of genius is to offset a shortcoming of German cul-

tural history. But there are traces of the project's violence in several formulations of Plessner's work.

The present book examines the curious dimensions of the anthropological principle, "man is artificial by nature." It reconstructs the principle's historical background, as well in its involvement in Nietzschean
aestheticism as in its affinity to the pronouncements of the European
avant-garde. The study questions how a brief alliance of this thought
with that of the legal theorist Carl Schmitt could have come about.
Schmitt found an anthropological basis for his political friend-enemy
formula in Plessner's texts of the 1920s. For his part, Plessner referred
to Schmitt in political questions. One of them became the crown jurist
of the Third Reich, the other took refuge in the Netherlands as an exile.
The codes of cool conduct form a hidden intersection of the various political camps in pre-Hitler Germany. Underneath the political differences
fantastic alliances developed: all of a sudden we glimpse a subterranean
link between Ernst Jünger and Bertolt Brecht, Walter Benjamin in correspondence with Carl Schmitt, Werner Krauss, a resistance fighter, in
touch with the dadaist Walter Serner.

All these unlikely neighbors venerated—and here is the secret center of this book—a conduct code of the seventeenth century: the *Art
of Worldly Wisdom,* written in 1647 by the Spanish Jesuit Balthasar
Gracián.

Cool Conduct in fact tries some sort of "border-surfing" to find out
whether this phase of Germany's classic modernity had a shared radical
core beyond the political rhetoric. Having defined this core in all its
strangeness, we can more easily dismiss a catastrophic epoch that held
us spellbound for so long.

Rostock, 22 May 1998
Preface translated by Caroline Sommerfeld

Acknowledgments

Without the friendly suggestions and criticism voiced in conversations with Helga Geyer-Ryan, Hortense von Heppe, and Heinz-Dieter Kittsteiner, this work would never have been completed. My thanks go as well to Inka Mülder-Bach, Regina Busch, and Ulrike Baureithel, who commented on drafts; and to Carl Wege, Richard Faber, Rüdiger Safranski, Hans-Thies Lehmann, Joachim von der Thüsen, and Bernd Weyergraf, with whom I had subsequent discussions. The book benefited from the advice and objections of Carrie Lee Asman, Friedbert Aspetsberger, Teja Bach, Susanne van Briemen, Jean-Luc Evard, Joachim Fischer, Dieter Hensing, Tony Kaes, Volker Kaiser, Reinhard Kapp, Martin Lindner, Crystal Mazur, Helga Moser, Manfred Moser, Peter Oesterreich, Klaus Rathschiller, Friedrich Rothe, Georg Scherer, Renate Schlesier, Nicolaus Sombart, Caroline Sommerfeld, Frank Trommler, Renate Voris, Waltraud Wende, Hannes Wendt, Ernest Wichner, Hubert Winkels, Heinz Wismann, Temilo van Zantwijk, and Carsten Zelle. Karl-Heinz Barck was kind enough to arrange access to the Werner-Krauss Archiv in the former Akademie der Wissenschaften, where I enjoyed the assistance of Horst F. Müller and Karin Preisigke. I thank my colleagues Jattie Enklaar, Gregor Laschen, and Peter Wessels for having helped make this book possible.

At the invitation of Herbert Wiesner, I was able to present a few of my ideas at the Literaturhaus Berlin. Winfried Menninghaus encouraged me to publish them.

The work was written under the auspices of the research program of the Onderzoekinstitut voor Geschiedenis en Cultuur at the University of Utrecht and would never have been finished without the remarkable assistance of Lilo Roskams.

Nearly all the persons named raised serious objections to the afterword, which, consequently, is the only chapter short enough to be my responsibility alone.

CHAPTER ONE

Fending Off Shame:
The Habitus of Objectivity

THE NORTH STATION

At about 11:00 A.M. on the first or second of November 1918, a thirteen-year-old boy waited at Vienna's North Station for his father to return from the front. He waited for some hours, enduring the ice-cold wind blowing across the tracks. Decades later the boy will recall seeing, among the disembarking passengers after the train finally arrived, an officer shouting at his orderly to pick up the pace. The *Putzfleck*—to use the Habsburg imperial army's label for such a servant—was loaded and overloaded with baggage, bathed in sweat despite the cold, barely able to lift his head. Still he mumbled all the while, "Yes, sir, your most obedient servant, sir, at the ready."

Suddenly his path was blocked by a young soldier. "Comrade," said the soldier, "what are you running for? There's plenty of time. We all have plenty of time." The soldier began taking suitcases out of the servant's hands. The servant motioned silently, warning of the presence of a superior officer who, for his part, was already preparing a fitting response to the mutiny. Coming closer, however, the officer noted that a band bearing the Polish national colors had replaced the imperial cockade on the soldier's cap. His resolve began to waver, and now he found himself surrounded by other hostile parties, one of whom knocked the hat off his head. He reached for his saber, but already the *Putzfleck* had thrown off what remained of his load and pulled himself erect. Taller now than the officer, he boxed the latter resoundingly on both ears.

Clearly the officer had realized by now, in the storyteller's words, that "some weirdness" was afoot. The underlings all around him appeared suddenly as unpredictable as "monsters in a nightmare." They were laughing at him. Leaping over the tracks, he fled the scene.[1]

It is tempting to add to this story of a lightning-quick metamorphosis at the Vienna train station the inscription *natura facit saltus.* But it has been retold to us as part of the introduction to Manès Sperber's *Sieben Fragen zur Gewalt,* his reflections on political violence, offered in opposition to strategies that would seek to accelerate the historical process. Sperber's emphasis therefore falls on the necessity of slow evolutionary development. Recalling the incident from sixty years' remove, he inscribes it with the words *natura non facit saltus.*

The scene at the North Station will remain in Sperber's memory all this time, functioning as a mythical image informing his thought: he will come to understand institutions as no more substantial than a feather, as fragile as a house of glass. The child waits for his father to return in the more or less heroic garb of a soldier and instead experiences this scandal. It leaves its mark. Sperber does not question the authenticity of the tale. He even accords it a certain historical legitimacy, given the dubious status of the Habsburg monarchy. More generally, however, his recollection of the scene casts it in the form of a compensatory daydream. A subject suddenly finds itself inhabiting a space where the law of gravity has been annulled. Traditional entanglements are simplified to the point of vanishing. The dense past, which has been bearing down like a knapsack on a servile back, is easily tossed aside, to be forgotten like so much castoff baggage. Sperber describes here a time in which the desire to be freed of the gravitational force of one's own mentality finds expression even in the jargon of soldiers.[2]

There are a number of perspectives from which we might describe such acts of instantaneous transformation. History, theology, the dramatic arts, and finally sociology all have their explanations of the incident at the North Station. Encouraged by the French *annales* school, historians distinguish between "long" activities, events repeated in succession over time, and "short" ones, occurring once or only a few times.[3] From this historical perspective, the latter are exotic rather than typical, and consequently of little value as knowledge. Of greater interest is the structure of long-term or conjunctural processes. In any case, a train station—like the Pyrenees or a bend in the Loire River—is not the sort of context that remains constant over time.

The "historical moment" nevertheless remains a historical category that helps us understand the incident at the North Station. Historians conceive of such moments as an "empty field," across which consciousness draws a caesura. As it appears in the consciousness of an observer, the historical moment resembles "a collision between two billiard balls; having no materiality of its own, it is rather the result of complicated physical processes going on all around it."[4]

By the time the event at the North Station moves into the range of the young boy's consciousness, however, it is already a repetition. By the time his memory recomposes it, it has already been rendered in dramatic form. Were this not the case, those present at the station would not be able to recognize in concert its farcical element, which is the condition of the fun they have with the officer.

We could rest content here with a note to the effect that the notion of the farce comes from Marx, writing about Bonaparte in the *Eighteenth Brumaire*. Since a farce's subject is always someone other than the observer, this is one of a small number of Marx's statements that generally goes uncontested. But the larger point is that the historical understanding of the incident suggested by the physical analogy obscures a critical element. The two billiard balls—the subject of the instantaneous metamorphosis, their collision constituting the historical moment—remain beyond the reach of our analysis. Having arrived at the point of collision, they take a course we can describe in the language of stimulus and response, but only at the cost of leaving unanalyzed the inner structure of their motion.

Examined in detail, the train station scene is more differentiated than the billiard ball analogy suggests. Since the observers' reaction at the train station is coherent and collective, it suggests that they experience in the moment of their reaction a high degree of shared awareness. But Sperber's telling of the story attributes this differentiation only to the officer. He is acutely sensitive to the "weirdness" inherent in the scene as soon as he gets an unmediated glimpse, through the glasshouse of etiquette, at the "animal realm" of rebellion. The macabre aspect of the situation, with the exception of the boy waiting for his father, escapes the rude public. Yet, even given this capacity for nuance in the officer's consciousness, neither he nor his servant can function as anchors for the sort of cunning we know from Hegel's master-slave dialectic, which comes of the attribution of a psychological disposition to anonymous processes. Individuals act and are utterly realistic in doing so, with no thought of snatching chestnuts out of the fire for the world spirit.

Although a theory of the historical moment can help clarify dramatic instants, it leaves us wanting as soon as we inquire more deeply into the nature of the actors. The scene at the North Station raises questions that we can answer only if we know more than the tale tells us about their psychological dispositions. For example, is the transformation reversible? Can the rebel be turned back into a *Putzfleck?* We must look elsewhere for answers to questions such as these.

When the social sciences look for guidance to psychological theories of individual behavior, they run into problems explaining behavior in exceptional circumstances. Pointing out that "the meaning of the exceptional condition for jurisprudence is analogous to that of a miracle for theology," Carl Schmitt suggests an alternative approach.[5] Theology, however, conceives of transformation as a sudden awakening. The light of theological revelation comes to the individual from outside, "like a bolt of lightning" in a moment "of crisis for the arts of human enactment."[6] The directionality of this kind of change thus runs counter to what we see when the *Putzfleck* suddenly comes alive. Since a theological approach presupposes the failure of individual sovereignty, we can apply the model of revelation to the North Station only by labeling the *Putzfleck* a model proletarian suddenly illuminated by the spirit of revolt.

Our question pertains more to the nature of the underlying anthropology that warrants a theological assumption of abrupt changes in personal orientation. Here we come on the notion of the garment, which served for centuries, in the evidence of the *Reallexikon für Antike und Christentum,* as the prevailing image of radical changes in an individual's conviction and temperament as a change of clothes. "After he had laid aside persecution and joined the Apostles," we read in a description of the converted Paul. Or, also in the context of rebirth: "to doff the soldier and don the sophist"; "to take off the purple robes of darkness and put on a new man."[7] We shall see that the aesthetic prevailing among the new objectivity generation in the 1920s preferred the reverse procedure. It liked to take off the expressionistic garment of the new man in order to wrap itself in Lucifer's cloak.

It is part of the cultural history of the modern conscience that such changes of persona, orchestrated by the Pietist clergy as late as the eighteenth century, met with skepticism from the bourgeois classes. The problem lay in not being able to discount the possibility of a merely external change in attitude.[8] The Pietists, forerunners of our own "long-term conscience," welcomed signs of instantaneous awakening but could not resist tormenting themselves with the problem of how to maintain a transformation over the long run. They put considerable stress on inner motivation, so, even while compelling the conversion of lower-class types bound for the gallows, they viewed with mistrust any signs of overly rapid changes. They could not altogether still their suspicion that what motivated the sinners was the prospect of being led to their execution in the white robes of the converted. The idea of a complicated mechanism of self-direction as part of individual psychology—David Riesman's inner compass, which resists any sudden change of orientation brought about by an external stimulus—is a later product of bourgeois modernity, laid superficially over an archaic constitution but never entirely popular with the lower classes.

The phenomenon of a prebourgeois "rational type"—a person who was able to adapt personal behavior to external influences with no feelings of guilt—was the parallel discovery of a number of historical anthropologists in the 1930s. Norbert Elias, reconstructing martial scenes from the Middle Ages, depicts the psychological apparatus of self-control as scarcely developed. "Rather sudden transformations," he finds, are common, and threats of physical force always accompany the disciplining affects.[9] After the First World War, of course, it was hardly necessary to reach back to medieval times to reconstruct a military society. What Sigmund Freud termed the "artificial groups" formed by institutions like the army and the Freikorps were in evidence all around, and within them there was nothing extraordinary about quick changes of persona.

Finding evidence of rapid reorientation on the part of soldiers leads us back to the behavior of the character allotted the more differentiated role in our scene at the North Station, namely, the officer.[10] Failures of conscience or nerve may have been most commonly attributed to the masses, but we are not dealing here with an exclusively lower-class phenomenon. In accomplishing sudden shifts from the formality of etiquette to barbarism, leaders did not distinguish themselves from the team; it would be more accurate to say that it was incumbent upon officers to be able to make just that shift expertly.

Psychoanalytic explanations of such sudden transformations assume that the institution of the army, in the midst of industrial society, represents "cold culture."[11] It encourages the hibernation of the ego, which is responsible for psychological self-direction. When the ego, the supposed guarantor of coherence, balance, and continuity, loses its direction, quick transformations and discontinuities of motion become possible. The military has need of people who are specialized in quick adaptation to extremely rapidly changing situations.

There is an extensive literature in which officers, indulging the aesthetic appeal of "horror," depicted their own enactment of "behavioral dissonance" (to use a contemporary term). They had no need to reach back to prebourgeois sources in their search for representational devices; images of a more archaic individual constitution, wholly suitable for producing uncanny effects, were ready to hand in the horror literature of the eighteenth and nineteenth centuries and keep us relatively well informed about such changes of persona in the upper class.[12]

But when we turn to the proletarian literature of the time, it disappoints our expectations. Since the characters of proletarian literature are more often rooted in notions of a shared mentality, the few quick shifts we do find tend to be bound more to the image of betrayal or ascribed to the anarchism of marginalized groups. The functionary, on the other hand, although belonging to the other-directed type, presents us with an exemplary model of long-term internal affective stabilization: the functionary is required to practice the art of executing changes in policy as if they were not changes.

Nevertheless, it is finally in the literature of the avant-garde that our findings become really rich. In the decades separating the first futurist manifesto from Ernst Jünger's *Der Arbeiter* (1932), the avant-garde gives shape to a type displaying all the essential elements of a prebourgeois subjective constitution.[13] This reach back to a "subcomplex" subject distinguishes the avant-garde from modernists like Robert Musil, Thomas Mann, or Hugo von Hofmannsthal, whose intricately difficult subjects are able to endure the process of historical acceleration only from a healthy distance. The artistic figure of the prebourgeois subject was as if magnetically drawn to the military, less in pursuit of enlightenment than a kind of wake-up call. We find characters here ranging from those beset by "an electric bell going off nonstop inside them" (Ernst Jünger) to mechanical men in the paintings of the Italian *pittura metafisica,* to the constructs of the Proletkult.

It is tempting to draw into our discussion at this point the aesthetic of "suddenness," with which Karl Heinz Bohrer illuminates the avant-garde's fascination with decisionism.[14] The sign of suddenness, according to Bohrer, comes in for particular dramatization toward the end of the nineteenth century. For a generation of Nietzsche readers, temporal awareness had concentrated on the "dangerous moment": an instant in which the "eruption of the irrational" becomes an aesthetic phenomenon that is no longer embedded in any causal explanation.

But a simple transfer of Bohrer's theory of suddenness to our scene at the train station would force a drastic change in it. Sperber, the theorist of evolutionary historical change, composes the scene as a panorama. To turn the tale into a document in the history of the horror aesthetic, we would have to limit the narrative perspective exclusively to the officer's perception. Encapsulation of the gaze in a single figure still believing himself to be king of his castle makes it possible to see in the phenomenon of rebellion a "horrifying cancellation of the reality principle." But the account would leave out the singularity of the officer's horror, which makes up only one element of the farce, whereas it is the farce as a whole that serves as our medium of reflection.

Thus we can frame the anecdote in a way that directly counters the theory of suddenness; in the end the theory serves only to double the perspectives of the self-assured actors it describes. And yet we could, from Bohrer's standpoint, raise an objection to Sperber's recall of the scene from memory: his recollection presupposes an epic sovereignty that is wholly removed from the shock experienced by contemporary eyewitnesses; it reduces the stuff of dramatic fascination to material diced neatly into moral categories.

What best serves our purpose here, however, is a closer look at the rebellious young soldier's statement. Against the backdrop of the era's characteristic speed fetish, his intervention may have been sudden, but the burden of it was not: "We all have plenty of time"—as if time had volume and could be divided into parts. For Marx, revolutions were the speeding locomotives of history, but the soldier asks, why hurry? Unlike the avant-garde, the soldier is not obsessed with tying his action to the forward point of the arrow of time. He acts instead from the standpoint of a multinational *space,* and his subversive action lays no claim to harmony with the accelerating thrust of modernization. With the disintegration of a larger transnational political space, the factor of national space comes to play a critical role.

The discipline of history, taking the categories of repetition and space as its primary interest today, attributes a merely novelistic character to

narratives of historical leaps. Fernand Braudel remarks dismissively on
the "myth" of the barbarians' impact on Europe; they tarried long, he
says, at the door to the house of higher culture, knocking repeatedly, before they were ever allowed in. "Their triumph was short-lived, and they
were quickly reabsorbed into the very spaces they believed they had conquered." And then, he summarizes, "the door of the conquered house
slammed shut again."[15]

Did the European avant-garde, in the decades from 1910 to 1930,
suffer a similar fate? Do the spatial categories with which Braudel operates even retain any validity for bourgeois modernity? What seems to
comprise the larger space today is the world market, which reincorpo-
rates the other that it itself produces.

THE DRAMATURGY OF DISGRACE

Shame isolates. It operates on the "dark side of life, where an embarrassed silence descends over a feeling of having been wounded in one's
dignity."[16] The acute breach of self-esteem the officer must have experienced makes him the focus of a crowd, in which some members are
hostile, some indifferent. The sociology of shame tells us that his mood
at this moment is shot through by two simultaneous sensations, both
dreadfully certain, of being discriminated against, on the one hand, and
of being exposed just as ruthlessly, on the other. Shame is a reaction to
the perception of having been degraded in the eyes of others. The captain, in the language of the warrior caste to which he belongs, suffers
"disgrace."

In Sperber's scene, all the elements of a theatrics of disgrace are visible. The signs of disgrace are bound to bodies in action, so that few
words are required for its expression.[17] "In a shame-based culture, the
subject is engaged in a never-ending drama," "in a scene of projection,
mirroring, and remirroring, which is fundamentally distinct from the
theatrical form of the tribunal characteristic of a guilt-based culture."[18]
Attitudes, gestures, and motor reactions are arrayed in opposition in the
enactment of shame at the station: excess and restraint, aggression and
flight, the sword and the hand, panic and calm, sovereignty and subordination—gradations are neither necessary nor present; attitudes change
abruptly, with no transition between being bowed and erect, between
being concealed and exposed. The nearly mute constellation of power is
static, like a woodcut.

But from the narrator's perspective, the scene belongs to the genre marked most essentially by instability. From the angle of the "raw" public, it is a farce: resounding laughter accompanies the flight of the captain. There is a tragic quality to the events from the viewpoint of the officer and those who sympathize with him; paralyzing horror, however, is reserved for the boy waiting on the platform. Every disgrace seeks its genre, the most popular of which is the farce.

The sociology of shame could take the scene at the North Station as a textbook example of the way external regulators of social behavior function. The mechanics of the interaction proceed without a hitch; internal guides to behavior are imperceptible, though their concealment in no way interferes with understanding the scene. Among the antagonists in the critical instant there is no misunderstanding. Such communication in exceptional circumstances is as unfamiliar to the officer as it is to the servant, yet both react automatically with the respective gestures of their stations. The captain reaches for his sword, the underling strikes a blow. The *Putzfleck* responds with an action that an officer in more stable times would reserve for punishing an insult delivered by someone unworthy of offering further satisfaction. By boxing the officer's ears, the servant manifests the sudden exchange of power positions.

The officer's disgrace consists in having lost face, having been relieved precipitously of the command he was in the act of exercising. And there is no conceivable ritual that could restore his wounded honor before this public. The diffuse gathering of the urban masses here is as typical as it is accidental and formless; nevertheless, its laughter suddenly lends it the appearance of homogeneity. Only the laughter makes it possible to talk of a collective subject: the mutineers.

The officer persists in his domination past the moment of the train's arrival: he parts the masses like a snowplow. In being shamed at precisely that moment, he suffers a paramount disgrace. He is deluged, swept away, in his defeat by the perceptions of countless witnesses. His habitus—his constitution or demeanor; in this case the unstoppable momentum of his stride, the watchful gaze he tosses back at the crowd—is subverted, violated: he becomes the object of an enactment of humiliation. Perhaps the boy blushes in his stead, but the officer, in the grip of his reflex to flee, spares himself the sight.

As we know, the scene is a harmless prelude to disgrace of a wholly different caliber. Disgrace—*Blamage*—is one of the key words of the postwar turmoil, and the officers' revenge was not long in coming. It turns out that the instantaneous metamorphosis of the *Putzfleck* was reversible, even if the system of resubjugation worked more slowly than the original transformation. From the battles that took place in the Berlin newspaper district in 1919 to the Reichstag session in 1933 that passed the enabling acts of the dictatorship, we find scenes of horrific shaming and disgrace. To overcome shame, the offended parties donned the masks of the new political movements. "In fact, the forms of humiliation to which the masked bands resort with impunity are endlessly manifold," as Léon Wurmser remarks about the Shrove Tuesday processions.[19] They would ultimately amount to something like a fascist carnival.

"Status inconsistencies," we learn from sociology, "are hothouses of social shame."[20] If that is accurate, the constant threat to distinct boundary markings in the Weimar Republic generated considerable warmth. People, seeking escape from the heat of shame, trying to establish themselves as separate from it, assumed a variety of attitudes marked by their "coolness." In doing so, they were obliged to elaborate doctrines of cool behavior.

Members of the intelligentsia sought—as the young Sperber did in our scene—to remove themselves from the mechanisms of disgrace by becoming observers. Their success in doing so depended largely on being able to distinguish their own self-image from the frightening image they constructed of the masses.[21] We see this at the North Station. The soldier's mutinous act does not transform the crowd into a revolutionary mob but into an audience for a theatrical event appealing to "vulgar" tastes. "Gesture—not being," says Karl Jaspers of the "masses" in 1931, and in this incivility he will glimpse an essential characteristic.[22] Inhabitants of the hothouse culture of shame who manage to cool themselves will take every opportunity to note with fluent disdain the distinction between themselves and the visible gestural language they see all around in their environment. "Experience rather than existence, endless mimicry"—this is Jaspers's critique of the masses' existence.[23] In the play of gestures offered to them on the platform, such masses get their money's worth. Like the officer, the readers of Gustave Le Bon's 1895 study of mass psychology will learn to see in the servant a mere automaton with no will of his own, dominated by base drives and destructive energy.[24] And—if they happen to be of a humanistic disposition—they will identify with the boy, who involuntarily assumes the role of an ethnographer observing savages engaged in a primitive shaming ritual, while waiting for the glorious father.[25]

FORSAKING THE CULTURE OF CONSCIENCE

Among the distinguishing characteristics of the reaction to the shocking experience of slaughter in World War I is an absence of tribunals, which are among the rituals of a culture based on guilt. The fact that civilized nations could engage in such horror, that individuals were able to suspend conscience for the sake of military operations neither informed introspection nor generated confessions. We would be much nearer the mark in saying that the collective gaze following World War I was averted from the complex of issues identified by a guilt culture.

Perhaps, in this averting of the gaze, a marginal artistic movement such as dadaism coincides with the postwar mood of the simple infantryman. Certainly, research identifies more and more signs that the peripheral current of dadaism lent expression to a widespread unwillingness to go on applying the internalized lash of a guilt culture. "All the symptoms of a bad conscience (ding!), guilt (dong!), like blushing, paling, stuttering, shifty eyes, a compulsion to utter the revealing word, and so forth—*per procura*, nonsense," we read in Walter Serner's dadaist manifesto of 1920.[26] From another angle, Helmuth Plessner warns against the fatal consequences for morality itself of an overemphasis on conscience.[27] Brecht's "Report on a Tick," in his *Hauspostille* (Devotions), describes the torment of an internalized guilty conscience created by Christian religion:

1
Through our dreams of childhood
In the bed of milky white
Round apple trees there haunted
The man in violet.

2
Lying in the dust near him
We watched how he sat. Idly.
And stroked his pigeon
And basked by the pathway.

3
He swigs blood like a tick
Cherishes the smallest gift
And all that is yours he'll take
So that he's all you have left.

4
And you who gave up for him
Your joy and others' too

And lie, a beggar, on the ground
He will not know you.
5
To spit right in your face
Is splendid fun, he'd think
And he will lie in wait
To catch you on the blink.
6
After dark he'll stand and pry
Over your windowsill
And go off huffily
Remembering every smile.
7
And if you feel joyful
And laugh however low
Upon his little organ
A mournful tune he'll play.
8
If someone mocks at him
He'll plunge in heaven's blue
And yet he made the sows
In his own image too.
9
Of all besides he loves
Most by deathbeds to sit.
He haunts our last fevers
That man in violet.[28]

The crisis of conscience produces a longing for the externalities of a shame culture. This is not a new motif, and certainly Friedrich Nietzsche had been there all along to reinforce it. Now, however—following the debacle of the guilt culture in the world war—the motif falls on particularly favorable ground. The desire to throw off the "enormous complication of the guilty personality,"[29] in which nineteenth-century psychology had entangled the image of the subject, finds expression in the writings of the new objectivity. In new objectivity's images, individuals are no more than motion-machines, feelings are mere motor reflexes, and character is a matter of what mask is put on. External judgments and rules guide individual behavior, and response to the web of others' perceptions helps define the self. The noise of the street penetrates into the house of the psyche. Benjamin notes in 1921,

> It is not possible to define a concept of an outer world in juxtaposition to the bounded concept of the effect-producing individual. Interaction characterizes everything between the individual and the outer world; the respective

spheres of activity between inner and outer cross over into each other. . . .
The outer found by the acting individual can in principle be referred back in
whatever degree one likes to the inner, the inner in whatever degree back to
the outer.[30]

Critical contemporaries trace the change in norms to various factors. In
1915 Freud spoke in his *Reflections on War and Death* about the disenchantment born of the experience of seeing the lofty ethical norms of civilized states lose their validity overnight, of learning that people were capable of "deeds of such cruelty, maliciousness, betrayal, and brutality"
as would not have been thought possible for nations of that level of cultural development.[31] It was easier, on the basis of an observation like
that, to conclude that conscience owes its existence to external force and
social anxiety, that its purported moral framework could be thrown off
"like a coat" upon a change in the social constellation, and that the pro-
pensity for cruelty must be among the most basic of human drives: "The
war causes the primal self in us to make its reappearance."[32]

If, however, the conscience is nothing but the internalization of a violent external authority, if the superego, which is supposed to hold aggression in check, is capable of suspending judgment in favor of external authorities such as the military command, there seems no point in seeking
the source of personal "guilt" in a conflict of conscience. The gaze turns
outward; attention turns to the origins of moral norms and the genesis
of the conscience as their supervisory apparatus in violent society.

Here in 1915 (and again in 1930, at greater length in *Civilization and
Its Discontents*), Freud maintains that the conscience, which in a guilt
culture acquires the function of an internal regulator, actually develops only in an advanced stage in the history of civilization. This insight,
the late internalization of external authorities, inspired the cultural anthropology of the interwar years.[33] Freud's idea honed the perception of
ethnologists. It guided their search for examples of societies still in an
earlier evolutionary stage, in which individual consciousness of guilt, a
result of the tension existing between a strict superego and a subordinate
ego, had not yet taken form. The American anthropologists Margaret
Mead and Ruth Benedict found cultures of this type in their field research and termed them "shame cultures."

Although research since the Second World War has made it evident
that the strict polarization of guilt cultures and shame cultures cannot
be maintained on empirical grounds, it remains instructive for our purposes as a historical model. The polarization is itself interesting as a
myth, the reality of a wish projection that was persuasive to a genera-

tion of critical intellectuals. The construction of the antithesis in pure
form will enable us to see anew certain cultural aspects of the period following the First World War. Looking at these aspects in combination
with the other reigning dichotomy of the Weimar period, between culture and civilization, we see a shift.[34] If the new objectivity intelligentsia
has a single common trait, it is a provocative decision in favor of the concept of civilization.

The concept of culture, as developed in the German tradition, encom-
passes the intellectual, religious, and moral sphere, in sharp distinction
to the sphere of the economy and technology. The concept of civilization, in contrast, favored in the English and French traditions, encom-
passes technology, science, and more diffuse worldviews. Alongside these
collective human accomplishments, the concept of civilization also includes behavior. During the war, the opposed "signal concepts" of culture and civilization had been supposed to stabilize the self-consciousness
of the national collective;[35] Thomas Mann's reflections of a nonpolitical
man are to be counted among the symptomatic texts offered in opposition to the concept of civilization. From the perspective of culture,
"merely civil behavior"—and societies that appeared to content themselves with it—was judged deficient. As a cultural ideal, civilization
seemed to negate interiority, authenticity, and the subtleties of truth that
are not manifest in behavior.

In the decade of this new objectivity, from 1920–30, the disappointment caused by a culture at war informs the intelligentsia's critique,
which stresses the uncivilized nature of a culture capable of conducting
war. In the ideological sphere, the critique exposes the degree to which
culture allows barbarism and owes its existence to violence; in the sphere
of the sociology of knowledge, it concentrates attention on the functional accomplishment of cultural values within civilization.

The turn of the new objectivity from a concept of culture, with a focus on the superego, to civilization keyed to behavior, does not escape
the polar tension; the exaggerated welcome bestowed upon civilization
itself betrays the unbroken presence of the German culture complex. A
further expression of the persisting tension is the hybrid structure of new
objectivity jargon, which continues to betray the pull exerted by two
poles, even if its typical formulations blatantly discount culture:[36]

> Radio, Marconigram, and telephoto release us from national isolation into
> the world community. Our dwellings will become more mobile than ever:
> the mass apartment complex, sleeping car, houseboat, and transatlantic
> liner undermine the local concept of *Heimat*.[37]

The specific energy channeled by Emil Fischer in synthesizing grape sugar is a match for the greatest human accomplishments [1924].[38]
The most trivial fact concerning the connection between character and endocrine balances offers a better view of the soul than a five-story idealistic system [1923].[39]
The proof that a newspaper is right is that someone buys it [1926].[40]
The way a man moves mirrors the meaning of his life [1930].[41]
The characteristic gaze of today, the mercantile gaze into the heart of things, is the advertisement [1928].[42]

Looking at the turn toward a code of civil behavior in terms of a schematic polarization between guilt and shame cultures, we can glimpse aspects of postwar German thought that its practitioners were less aware of as they focused on civilization. Their exaggerated affirmation of a culture of exteriority, rooted in shame, could not nullify the effects of a persisting internalized culture of guilt. As contemporary anthropologists defined it, a shame culture amounted to a transparent complex of conventions, in which the external compulsions regulating behavior are visible.[43] The individual follows a self-enacted dramaturgy intended to secure the respect of others for his or her person. Dignity is the keyword. The appraisal of others' visible behavior and reactions takes the place of self-knowledge; subjective motives carry little or no weight for purposes of public judgment, which, when it is negative, plunges the individual in question into a profound sense of shame.

During the interwar years, critical minds found variants of a shame culture captivating for a number of reasons. Fixing the genesis of internal authority in social violence, a shame culture enabled them to subvert the fiction of the self-made individual that is part of the concept of a guilt culture; and it offered a context for the construction of a self more able to bear the immense pressures that rapid modernization placed on the bourgeois individual.

What we would now describe as a mythical wish projection was made up of both destructive elements and aspects of a necessary adaptation to modernization. The image of a society that had moved beyond a culture of conscience held out to new objectivity intellectuals the considerable and widespread appeal of suggesting the possibility of realizing social civility. Thus we find surprising correspondences between the cultural anthropologists' polarized schematic and the polarity that Peter Suhrkamp and Bertolt Brecht proposed as the foundation for epic theater.[44] Brecht's involvement in classic Japanese No theater, which itself owes its origins to a cultural tradition of shame, offers a valuable hint.

In both cases, attention is turned to external influence of convention, which has the virtue of appearing artificial and potentially subject to change.

In a culture based on shame, "perceived being" (Pierre Bourdieu) predominates over other possible constructions of existence. Interior signs refer back to where they are grounded in the body; feelings are expressed through physical gestures. By causing the self to appear as the object of others' perceptions, "shame documents itself through the body."[45] These various qualities recommend a shame culture to the new media:

> In reality, what film requires is external action and nothing in the way of introspective psychology. . . . Seeing from outside is appropriate to film and is what makes it important. . . . If the individual appears as an object, causal interrelations become decisive. The great American comedies also present the individual as an object, and might as well have audiences made up entirely of reflexologists.[46]

Since this "visible individual" (Béla Balázs) can be photographed, the cinema can establish as its domain the once dark archive of the soul enacting itself through gesture. In the context of a shame culture, the arts can engage directly on the practical level in debates concerning the meaning of "perceived being."

If the projections of the civilized shame culture tend toward the exclusivity of an isolated observer, they have the merit of offering insight into the mechanisms of mass society, which can be studied with relatively little anxiety. Karl Jaspers's frightening image of the masses ("gesture—not being") acquires a certain value. In the eyes of new objectivity artists, the masses at least have the advantage that their being is easily decipherable, appearing to them in the status of an open book of gestures.

It is at this point, however, that minds begin to diverge. A comparison of images of a shame culture arising in the German context with the even-tempered registration of mass social phenomena on the part of American sociologists such as George Herbert Mead, David Riesman, and Erving Goffman reveals that German writers, as a rule, present shame culture as a model of modern behavior in a heroic world and conceive of its inhabitants either in the context of a prebourgeois anthropology or in anticipation of a futuristic machine man. The achievement of American sociologists in the 1920s consists in perceiving the phenomena of mass society without deploring the loss of the subject or referring to a heroic past and future while keeping an awareness of the genesis of ethical norms in social force.

There are two explanations for the typical German weakness for heroism. First is the Nietzschean will, which operates in the realm of the heroic: a future humanity will be made up of "barbarians" who courageously set themselves back a step on the evolutionary ladder in order to attain civilization. Second is the felt experience that heroism is necessary: when hopes for the positive forward movement of history are at an end, half-measures will accomplish nothing.[47] So it is that the new objectivity comes into being in the aftermath of expressionism, which it sees as turbulent inner experience of loss stemming from the memory of defeat and entangled in a culture of guilt. It bears the marks of a heroizing shame culture. A favored slogan in this context, which can be read in schematic polarization within the opera *Mahagonny,* runs *natura facit saltus.*[48]

The sentimental jargon of new objectivity thinkers, however, cuts both ways, and in this it becomes apparent that their forthright attitudes could do no more than draw a thin veil over the culture of guilt.[49]

CODES OF CONDUCT

Remarkably enough, the Weimar Republic, a time of extreme instability, burgeoning status insecurity, and dramatic oppositional tension, offered fertile ground for highly artificial elaborations of shame-based cultures. The loss of undisputed legitimacy on the part of social institutions was compensated for by the proliferation of codes of conduct, which in times of normative transformation are generally produced in great number. When social crisis takes hold, the external voices to which individuals have attended are no longer clearly audible and the interior seat of judgment is no longer credited. In such circumstances, codes of conduct operate as written receptacles for external directives to guide individual behavior. They appear in a number of forms: as paeans to the objectivity of the scientific attitude or how-to books on marriage; as the catechism of this or that political camp or Walter Serner's *Handbrevier für Hochstapler,* a guidebook for the confidence man; as the pedagogical doctrine of architects or city planners; in the form of anthropological theory or Brecht's lyrical *Devotions;* or in the principles of the philosophy of law. The dynamic element in these codes of conduct is a desire for masking and concealment, which, in situations threatening shame, offers protection:

> The mask transforms a person who has been exposed in a shaming way into a shameless performer; it turns one who is afraid of being perceived as weak into someone who is seen and feared as being strong.[50]

Amid the unmanageable complexity of postwar society, in situations of economic insecurity and uncertain social status, the rules inscribed in codes of conduct operate to draw elementary distinctions: between what is one's own and what is other; between inner and outer, male and female. They mark separate spheres; they regulate forms of expression and realize the self's equilibrium. They recommend and describe techniques of mimicry in the face of a violent world, subordinating everything to the protection of an individual's defenseless objectivity. They promise to lessen vulnerability, suggesting measures that will immunize people against the shame to which the collective subjects them.

Modern codes of conduct encourage people to acquire the skills they need for strategic self-enactment; the aim is the training of a functional ego. The codes represent an attempt to turn the effects of social distinction over to the personal direction of the individual, transforming the convivial arts of separating and combining into learnable techniques. In doing so, they generate two paradoxes, which typify the dual nature of objectivity. On the one hand, codes imply an acceptance of the individual's status as an object; on the other, they stubbornly hold out the possibility of making that same individual the master of his or her fate. Their affirmation represents a desperate attempt on the part of the new objectivity generation to restore to itself a sense of agency by exploring possible interventions into the workings of external influences. The goal is, through the cunning of concession, to participate in the forces that drive the historical process.

The strict observance of rules designed to vouchsafe distinction, however, necessarily causes the individual to lose hold of the levers of direction. Because the essence of the culture of conscience consists in the expectation that people will behave according to norms even without the threat of external sanctions, the new rules of behavior must keep consciousness alert to the uninterrupted presence of the supervisory gaze of the other (see Figure 1). The rules' promise of relief from self-directed responsibility easily gives way to an imperative of absolute alertness, and, as we shall see, in most cases the codes of conduct of the period set a mood of "chronic alert." Shame cultures never come into existence to benefit individuals; they lead naturally to the next step, which is absorption into an institution: outside institutions, codes of conduct accomplish little. While suggesting the possibility of successful individual interventions into the social power struggle (through the mediation of rules), all codes actually occasion is the self-expression of a lifestyle. Codes of

1. The uninterrupted presence of the supervisory gaze of the other
(Herbert Bayer, *Einsamer Großstädter* [Lonely city dweller], 1932. With the permission of VG Bild-Kunst, Bonn, and Bauhaus-Archiv, Berlin.)

conduct thus become what their new objectivity creators want most to avoid: they become documents of the expressivity of objectivity.[51]

In the 1930s the description of the great shaming theater of social struggle rises to its literary high point. Elias Canetti's *Crowds and Power* offers a panoramic depiction of the mute constellations of power. Here is a comprehensive interpretive analysis of body positions that builds on descriptions of the shame culture by writers in the 1920s.[52] Canetti deciphers the sign language of subjugation and subordination. Fearing con-

tact with others, individuals flee into the masses, where they find protection against shame. They are relieved of the discipline of distancing
themselves; there is no need to practice personal techniques of separation to mark off areas of trust from areas of otherness, because that task
is taken over by the mass formation itself, which simultaneously holds
out the promise of an enormous expansion of the boundaries of individual personality. Canetti describes forms of mass behavior, but his observations apply much more readily to the mechanisms of "artificial
groups" (Freud), such as the army or a party apparatus. His book
on gestures becomes in fact a contribution to natural history. What
he holds up to view are creatures failing to escape the dictates inscribed
schematically in their bodies.

In the image of the creature, the cool persona's central ambition to
become a self-conscious agent of history deteriorates into its opposite.
The suppressed sense of remaining subject to blind fate is the underlying motivation for its magical thinking. What the present book demonstrates is how uncannily close the two images are: the heroic images of
the self-confident subject striding across the civil war landscape, carrying its slogans—*natura facit saltus* and *distinguo, ergo sum*—and the
images of the creature, whose bodily existence dictates its perceptual
and behavioral range.

CHAPTER TWO

The Rapture of Circulation and Schematicism

Beauty is either the end result of a parallelogram of forces, or it does not exist at all.

Theodor W. Adorno, *Funktionalismus Heute*

On 11 March 1932, the *Frankfurter Zeitung* published a sketch by Siegfried Kracauer of a gloomy railway underpass near the Charlottenburg Station in Berlin. The ceiling, constructed of countless riveted iron girders, appears to the author to sink gradually deeper and deeper into the earth, prompting comparison to a nightmare. Pedestrians passing through the tunnel seemed gripped in permanent displeasure. A few chronic inhabitants—a baker in white, a beggar with a harmonica, an old woman—are reduced to reliefs against sooty brick walls, absorbed into the functionality of the underpass while others, bent on their individual courses, lacking the purposefulness of a crowd, quicken their steps.[1] Why does this cellarlike passage made of bricks, iron, and concrete horrify the observer, although its usefulness is not in question? "Probably the contradiction between the closed, immovable construction system and the streaming human chaos produces the horror," Kracauer speculates. What strikes him is the junction of the compact functional structure and the fragmented crowd, the systematicity of dead material and living chaos, the claim the underpass itself stakes on brute endurance, in contrast to the transience of generations passing through it. Sixty-five years later it is still there, as a trip to Stuttgarter Platz will confirm.

Kracauer's sensitivity might point to a bad case of claustrophobia if the philosophical element in the sketch were not also evident. As a symbol of the "sovereign indifference of actual history toward the demands

of its significatory logic" (Max Scheler, in 1926), the underpass reflects
the anxiety of an intelligentsia tuned for dialectics, confronting the un-
dialectical coarseness of history. People who count on the dialectic of the
historical process find themselves horrified when the course of things
deteriorates into a pointless muddle of functional "system" and random
anarchy.

Still, the plunge into childish fears the author reports, from simply
crossing through a cellarlike passage, scarcely seems an adequate ground
for his horror. His discontent stems more from the experience of his perception of urban phenomenon suddenly splitting into "construction"
and "chaos," which he had previously been able to blend together in an
image of a pulsing urban life. A polarity Kracauer believed he had long
since overcome in his encounter with philosophical vitalism confronts
him anew from without, as the irrefutable power of the object world.

The crass polarization of Kracauer's sketch reflects the specific coloration of thought in the year 1932. The sketch is informed by a vision.
Kracauer calls for "more beautiful constructions"; he demands that they
also be made "to a certain extent of people." But what can he have
meant by that? Crystalline housings, phalansteries in the spirit of the
French utopians a century past? Marching columns? What mass ornaments could he have had in mind that would promise an anxiety-free
passage through history, apparently transcending the indifference of metallic systems and lived meaning?

POLARIZATION: PERSONA VERSUS CREATURE

Berlin in the 1920s is a "focal point of social disorganization."[2] The
trusted schemata of Wilhelmian social orientation are put to an extraordinary endurance test. If a power structure is rocked by social change
and if, as a result, the conformity-inducing pressure of established living schemata suddenly declines—then there will be some recoil. When
the external moorings of convention relax, when the blurring of familiar boundaries and roles and ideological constellations stimulate fear,
elements of ideological stabilization and schematicism come more force-
fully into play.[3] In a classification mania, contemporary observers of the
social field categorize phenomena ranging from body type to moral character, from handwriting to race.

Thus the 1920s appear to us both as a period of overheated social
mobility, blurred class distinctions, and exaggerated reassertions of old

orienting values and as a decade in which distinctions between friend and enemy, between opposing fronts, are very clearly drawn.

If we had hopes that literature in such times managed to avoid the schematicism of public discourse, the literature of the new objectivity quickly disappoints these hopes. The arts of the new objectivity respond to the times with a paradoxical maneuver. They react to schematicism, on the one hand, by affirming the transitory reality of life in the industrial world, which continues to go without its appropriate symbolic representation. The arts formulate their opposition to the rigidity of the old symbolic order by mimetically appropriating the forces of social disorganization, particularly whenever it appears in the form of the capitalist market. On the other hand, they respond by formulating a logic that outbids the popular mania for classification, raising schematicism to the verge of dead rigidity. Doing so, they expose the dubiousness of the maneuver.

The images of human being conceived under the sign of the new objectivity are marked by the climate of polarization. The converse is also true: new objectivity images lend impetus to polarization. The "naked contemporary" as drawn by the literature of the decade swings between extreme poles: between armoring and exposing; between fantasies of unbridled agency and pitiful creatureliness. We see humanity represented in the form of media idols and earth spirits, as isolated moralists or collective beings unburdening their conscience in social groups. Like flaneurs, they display their eccentricities among the crowds, appearing lost in the anonymity of a sociological type. The "photograph faces of modernity" (Inka Mülder-Bach) make their appearance in the new objectivity decade; in them the signature of individuality is assimilated to the homogenizing conditions of technical reproduction.

The icons of an armored ego go on parade (see Figure 2). A new type joins them, the white-collar employee. As models for sociological construction, these figures turn up in billboard simplicity and in intricate dialectical images: in all of them the subject reveals itself armored to the extent that emptiness is all that remains to be protected. The representational maneuver signals at once a defense against and a lust for the decentering of the subject.

The climate of polarization has a complex relation to the ideology of vitalism, which is widespread among intellectuals at the time.[4] The assumption here is that any particular life currents, viewed in sufficient depth, are characterized by absolute continuity, even if what we see on

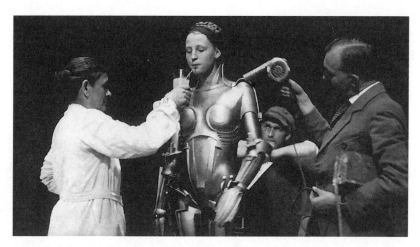

2. The icons of the armored ego go on parade
(Publicity still for the film *Metropolis*.)

the surface are discontinuous and contradictory rigidified forms. Life, in
this sense, has a polar structure, whereby polarity implies neither mechanical separation nor dualism. It is comparable instead to the polar opposition found in magnetic fields, which, in their very polarity, represent
an indivisible unity.[5] As Felix Weltsch had written in the *Weiße Blätter*
of 1913–14,

> The most primal being of the individual is polar: duality and the desire for
> unity: the tension of contradiction and the longing to overcome the tension.
> ... The tension between these two poles gives birth to the horrifying abyss that
> appears at times in the relation of man's spirit to its surroundings, that un-
> canny strangeness of the object, that profound experience of the "something-
> other" status of the world—which, as one side of a polar tension brought to
> its highest pitch, drives toward some kind of overcoming of the tension.[6]

This testimony from the decade of expressionism allows us to identify a sense of life's dynamism as an oscillation between two poles. But
in the new objectivity decade, when "polarized thinking" (Theodor Lessing) had in fact reached its high point, we learn that the pendulum motion can get stuck uncomfortably between the extremes. A central characteristic of the cool persona's habitus is its marking of boundaries
between spheres, causing the polar attraction to operate secretly beneath
the surface. Before the new objectivity construction, polarization was a
surface aspect of the life stream; now, as either a gradual development
of the concept or an abrupt effect of the shock of world war, the polarity has worked its way into life itself, splitting it in two. Whatever idea

of a unified life remains in the arts of the new objectivity has so little force as to rule out any chance for synthesis or any pleasure from oscillation between the poles.

Moreover, phenomena produced by radical separation, in contradiction to the idea of wholeness, begin now to exert a great aesthetic appeal. Literary characters carry about with them the shadow of their counterpoles: the "ice-cold" functionary stands out against the "warmth" of traditional working-class culture; the creature in need of warmth exists in contrast to the "glacial" types of civilization. A complex man is depicted in flight through a gallery of women. The restless street poet is surrounded by sedentary hordes. The pressure to polarize divides characters among mobile inhabitants of the cold system and those still living in the world, among practitioners of the art of distinction and others mired in their own being, among questing "gents" and clutching innocents. The arsenal of human images compiled by new objectivity artists lives off contrast:

> On the one hand, glass—on the other, blood. On the one hand, fatigue—on the other, ski jumps. On the one hand, archaic—on the other, contemporary, with a hat from Bond Street and a pearl tie tack from the rue de la Paix.[7]

If the "phenotype" of modern literature, described here by Gottfried Benn, retains contradiction within itself—revealing the action of diverging force fields through fissures in the character—the literary inhabitants of the new objectivity still show the scars but behave as if they had overcome the split. Should a character, contrary to the rule, appear as a torn and problematic individual, what the narrative represents is his inevitable downfall. Characters conceived as survivors lose all trace of individuality.

What follows is a depiction of aesthetic figures, the "cool persona" (see chapter three) and the other-directed "radar type," as David Riesman would name it two decades later (see chapter five). What we shall see in the two images are symbolic sleights-of-hand designed to free people of the anxieties induced by the process of modernization, to open up for them areas of free movement.

But anxiety falls away from the figure of the cool persona only to return in that of the *Kreatur*. The image of the creature was known from primal sources; it was readily available for reuse. The process of thinking it through once again, in the absence of institutionalized amelioratives (not even social welfare or therapy) represented a new challenge.

The peculiar positive revaluation of the creatural in this decade, in which, under the sign of objectivity, the dominant character is some variant of *homo faber,* serves to open a "sally port out of history."[8] "Natural characters" suddenly appear, distracting attention from the dark side of the historical process.

TRAFFIC AS A PERCEPTUAL MODEL

The central topos of new objectivity literature is "traffic" (*Verkehr*), which transforms the avant-garde's understanding of motion. The arrow of progress now turns back on itself, describing a circle. The new topos redirects wartime mobilization to civilian tracks; when the period of stability and neutrality runs its course, the traffic flow will be militarized once again.

Yet for the time, in the peaceful middle years of the republic, traffic suggests the civilian sensitivity that blends functionalist perception and the idea of systems with revaluation of codes of conduct and a delight in urban circulation. In 1924, Helmuth Plessner contrasts the deadening air in a community to society's "open system of traffic among unconnected individuals."[9] In the space of this public medium excessive demands imposed on individuals by fundamentalist values lose their force:

> In every aspect of the traffic system, the lawfulness of pure values must be sacrificed to the idea of a completely realizable order. The medium, the clear light of which both distracts and obscures, is the inescapable disconnectedness among individuals operating in the existential sphere bounded on the one side by familiarity and, on the other, by objectivity.[10]

Intersubjective traffic systems may be mechanical, but they safeguard distance, which is to say, freedom of movement. The functional topos of traffic promises to vent some of the heat generated by the oppositional constellation of the postwar years.

The traffic image is neither self-evident nor self-supporting but appears instead in alliance with the provocative appeal of Fordism, as evidenced by Ezra Pound's "Definitions," published in the January 1925 issue of *Querschnitt:*

  1. A good state is one that impinges least on the activities of its citizens.
  2. The function of the state is to facilitate traffic, i.e., the circulation of goods, air, water, heat, coal (black or white), power, and even thought; and to prevent citizens from infringing on one another.[11]

And the effects of the topos are considerable: traffic transforms morality into objectivity, compelling behavior appropriate to function. Taking
part in traffic is a provisional status; inserted in the prescribed current,
the individual derives from it a feeling of freedom. It is not a place to put
down roots. Expressive behavior, moreover, is of interest only as the play
of gesture. In traffic, an arena is identified in which every sign is a signal
guiding motion: stopping, jamming, releasing, regulating. Points of rest
are provisional: the waiting room, foyer, railway compartment, subway,
elevator, bus stop, reloading depot, planning office. What causes discontent is the sudden interruption of the flow, the occurrence of tedious traffic jams. Such blockages, in turn, can be referred back to some disturbance, the elimination of which can be effected by technical means. That
the traffic circulates around an empty center is all right, is not a distraction. On the contrary, the loss of a center is animating; it allows the
senses to focus on circulation itself.

> To be mentioned above all in this connection is the penetration from all sides
> of rhythmic processes, and then the ensuing changes, how they give rise to high
> speeds. There are already major areas in which our actions are becoming in
> creasingly oscillatory, becoming reflex; this is true in particular of traffic.[12]

Kracauer observes an astounding array of communicational forms
in the signs of traffic in 1926. The simple gesture with which a greeting
is exchanged between taxi drivers and traffic police, for example, transcends the familiar categories we usually use to describe relations between state agents and private persons:

> It is scarcely possible to measure how fleetingly the greeting is accomplished.
> The policeman is occupied with difficult arm movements, which he must exe
> cute according to rigorously standardized stipulations. The driver, let us call
> him A., must divide his attention between the steering wheel and the official
> arm movements of the policeman.

Neither a hierarchical nor a collegial relationship characterizes their
greeting; Kracauer is more concerned to emphasize the context of the
encounter as effected by the system:

> What connects the driver with the traffic police is the constant utilization of
> the roadways for the sake of the generality of traffic. These two categories
> of work contribute more to maintaining the flow than any others.

Traffic is not a dreadful image in the mid-1920s; the egalitarian joys of
circulation ("Everything traffics with everything else; all the barriers are
down") echo the relief in an end to the horror of Wilhelmian rigidity.[13]

New objectivity writers always observe traffic with an ambiguous grin; nothing must escape the functionalist gaze. Thus the term *Verkehrsro-man* (traffic novel) accounts for a good portion of the prose, and we can view both Kästner's *Fabian* and Bronnen's *O. S.* from that category's perspective. The designation *Verkehrsdramen* casts light on the stage of new objectivity behavior, which twists communication, as in plays by Ödön von Horváth, Marieluise Fleißer, and Bertolt Brecht, to the requirements of the traffic paradigm.

The motto of the new objectivity—"Not expression—but signals; not substance—but motion!" finds in traffic both a milieu and the necessary latitude for movement. Whether behavior is appropriate or not, extending all the way through to entire lifestyles, is judged according to the model of traffic. "Streamlining" makes it possible "to overcome resistance elegantly, not by increasing exertion, but by adapting smoothly to the nature of the resistance."[14] From major urban squares to the living room, arrangements are tailored to the traffic paradigm, as a functional "system of movements" (Hannes Meyer). There is no room left here for an alternative to a functionalist descriptive vocabulary. When the Berlin city planner Martin Wagner defends his concept for the reconstruction of Alexanderplatz, his new objectivity squares render excellent service:

> The major urban square is a nearly continually busy traffic channel, a clearing-point for a network of arteries of the first magnitude. . . . The capacity of a square to bear traffic is in turn a function of the traffic capacity of the streets leading into and out of the square. . . . Traffic flow on the square must be set in relation to stationary traffic, which attracts the consumption power of the masses of people crossing through the square (shops, bars, warehouses, offices, and such). . . . A major urban square is both a stopping-off point and a channel for flowing traffic.[15]

Motion diagrams also set efficient mobility patterns between table, stove, and pantry. Making work easier is equivalent to accelerating the pace.

Traffic does not oblige its participants to a heroic pose: the "achiever's face should remain unmoved," runs the advice in 1932. "The modern smile has, among other functions, that of concealing all inner tension. The lady at the wheel of a car must at every moment maintain her elegance unblemished by exertion."[16] If the avant-garde goes on declaring the *de*automation of perception and behavior as a goal, nevertheless the choice of traffic as a topos identifies a context that calls for reflex-driven behavior. The acceptance of reflex goes hand in hand with another insight: "The human stream is also guided by habit. The power exercised by habit exceeds that of the great revolutions."[17] The traffic model serves to bring to mind the superiority of the supra-individual system that directs the behavioral forms. The simple observation of a traffic signal leads to penetrating insights:

> On the most important intersections in Berlin, as we know, colored signal lights regulate traffic. The red stoplight does not, however, switch immediately to green, which signals the right of way, but changes first to a glowing yellow. Yellow signals a transition from one determinate state to another. It admonishes pedestrians and drivers to pay attention and relieves them of the need to consider people and vehicles that a sudden change of signals would otherwise require. To a certain extent, the use of a transitional light objectifies consideration and takes the initiative out of human hands.[18]

Police, no longer carriers of sovereignty, turn into "traffic officers"; the contents and typography of newspapers are determined by traffic, as is evident in any streetcar; the market in signs and symbols adapts itself to traffic; people are separated into "pedestrians" and "drivers," and the solitary figure moving against the flow is granted the special status of the flaneur. Not only the engineer in general but the traffic engineer in particular becomes a prominent figure.

When traffic becomes the central topos, beings who want to put down roots do not fare well: asphalt streets are taken for granted as the condition of the modern traffic system. "Street poetry" is a medium that, on the one hand, invents the mobile type, probing at the same time the extent to which an individual in this mobility system can represent a disturbance factor. In a certain sense, the civilian traffic topos of the middle phase of the republic had a moderating effect: neither too much armoring nor complete decenteredness is suited to traffic conditions.

The attack on the idea of the republic as a neutral space for traffic ensues from two sides. Carl Schmitt complains, in the tradition of Rathenau's cultural criticism, that in the "age of traffic" society is conceived on the model of the factory, as a "plant, as the gigantic functioning means to some miserable and senseless end," as a system that wreaks such destruction on individuals that "they do not even feel the way they are being annulled."[19] The Marxists, who label the entirety of the social conditions of production and exchange *Verkehrsform*,* use the traffic paradigm in the first instance because it encourages a perspective according to which all ideas can be first tested out in their functional as-

---

* Literally, "traffic form." *Verkehr* has multiple English meanings, including "exchange," as in this instance, but also communication, intercourse, circulation, and dealings.

pect. Likewise they relate language to the "necessity of traffic with other people"; it is "practical and, for other people, existing consciousness." People are to materialize their powers in the forms of traffic. At the same time the Marxists—especially under the influence of Georg Lukács's vitalist update of Marx's writings—lump together all the forms of social traffic in relation to claims raised from the angle of their conception of humanity. They warn against the "domination of objective relations" over the individual and come to the conclusion that the modern forms of *Verkehr*, in a society dominated by private property, will necessarily become "destructive forces."

By the beginning of the 1930s, new objectivity writers are themselves discovering the traffic paradigm's dark side. Images of life pulsing through rationalized traffic constellations, unified and coherent in their mid-1920s presentation, now fall apart again. The vitalist ideal of a dynamic flow, the sense of civilization as the circulation of commodities, labor power, and money, which had for a moment blended seamlessly together, now fractures irreconcilably. Kracauer's image of the underpass introduces the split.

Does the traffic topos form the background structure of modernization, with the agonistic images of polarization, armoring, and schematicism occupying the symbolic foreground? The decade of the republic offers no bounded horizon within which homogenous images could ever arise. What it produces is much more in the way of a mixing. In the literature of the new objectivity, the distant structure of circulation—which is indeed impartial but also civil—moves for a historical moment into the foreground. Literature represents a place where images of armoring and polarization, amid the "frenzy of circulation" (Klaus Heinrich), can be mixed up, and the schematicism of the symbolic order destabilized. At the beginning of the 1930s, a militarization of the traffic paradigm begins. As Arnold Bronnen remarks in 1930,

> The German, whose warrior nature embraces all its mutations, such as ambition, a challenging disposition, greedy commercialism, and contempt for death, apprehends traffic, in the first instance, as a warlike state.

And, he continues, the German

> climbs into the subway and streetcars as if they were transport trains to the front. He scouts out suspicious signs of hostile intent in every passerby, in order to be able to reciprocate immediately.[20]

In disastrous fashion, the dictatorship realizes the synthesis of people and traffic constructions Kracauer hoped for.

Even before that point, in the middle phase of the republic—the time of "exchange cynicism," as Peter Sloterdijk terms it—the civilian topos of traffic models possible images of human being. Quite understandably, the externalities of visible behavior attract attention. Surface psychology comes to dominate the field.

SURFACE PSYCHOLOGY

In the expressionist portrait of the individual, contours fragment, as if the body's surface were splintering under the force of energy radiating out from a central stimulus. In the new objectivity model, contours hold. Eyes peer out like spotlights from beneath a shielding brow, to interrogate space; the body (usually encased in a uniform, for quick sociological ranking) presents an occupational and class affiliation to the gaze of others, who similarly present and interrogate others' performance. The dadaists had prepared the change of perspective. Setting aside the expressionist representation, in which the head stores expressive energies, they opened skulls and put newspapers inside; they networked brains with signs from the print and electronic media. The decade of the new objectivity introduces a figure with his hat pulled down over eyes that, in their expressive dimension, are no longer of interest. The pose of indignation—raised head and steady gaze lending expression to the figure's discontent—becomes antediluvian, an object of parody:

> He strode down the street with his hat tipped back!
> He looked each man in the eye and nodded
> He paused in front of every shop window
> (And everyone knows he is lost).
>
> You ought to have heard him explain that he'd still
> Got a word or two to say to his enemy
> That the landlord's tone was not to his liking
> That the street had not been properly swept
> (His friends have already given him up).
>
> All the same he still intends to build a house
> All the same he still intends to sleep on it
> All the same he still doesn't intend to rush his decision
> (Oh, he's lost already, there's nothing behind him).
>
> (That's something I've heard people say before now.)[21]

In new objectivity contexts the individual appears primarily as agent. The category of social interaction models the characters of literary representation. "Man," in the definition of Plessner's anthropology, "must act in order to live. A single deed is not enough; instead, the restlessness of constant activity."[22] To keep this energy directed along the proper tracks, codes of conduct come into being in the decade of the republic. The codes' schematicism keeps people from getting lost in the frenzy of circulation.

Observing processes of repetitive motion and specifying radii of action move to the forefront in new objectivity literature: attack and defense; crash and rise; circulation and exchange; boundary violations and containment. Rather than introspection, the motto now is movement. As everyone has learned by now, "The way a man moves mirrors the meaning of his life."[23]

"Study ritual—not belief" (Bronislaw Malinowski): the modern ethnologist's methodology characterizes advanced literary discourse; it assumes that perception of habitual behavior offers deeper insights into the mentality of characters than study of what they believe. And the new medium of film intensifies the shift we trace here. Film promises to restore "visibility" to reality, which seemed to have been on the verge of vanishing into the medium of the printing press.[24] The break from dark familial deposits of the soul to externalities of human action proceeds by way of polemics against psychology, which its critics take to cover everything from depth psychology to cognitive approaches. "Psychology hullabaloo," in their words, soaks up attention and almost succeeds in making the physical environment invisible.[25]

The dispute has no place for subtleties: "Personal destiny, the private orientation of the personality is unimportant. Psychology is cowardice. The turn inward has become a turning out."[26] The crude formulation almost conceals the elemental aspect of the shift: the unconscious id has moved from the inside to the outside. An exploration of the orienting mechanisms of the outside world emerges as the reversal of psychoanalysis. A street had been run through the house of the psyche.

Instead of answers to inquiry into the nature of human beings, our investigation of the period leads to a telling disappointment. There is no anthropology to be found; instead, codes of conduct.

CHAPTER THREE

The Conduct Code
of the Cool Persona

Outside an earl, inside a pariah.
       Gottfried Benn

The historical avant-garde of the years 1910–30 is fascinated by characters with simple contours. Free of the complexity of deep psychological structures, these characters appear as "metallized bodies," innocent of organic frailty. Armored, they hold their own in the "force field of destructive currents."[1] They strive for the greatest possible mobility and are constantly alert, "as if they had an electric bell going off nonstop inside them."[2] They avoid public displays of emotion. If they should happen to suffer fatigue, they say only, with Charles Lindbergh in Brecht's *Ozeanflug:* "Carry me off to a dark hangar, so no one sees my weakness."[3] Walter Serner adds a laconic corollary in the *Handbrevier:* "When you're not doing well, make an effort to conceal it."[4]

Characters with simple contours may indeed be "subcomplex," but they have the virtue of being able to make decisions. What they decide on remains in the first instance abstract; what they want is to be in motion inside a process that compels mobility. Avant-garde literature fills out the image, testing out how it will function in the organic world defined by the body.

THE RETURN OF GRACIÁN'S COOL PERSONA

THE PRISONER'S MOBILITY DOCTRINE

"Man has one purpose: life, that is, to move," notes Werner Krauss, a specialist in romance literatures. It is 1943; he is awaiting execution in the Plötzensee prison.[5] "I found myself in a unique situation," Krauss reports later, "without any consideration of its effect on a real or imagined public, to capture the whole of my life in the presence of the word. Ultimately I began an academic work about [Balthasar] Gracián's life precepts, which shortened for me many a dreadful hour."[6] So it is that an appearance is put in at the prison by Fortuna, who (Krauss is quoting Gracián) is not blind but has "the eyes of a lynx" (75), and can be moved by an intellectual appeal.

Our question now concerns Krauss's interest in *The Art of Worldly Wisdom*, Gracián's midseventeenth-century code of conduct, which he reconstructs in the extreme isolation of his prison cell. What he finds in the Jesuit's precepts is first of all a challenge of intellectual engagement in the "border area between humanism and barbarism." Gracián appears to Krauss as an advisor on how to behave in mined territory, where the placement of every step requires caution. In this situation, morality is not a compass you grip in your hand. If threats rain down from all sides, Krauss learns from Gracián, "the whole of morality comes down to tactical rules." Gracián's book offers guidance for situations in which existence has been rendered "incredible" and the truth, afflicted by "signs of a severe flu" (83), has withdrawn to a distant corner.

These few words from Krauss's *Lebenslehre* (1947) may suggest the reason for the resistance fighter's interest in the Spanish Jesuit. In a letter of 26 March 1946 to Erich Auerbach, who was living in Istanbul in exile, he offers a succinct account of the reasons for his imprisonment:

> At the instigation of the former Dean Träger [dean of the Philosophische Fakultät at the University of Marburg], who wanted to get rid of me, I was conscripted into the army in 1940. *Ad arma cucurri,* and I made it all the way to lance corporal. But my brilliant career met a sudden end when I was arrested at the end of 1942 for my part in the Harnack-Schulze-Boysen conspiracy. In January 1943 I was sentenced to death, along with countless others, by the Reich war tribunal. In May, after the judgment had been confirmed, I was moved to Plötzensee for execution. . . . It was possible to manage a transfer and, with the assistance of one of the tribunal justices (who committed suicide after 20 July 1944), to arrange for my psychiatric examination. I was moved from one prison to the other. Only at the end of 1944 was the death sentence commuted to confinement in a penitentiary. New danger from the Gestapo, which wanted to get me out of the military sentence and send me to Buchenwald. My salvation was the hasty evacuation of the Torgau fortress, when I was able to take advantage of the confusion and flee in a hospital train.[7]

The commentary on Gracián took shape in this context.

A list of fourteen of the three hundred behavioral precepts from the *Art of Worldly Wisdom* will help clarify the reasons for Krauss's attraction. The criteria of selection reflect their astounding correspondence with precepts current in the 1920s:

Hope is a great falsifier of truth; let skill guard against this by ensuring that fruition exceeds desire. (no. 19)

Know how to withdraw. If it is a great lesson in life to know how to deny, it is still greater to know how to deny oneself as regards both affairs and persons. (no. 33)

Think with the few and speak with the many. By swimming against the stream it is impossible to remove error, easy to fall into danger. (no. 43)

Never be put out. 'Tis a great aim of prudence never to be embarrassed. It is a sign of the real man, of a noble heart, for magnanimity is not easily put out. The passions are the humours of the soul, and every excess in them weakens prudence; if they overflow through the mouth, the reputation will be in danger. (no. 52)

Observation and judgment. A man with these rules things, not they him. He sounds at once the profoundest depths; he is a phrenologist by means of physiognomy. (no. 49)

Find out each Man's Thumbscrew. 'Tis the art of setting their wills in action. . . . Have resort to primary motors, which are not always the highest but more often the lowest part of his nature. (no. 26)

Do not wait until you are a Sinking Sun. 'Tis a maxim of the wise to leave things before things leave them. One should be able to snatch a triumph at the end. (no. 110)

Get used to the failings of your familiars, as you do to ugly faces. It is indispensable if they depend on us, or we on them. There are wretched characters with whom one cannot live, nor yet without them. (no. 115)

Never complain. To complain always brings discredit. Better be a model of self-reliance opposed to the passion of others than an object of their compassion. For it opens the way for the hearer to what we are complaining of, and to disclose one insult forms an excuse for another. (no. 129)

Never contend with a Man who has nothing to Lose; for thereby you enter into an unequal conflict. The other enters without anxiety; having lost everything, including shame, he has no further loss to fear. (no. 172)

Make an Obligation beforehand of what would have to be a Reward afterwards. The same gift which would afterwards be merely a reward is beforehand an obligation. (no. 236)

The Art of getting into a Passion. If possible, oppose vulgar importunity with prudent reflection; it will not be difficult for a really prudent man. The first step toward getting into a passion is to announce that you are in a passion. By this means you begin the conflict with command over your temper, for one has to regulate one's passion to the exact point that is necessary and no further. (no. 155)

Nothing depreciates a Man more than to show he is a Man like other Men.
As the reserved are held to be more than men, so the frivolous are held to
be less. (no. 289)

Be able to Forget. It is more a matter of luck than of skill. The things we re-
member best are those better forgotten. Memory is not only unruly, leaving
us in the lurch when most needed, but stupid as well, putting its nose into
places where it is not wanted. (no. 262)[8]

All the core ideas of the 1920s cult of objectivity are present here: the
prohibition of ritual complaining; the disciplining of affect; the knack
of manipulation; the cunning of conformity; the armoring of the ego;
the practice of physiognomic judgment; and the reflection of behavior
within a parallelogram of forces.

Much of the advice is difficult of access. "Sitting over this work with
my hands in manacles," as Krauss later recalled, "I understood the paradox of my endeavor."[9] At first what interests the prisoner is only Gracián's understanding of the virtue of restraint (*retentiva*) and the art
of hopefulness (*espera*) — as well as cunning during interrogations, for
which the manual has advice to offer. "A player never plays the card his
opponent expects," states Gracián, adding: "and even less, naturally, the
card his opponent would like him to play."

Krauss's return to Gracián is not, I suggested earlier, an isolated
event. It corresponds to a broader tendency on the part of the European
avant-garde in the interwar years' "trench communities" (Marc Bloch),
namely, its Nietzsche-inspired skepticism about any sort of "organic
phantasm of the personality culture,"[10] which Gracián also calls radically into question. An early diary entry by Krauss, on 12 November
1932, shows how closely the scholar's protean ambition predisposed
him toward his reading of Gracián:

> Become what you are not. Thence man, rather than condition existence on
> change, draws change into his own ego, making of himself a monad deter-
> mined by laws of change specific only to itself, which transforms the outer
> world in the process into a space for personal development. The innocence of
> becoming, as Nietzsche nicely blasphemed.[11]

What interests us here is Krauss's interpretation of the subject in the
courtly codes of conduct. I want to build a bridge from his construct to
the philosophical anthropology of the 1920s and then to track the
codes' fate in new objectivity narratives. At issue for Krauss and his contemporaries is nothing less than an experimental attempt to *de*psychol-
ogize the modern concept of the subject.

The subject with whom Krauss becomes acquainted in Gracián's code has no internal compass to call on when it moves into life-threatening territory. The inner regulator, the conscience, is precisely what the Jesuit has removed from the subject, because the conscience restricts freedom of movement. Gracián has in view a subject that requires an external voice for the sake of orientation. The persona the code presents knows neither the bourgeois's "worldless interiority" nor its Protestant variant, the conscience. Introspection is available to the persona as little as is the direction of conscience, raising the question of how it can establish identity.

Here Krauss discovers in Gracián's code of conduct a procedure that George Herbert Mead and Helmuth Plessner defined in the first two decades of the century as the "reciprocity of perspective." The persona finds its identity by combining the perspectives of ego and alter ego. Gracián's persona acquires an instrumental image of itself by reading the perceptions of others, with which it is constantly vying. Since the shared world in which reflection takes place is "always merciless," and the stakes are survival, the image of itself the persona finds reflected there corresponds to perfectly realistic self-knowledge. The only guarantee of mobility is a high-strung alertness and readiness to cut ties at any time. The complete persona, therefore, must never allow others to affix any firm characteristics on it. A total absence of characteristics increases the radius of action.

Gracián's persona is a master in the art of distinction. All "idylls," which leave this (male) subject open to the wiles of passion, are to be avoided like "traps," as he puts it; arcadian voices stir the nerves; too many possessions "overburden the run," says Gracián, according to Krauss; for "man has but one meaning; that is, to move."

We might well expect Gracián to advise against "excessive individuation" (113). A strain of authenticity could in easier times serve both uprightness and distinction, or even garner prestige. But on a minefield it is clearly a defect, and Gracián warns against it: "Individuating does nothing but attract unhealthy attention!" Little wonder that his *Art of Worldly Wisdom* would be deemed appropriate to a period of total mobilization.

And the maxims of the courtly mobility doctrine reconstructed by Krauss do in fact reappear in the literature of the 1920s. The most extreme version of the code at that time is found in Brecht:

Whatever you say, don't say it twice
If you find your ideas in anyone else, disown them.
The man who hasn't signed anything, who has left no picture
Who was not there, who said nothing:
How can they catch him?
Cover your tracks.[12]

Why such audacity is useful emerges from a review of Krauss's book
in 1950, in the journal *Romanische Forschung*. "If life is a battle,"
concludes the reviewer, who was in equal parts impressed and perplexed
by Krauss's book, "then morality is choosing the most successful path
to triumph."[13] The secret of Jesuit spirituality would be, according to
Krauss, the conception of life as master strategy: the objective is to win
the whole world, with no damage to the soul. But when the Christian
goal starts losing its power to illuminate, the result can easily be double-
entry bookkeeping for the conscience. For if every political path to the
goal is justifiable, means and ends have no necessary ties between them.
The radical methodology of politics prevails, while the Christian goal,
"set on a distant altar," no longer interferes with the method's inner
laws. So goals become interchangeable, an outcome with unfathomable
consequences:

> Reading Gracián is no doubt a pleasure for a Marxist, if only because certain
> of Gracián's formulations all but invite him to strip away the life doctrine's
> mythical wrapping and reveal its valuable core, as the founding genius did
> with Hegel's dialectic.[14]

The possibility of retooling Gracián in this way naturally depends
on Jesuit theology, for which Christ represents not an ethical intervention into the wicked world but the doctrine of virtue's "crowning
achievement."

THE MODERNITY OF THE PERSONA CONCEPT

Krauss's modern analyses of Gracián's concept represent a greater challenge today. "Gracián's persona is faced with the ceaseless task of 'being
somebody' in a hostile and competitive world," writes an American reviewer in 1949, wishing to emphasize the book's contemporary relevance.[15] Krauss's reflections on the idea of a persona reflect the experience of the ego as an illusion.[16]

In 1938, when Marcel Mauss traced the development of the fundamental category of "person" from the masquerade presented in the sa-

cred dramas to the individual figure of moral worth, he had not ruled out the possibility that the same development could be accomplished in reverse. "We are charged with the defense of great good," Mauss warns at the end of his lecture; "with us it is possible for the idea of the individual to disappear."[17] By the time the idea of an "indivisible, individual substance"—an autonomous being with a moral consciousness—comes in for treatment here, various academic disciplines had examined and undermined it, without suggesting anything to replace it. One of the appealing games of the European avant-garde of the first third of the twentieth century had been to follow the developmental descent of the individual's moral understanding all the way down to "mask civilization,"[18] in which the participant manufactures his or her person in rituals. Writers eagerly took up the (dubious) etymology that derived *persona* from *personare*: the voice of the actor sounds through the veil; the ego becomes autonomous only in the consciousness of that which appears to the outside.

As Krauss elucidates Gracián's persona concept, he allows himself to be swept along the current of the new objectivity: self-knowledge, attending to conscience or the possibility of regret, is of little use as a procedure for maintaining an identity. Others' understanding of the self is the royal road to a secure self; for—the language of new objectivity pamphlets left no doubt about it—"the path of knowledge leads from outside in." Krauss borrows the "emphatic image" of the persona developed in 1925 by his teacher Karl Vossler, who was searching for a concept of personal being adequate for both individual and collective use: "From mask or specter, from body or face, departing, in short, from an individual's externalities, the [concept of the persona] aims at our most internal, inalienable self. One is a person to the extent of one's success in arriving at the self by way of roles and their realizations."

Another reference to Vossler's persona follows in Karl Löwith's 1928 book, *Das Individuum in der Rolle des Mitmenschen*. Here Löwith defines the individual "in the existential category of the 'persona'" as the otherwise bounded being whose essential existence derives from social roles, one who is "fundamentally and formally established for himself by means of his correspondence with others."[19] The evidence delivered by others' perceptions is also the source for Krauss's idea of a personal environment, which is the only medium in which affective development can take place. Existence in the form of a persona fixes the individual's reactive character and dependent status in relation to others:

Gracián compares the person with a swimmer who has learned his skill through the threat of drowning. An activating stimulus is necessary—for the only way a person can achieve value is by going into the world. And there is no existence outside this value. The existence of a person is grounded in the unconditioned processes of social behavior. (107)

In a militarized situation, this version of anthropology—in which we hear echoes from the 1920s of Scheler and Plessner and also find concepts borrowed from Vossler, Heidegger, and Löwith—is highly explosive. If the battle gets decided in the social world, which, we recall, is "always irreconcilable," then the individual is compelled to focus attention on matters of self-representation. Orientation—and this is fiendish advice—must be geared to the value judgments upon which social recognition and acceptance depend. There are serious consequences for the persona: under these circumstances, being and appearing do not form a pair of diverging opposites, and the difference between them can be altogether inconsiderable—when it is a question of success. Krauss takes the idea to its logical extreme:

Being needs appearance. What does not appear falls short of recognition. An increase in appearance does not reduce being; on the contrary, it doubles its substance. (111)

Behaving according to the laws of probability (*Wahrscheinlichkeit*) now comes to mean using appearance (*Schein*) to gain recognition for the truth (*Wahrheit*). In such circumstances, objectivity quite naturally gains the upper hand; for prudence in life often demands that the persona behave in a businesslike manner, calculating the value of things on the market (113).

Alongside this motif, with which anyone born in 1900 and educated in the decade of the new objectivity would be familiar, it is of note that Krauss also undertakes a revaluation of the concept of politics by way of Gracián, and that it also corresponds to ideas from the 1920s. Krauss lays considerable emphasis on the claim that Gracián's code of conduct exceeds the bounds of a noble's breviary, restricted to the rules of life around the Spanish court. Court for Gracián is only a model, at once a "gathering place for life's dangerous creatures" and a "tempting laboratory" (119). Court affairs proceed according to life's most comprehensive law, to the forms of mutual obligation that typify aggressive or defensive situations. Gracián, as Krauss concludes in the theological spirit of Carl Schmitt, removes the concept of the political from the autonomous sphere of specialists in the art of statecraft, turning politics into the art of distinguishing, drawing boundaries, making adjustments—which is what anyone engaged in combat needs to do (80).

The political persona cannot get by without a heroizing attitude, another idea that, we shall see, suggests the contemporary relevance of the seventeenth-century Jesuit. Having fenced to the point of exhaustion on courtly terrain, the persona is by no means able to regenerate itself in colorful popular activities, or take part in any history-making mass movement. It must distinguish itself. Gracián fears the people; there is no sign of latent sympathy in his intellectual bearing. "The people appeared to him an obstacle in the path, a harmful power in its lack of understanding" (79 ff.). At this point Krauss's reconstruction of the heroic persona begins taking on uncanny qualities. Gracián's hero must make his way on his own within an aristocracy riven with competition; there is no way to take refuge in a philosophy of history that values his deeds from the perspective of a meaningful progression; there is no getting lost in popular currents. Suddenly visible in the distant mirror of the seventeenth century are the essential features of a heroic attitude in the twentieth: the constructions of the philosophy of history lie in ruins; in the absence of group solidarity or autonomous historical processes, artificial apparatuses in the form of parties are forming; the people are not to be trusted.

Extremely isolated from historical forces that had ever offered reason for optimism, the Jesuit discovers the immediate relevance of theology. Since the exemplary bearing of the heroic individual has lost its anchoring in the "primal force of existence," a theological turn becomes unavoidable. The heroic bearing "requires transcendence, a radiation by supernatural powers, for it to maintain itself in its distance from the people" (79 ff.). What remains of heroism when transcendence no longer radiates?

As Krauss, condemned to death as a member of the Rote Kapelle resistance group, formulates these ideas, he is already thinking in terms of a "popular front" strategy, although his skepticism about popular attitudes at the time of his arrest must have been considerable, judging from his report on a pamphleteering campaign:

> Sch.-B. [Schulze-Boysen] thought it necessary to the cohesion of his group to undertake an action he himself regarded as of minor political significance. Of course it was not a question of using slogans to achieve a propaganda effect, but it quite likely did concern giving the population the feeling that we are

still alive and that power stands ready for mobilization inside. A representative of the KPD [German Communist Party] had been invited to attend the preliminary discussions as a nonvoting observer. Rittmeister hadn't even been informed of the meeting, since his rejection of the idea could be assumed from the outset. Professional obligations kept me from attending the discussions, so I sent Ursula Goetze to Thiel to represent a similar negative position. I thought that the time was conceivably a bad one, given the major offensive against the Russians slated for the summer, where early successes had to be anticipated. My further objection, that the effort was too great and too risky for a merely symbolic action, was dismissed with remarks that the posters had already been printed. Calling the action off now would completely demoralize the group. Once the question was resolved in this way, Ursula, as we had agreed for such an eventuality, declared our readiness to submit to group discipline and take part in the action.

Thiel took over distributing the posters. We pasted up a large number of them around Sachsendamm the night of 17 May 1942. The affair made a big stir in Berlin, but all attempts on the part of the police to track down the perpetrators were in vain. We were mostly hidden at military positions.[20]

THE CODE OF OBJECTIVITY

When social ties fail and extreme agonistic tension fills the space in which individuals interact, the time has come for rules to govern behavior. Alfred Döblin called the Weimar Republic "a republic with no instruction manual." In fact, however, there arose during this period a wealth of codes to guide conduct, from architecture to philosophical anthropology, from sexuality to theater. Each political camp had its own catechism. The disoriented subject was clearly in need of an external voice to tell it where to go and what to do.

In this situation Max Weber offered up his own *Art of Worldly Wisdom,* "Science as a Vocation," his famous address from 1919 that founds new objectivity codes of conduct and simultaneously reveals the dilemma inherent in them.[21] For what sparked further discussion in his impressive document was less the idea of the dialectic of disenchantment or the polytheism of values than the closed habitus of those who want "purely to serve the fact (*Sache*) at hand"—even if it is transient, even if the chain of progress of which it becomes a part is "meaningless," and its final evaluation falls entirely to fate. Weber proposes disenchantment and defiant awareness of fate's demonic power, which the results of the various rational intellectual disciplines cannot sublate. The intellectual style he recommends takes shape from within a particular habitus; because hope is no longer to be vested in the evolutionary process, atti-

3. No summer's bloom lies ahead of us

(Adolf Erik Nordenskjöld. Photo by Graf Georg von Rosen. With the permission of
Archiv Deutsches Schiffahrtsmuseum, Bremerhaven.)

tudes of defiance must counter meaninglessness; their icon is the North
Pole explorer (see Figure 3), as anticipated by Nietzsche. Weber also re-
sorts to this image when, in "Politics as a Vocation," he goes on to warn
against the lures of putative saviors and calls on society to rise to the
challenges of the day:

> No summer's bloom lies ahead of us, but rather a polar night of icy darkness
> and hardness, no matter which group may triumph externally now.[22]

Weber's scientific type of the cool persona also manifests itself in his acceptance of the hard world of objective fact, in which all principles are
relative and all developments are finally a matter of accident.[23] "Disillusioned realism" is the keyword. Karl Mannheim points out that this way
of looking at things is also grounded in fear.[24]

We find in Weber the signature of the new objectivity: "Complete dis-illusion about the age and yet an unqualified commitment to it" (Benja-min). Only one ethical law applies to the scientific guild, and that is the relativism of variant valuations. Yet this ethical law, rather than allow-ing scientists to adopt a more relaxed attitude, makes them tensely alert to any intrusion of ethical conviction into their scientific practice and willing to maintain a defiant stand on the platform of negativity.

The 1920s is a boom period for codes of conduct. But their effective ra-dius tends either to be restricted to expressions of the new objectivity it-self or overwhelmed by the mass of rules they promised to relieve, which are rules generated by surrounding institutions, parties, and political camps. We meet here a generation of intellectuals whose readings of Sorel and Nietzsche, Marx, Le Bon, and Kierkegaard had been influ-enced by experiences of war, the suppression of workers' uprisings, and inflation. They were only all too familiar with the idea that law's origi-nary violence lay hidden in every legal institution, that latently illegiti-mate powers are at home in the houses of parliament. A small turn in the wheel of fortune was all it took for "naked" violence—violence not adorned with the insignia of legality—to emerge from within the ma-chinery of the constitutional state.

In this intellectual context we can perceive the republic as "earth-quake territory" and uncover references to codes of conduct conceived in the violent world of the seventeenth century. As Krauss formulated it, there was a demand for a methodology that promised to "delve system-atically into the warlike character of existence" (120). In Gracián's cool persona observers recognized the figure of a mobile subject, without psychological depth, with a radius of action unhampered by moral intervention or the voice of conscience. Whether this figure merged with Nietzsche's ideal of the "intellectual nomad" or the nineteenth-century dandy, or—one of the tricks of the Weimar intelligentsia—appeared in the uniform of the soldier, the worker, or the Communist cadre, the cool persona had caught everyone's attention.

As Krauss reconstructs Gracián's code of conduct, it has three motifs that take decisive roles in the rejection of ethical commitment and the radicalism of its expressionist offspring:

> Radical expression, as well as all discursive rituals involving expo-sure, confession, and sincerity seem silly to the new objectivity; these forms disarm the self and, as Gracián remarked, have the

single function of provoking the evil latent in the enemy. Impotence, in the 1920s, loses the discreet charm it had enjoyed. "It would be ludicrous to believe," as Schmitt puts it, "that a defenseless people has nothing but friends, and it would be a deranged calculation to suppose that the enemy could perhaps be touched by the absence of a resistance."[25]

In codes of conduct such as Gracián's, the elements of feigning (*dissimulatio*) and "masking [were forms] of resistance to seventeenth-century Lutheran orthodoxy." The Lutheran formula for authentic personal salvation was bound to heartfelt contrition, the free expression of pain, and the activity of the conscience. The arts of prudence and diplomacy, as well as the particular way Jesuits of Gracián's stamp assimilated foreign cultures, were "of the devil," and at the same time fitting instruments in the world of appearance. Proponents of the new objectivity perceive in expressionism and its cult of the scream the tradition of Lutheran authenticity. They opt instead for Jesuit strategies, explore their fascination for the hybrid type of the dandy-soldier. They accept Gracián's slogan—"Appearance civilizes"—in an effort to transcend the traditional division of labor between the cultures of private salvation, on the one hand, and public wickedness, on the other.

Gracián relinquishes the plaintive cry over the loss of a more "authentic" community. In his *Art of Worldly Wisdom* there is no lament about how people have become estranged from some origin. His persona moves inside a space of "seamless estrangement" and accepts it as an inevitable condition.

In Gracián's words:

> Time has moved far from its origin. There is nothing left to do but to live as one can, rather than as one would like to live. It is necessary to regard what fate bestows upon us as superior to what it denies. (86 f.)

In Plötzensee, Krauss discovers his agreement with Gracián in principle. His personal experience of the origins myth of the National Socialist movement has scarred him. In opposition to that kind of fundamentalism, he forms his persona in terms of the necessity for self-defense. Its cardinal virtues are "absolute alertness" and cunning. Krauss uses Gracián's code of conduct to seal himself off from the temptations of irrationalism and the seductions of community. The man he becomes is an actor, a practitioner par excellence of the arts of distinction. The palpable effect of the practice of distinction is coolness.

THE COOL PERSONA AS BOGEYMAN

This figure's prospects could not appear less favorable today. In the last few decades whenever science has focused its attention on the armored subject, the examination has quickly turned into a tribunal. Perhaps in political and rhetorical terms the concept of the persona serves as a neutral technical category encompassing observation of the self and observation by others, but the addition of coolness as a qualifying attribute all but guarantees a negative resonance. From the viewpoint of a culture of sincerity, the cool persona makes a ridiculous impression, a judgment that, in its expression, easily recalls Rousseau:

> Cool temperaments and cool hearts are the active properties of the comedic character, which derives its artistic and reflective senses solely from the brain.[26]

Cool personas are recognizable by their *froids posés;* they are deaf to the heartfelt tones of lament, anaesthetized to all that is authentic. Their strong suit is the exquisite finesse with which they decline to lend their own voices to the *cri de la nature:*

> At the proper time, operating coolly and according to plan, in unchanging conformity to their own will, they bring into play whatever guarantees their self-interest.[27]

In today's climate, the only legitimate interest in the cool persona is antiquarian. As early as 1943 Krauss drew attention to a pair of obvious shortcomings in Gracián's code, identifying precisely the points that had been taken to extremes in the 1920s and that would disqualify it absolutely today: Gracián's precepts construct a purely male world in which gender polarization effectively silences the female voice; the people appear in it only "in the armaments of a major power," which is always hostile to the individual. The rule is "Always armored, never carnivalesque."

It is easy to levy judgment: the cool persona implies a "masquerade of virulent narcissism."[28] All truly human qualities—which, arguably, necessarily involve personal vulnerability—atrophy inside an armored ego.[29] So many easy reproaches beset Gracián and Krauss's new objectivity type nowadays that it would scarcely find life livable. Dissections of the cool persona, stretching over a couple of decades now, have produced ominous results. Studies range from Klaus Theweleit's psychogram of the *soldeska* and Michael Rohrwasser's diagnosis of the functionary to Nicolaus Sombart's illumination of the Schmitt syndrome, from Carl Pietzcker's exposure of Brecht's heart neurosis to Peter Sloterdijk's discovery that the armored ego is depressive at its core.[30]

Feminist research has both multiplied these judgments and rendered them more precise. It uncovers in protective coolness a variant of male self-reflection, identifying in the cult of objectivity and coolness a compensation for the loss of the adjudicating father, and in the code of discretion a patriarchal division of labor (Ulrike Bauereithel), whereby women are expected to do all the work close to the home, while men are allowed to choose work at a distance (Claudia Szcesny-Friedmann).[31]

Already in 1923, Otto Rank conjectured that the remarkable cult of coolness he was witnessing among Weimar intellectuals was simply a "heroic compensation" for the birth trauma arising from the sudden loss of symbiotic community. Others found compulsive behavior of one sort or another embedded in the drive structure of all variants of the cool persona. Concealed behind an obsession with the state or a fetishizing of the collective is, in the words of one author, "men's deeply rooted fear of the female," which stimulates a compulsive attempt to contain phenomena suggestive of chaos or fluidity.[32] Praise of coolness, an acceptance of alienation, the cult of distance, the courage to make decisions: in light of the Freudian teaching on neurosis, the characteristics of the cool persona appear as pathological symptoms. And the symptoms involve more than the deformation of individual beings. The armoring results from a civilizing process that links the idea of autonomy to the disciplining and "cooling" of the affects. The containment of the ego, as Theweleit claims, following Norbert Elias, goes hand in hand with the centralization of state power, so that the autonomous ego becomes something like "a centralized state power in miniature."

If we pursue the question of the self-image implied in the judgments levied today—on the armored self, the metallic ego, the bunker personality—we find code words such as "relaxation," "demilitarization," "meditation." According to this model, ideal individuals live in harmony with their moderate drives, have cast off all "illusions of perpetuation," and have no need to mark off bodily boundaries or zones of discretion. They pursue a policy of "active inactivity."

Thus does Diogenes of Sinope wander unwittingly into the civil war scenario of the Weimar Republic. He delights in the functioning of his organs, murmuring:

> Where we have done nothing, there's no tiger on the loose and difficult to get off of. Those who know how to let things alone do not get dragged along by out-of-control projects; those who practice abstinence do not get caught up in the automatic self-replication of unrestrained physicality.[33]

Is it possible to imagine that society's power plays actually stop short of some realm of "unrestrained physicality," as this image suggests? In this free space, can the human psychic constitution really be "tigerless"?

SEVENTEENTH-CENTURY ANTHROPOLOGY IN THE TWENTIETH CENTURY

From the standpoint of the therapeutically inclined anthropology of the 1970s and 1980s, the leitmotiv of the code of coolness sounds a bit shrill, the more so when set to the inimitably subtle lines from the "Ballad of the Inadequacy of Human Planning," a popular song by Brecht:

> Man is no good at all
> So kick him with your boot.
> If you kick him with your boot
> Then maybe he'll be good.[34]

Through the halls of the republic, from early dada pamphlets ("Man is not good; he's a beast"—George Grosz) to Brecht's *Flüchtlingsgespräche* ("Man is good, veal is delicious") resounds the scorn of new objectivity intellectuals for the idea of inborn goodness; it echoes, for example, in the title of Leonhard Frank's very successful 1919 collection of stories, *Der Mensch ist gut*. Robert Musil, examining goodness in the light of functionalism, comes to the conclusion: "For a good person does not make the world good in the slightest. He has no effect on it whatsoever; he merely distinguishes himself from it."[35]

The view of man as harmless, according to Carl Schmitt, is either the quaint touch of a naive anthropology or the symptom of an infantile disorder, such as expressionism or some other comparable radicalism. Max Scheler sees salvation only in an energetic embrace of asceticism, which he supposes might help repress and sublimate destructive drives.[36] Helmuth Plessner warns against the "inherent baseness" in human beings.[37] Sigmund Freud speaks ironically of those good sorts who deny the ubiquity of destructive drives: "For 'little children do not like it' when there is talk of the inborn human inclination to 'badness,' to aggressiveness and destructiveness, and so to cruelty as well."[38] We find the dictum, again in Carl Schmitt, that every "genuine" political theory, as well as every "genuine" political anthropology, must assume from the outset that man is by nature a dangerous, a "risky being."[39] And Ernst Jünger calls attention to "nature's dreadful sneering laugh at the idea of its subjugation to morality."[40]

Seventeenth-century ideas stressing the destructive potential of human drives, as well as remedies cooked up to tame them, surface among avant-garde writers of every description.[41] In political theory, whether delivered on the stage or propounded in scholarly treatises, they focus attention on the "tiger's leap into the seventeenth century." There is an undeniable appeal to the logic of extremes. The figure of the crude "wolf man," which appears amid the wars of religion, is as fascinating as the horrors perpetrated in opposition by the burgeoning state machinery. What attracts the radical intelligentsia here is the implicit "aura of artificiality" because, whatever violence it entails, it promises to keep man's natural impulses in check.[42] A corresponding image also emerges: the figure of the subject, awash in this aura, lacking in conscience, dependent on external voices for guidance.

Walter Benjamin reconstructs the "catastrophic landscape" of the seventeenth century in categories that describe the intellectual situation after the war:

> The beyond is emptied of everything in which there is even the faintest breath of the world, and the baroque takes from it a multitude of relentlessly formless things, at the high point of the period exposing them in drastic form to the light, so as to clear out this one last heaven and, as with a vacuum, make ready one day catastrophic violence to destroy the earth.[43]

A view from the perspective of this nihilistic landscape makes available the conceptual image of a negative theology that will prove critical to twentieth-century dialectics. Since the path to redemption has been set off on the detour of transcendence,

> German tragedy has buried itself in the inconsolability of its earthy state. If it knows any redemption at all, it is one rooted in the depths of this fateful development itself, rather than in the completion of some divine scenario of salvation.[44]

Philosophical discourse in the seventeenth century undermined the theological assumption of an internalized seat of judgment and control, drawing attention to the obvious conclusion. Only the external force of social control mechanisms, along with a mutual neutralization of the affects, could ever produce any measure of morality.[45] John Locke began with the assumption that the human soul holds no natural inclination toward the good or judgment capable of effectively checking dark impulses. Whatever it has in the way of natural drives, he noted, tend more to destroy than to enforce morality. Reward and punishment, the external means of encouragement and deterrence, are the only things capable of getting moral law a hearing. Nor did Thomas Hobbes, shifting control to the state, trust inner impulses or the subject's action in anticipation of state rationality. Carl Schmitt, who refers to Hobbes, claims emphatically that the retrieval of seventeenth-century black anthropology has nothing to do with exoticism or a taste for cruelty. It corresponds much more, as Schmitt puts it, to the "real nature of being" in the twentieth century. It may be denounced as a return to the "atavistic remnant of barbaric times," but postwar reality warrants no other alternative.[46]

In his polemic against the fixed idea of "inborn goodness," Schmitt reveals a dangerous aspect and leads us along another track. From Schmitt's perspective all the talk of goodness is not only a sign of naïveté and pious humanism—liberalism's rallying call—but, far more alarming, an index of anarchism, which lays the blame for perversions of goodness on the state. In both liberalism and anarchism he sees subversive forces working against the state: the one by demoting it to a mere instrument of the market and replacing struggle by never-ending liberal "palaver"; the other by dissolving it altogether, abandoning institutional restraint for the descent into chaos.

For Lorenz von Stein, the greatest threat is from political liberalism, the way it strives for the "blurring of boundaries between hostile elements," the "interpenetration of opposing forces" through the medium of parliamentary exchange. In the face of this danger, the armored ego opts for defiance (though Schmitt is eager, by way of a kind of "authoritarian liberalism," to cozy up to industrial capital).

In the course of retrieving the negative anthropology of the seventeenth century, the thirty years' war of modernism (1914–45) also involves a remarkable resurgence of rules of prudent behavior, likewise a growth industry in that catastrophic century. Having lost the mooring of an external metaphysics, people begin scavenging the ruins of historical systems for an orienting codex of conduct, which is to say, the tools of self-stabilization. The principles underlying Hobbes's precepts of rationality return in modern variations:

1. Always follow that system of rules which, if enacted, promises you the greatest personal advantage.
2. Follow these rules even in situations in which violating a rule promises greater personal advantage than conforming to it.
3. It is unreasonable to continue following this system of rules when generalized nonobservance transforms the greatest advantage that would pertain given general compliance into the greatest disadvantage.[47]

The fundamental right in a violent world is the right to dissimulate. "Open-heartedness," as the decade of expressionism finally learns, is an unerring index of self-surrender. This explains why the time is so favorable for the political-pragmatic genre of conduct codes and the associated rhetoric of dissimulation. In the decade of the new objectivity the idea dawns that seventeenth-century rhetoric was far advanced over the critical concepts of the eighteenth, "because it reflects the mediation of communication, the polyvalence of signs, and the opacity of relations."[48] This discovery, of course, goes hand in hand with a fatal underestimation of the modernity of the eighteenth century, in particular its discovery of "history."

Along with the use of external force to rein in dangerous drives and a set of behavioral roles to enhance stability, the new objectivity reclaimed a third element from the world of eighteenth-century thought. This is the construction by Hobbes of physics as the scientific foundation of ethics and his conception of man as a motion-machine.[49] "Coolness, as a tendency," Osip Mandelstam reminds us in his 1930 commentary on Dante, "stems from the incursion of physics into the moral idea."[50] Hobbes's perception of reality is physicalist in tone: the world consists of moving bodies; mental processes are an element in this system of mobility. Subjectivity appears to him as a "thing among things" and results in an increase in the reflexivity of behavior. Reason is a kind of compensating apparatus within the mobility system of the individual person; it harmonizes the dynamics of personal drives with state power.

The avant-garde greedily took up these aspects of an anthropology that had been overwhelmed by the nineteenth-century cult of psychology; they also filtered out the last traces of humanism in which Hobbes's anthropology was embedded. While few today would assert that Hobbes had reduced social action to the "reflected reciprocity of instrumentalization" (K. O. Apel), we can barely imagine the aesthetic appeal in the 1920s of the behavioral liberation implicit in that standpoint.[51] The idea of all actors' awareness that their counterparts were equally interested in harnessing others to their own private aims inspires Serner's scenarios of the gangster world and structures a few of Brecht's plays. Hobbes saw a world in which closed-off individuals compete with one another to increase their power and in which nothing, neither consensual understandings nor talking cures, could draw them out of their "private opacity." To a generation of the avant-garde, for whom nineteenth-century psychology did nothing but point toward impotence and paralysis, here was a welcome environment.

HELMUTH PLESSNER'S ANTHROPOLOGY: CLOAK-AND-DAGGER, NEW OBJECTIVITY–STYLE

"This radical thought of modernity, the Weimar symptom," Peter Sloterdijk concludes his analysis of cynicism,

> uncovers emptiness at the pole of the self and otherness at the pole of the world; but how an emptiness is supposed to recognize "itself" in an otherness is something that our reason, with the best of wills, cannot imagine.[52]

At the beginning of the 1920s, Helmuth Plessner could well imagine a form of self-knowledge that specifically did not opt for the path of introspection Sloterdijk has in mind. Plessner's assessment of the intellectual situation corresponds to Sloterdijk's dictum: the heavens of metaphysics, following the world war, are "cold and empty." "Vacuum" was a popular scientific term at the time, used to designate that condition; the 1918 revolution had been termed a "vacuum cleaner." Plessner captures the disillusion in a statement that many of his contemporaries would have underwritten: "Nothing may be expected of an arch, except that it will collapse."[53]

Where the heavens no longer arch protectively over the individual, where the "endless cooling" of modern society provokes fright, "the warm glow of community," in Kracauer's words, looms as an ideal haven.[54] But he, like Plessner, warns against a panicked flight into security. Plessner outlines a code of conduct suited to the "coolness of society" (11–133). His *Grenzen der Gemeinschaft: Eine Kritik des sozialen Radikalismus* appeared in 1924.

Combining the concepts "community" and "radicalism" in a single title, Plessner addresses himself to one of the central aspects of German ideology. Community (*Gemeinschaft*) stood as a polemical term opposed to society (*Gesellschaft*) during the 1920s, suggesting a return to a lost "original and natural condition" of unity, which Ferdinand Tönnies had already formulated as early as 1886 as a contrast to the dispersion and fragmentation of civilization.[55] Sociologists of the 1920s also gave considerable analytical credence to this distinction. Theodor Geiger recognized in community the regulative idea of that legendary symbiotic "form of being, in which I am aware of not being separate from others."[56]

With the term "radicalism," Plessner attacks worldviews based on a conviction that there was any good to be had from "a return to the roots of existence." To the wish projections of "primary unity" and radical therapies, Plessner opposes his behavioral doctrine of distance and bases it on the anthropological principle that every human being, from the moment of birth, leads an incomplete existence. "That is why man is 'by nature' artificial and never in balance."[57]

Plessner's text draws its polarity schema from a long iconographic tradition that associates images of community with the warm pole and those of society with the cold one; in this dualistic model, society is a sphere of permanent separation.[58] Plessner resolves to make his "way into the glacier" of society (Theodor Lessing). In this glacial space, the point is to save face.

Plessner understands the reasons people would wish to immerse themselves in a "warming sphere of trust," but he sees what he believes are fatal shortcomings in communitarian ideology.

> The idea of community harbors the illusion that it can overcome its inherent violence. It masks the life-saving function of differences among individuals, obscures internal hostilities and the necessity for spheres of mistrust, which it projects outward. Community forgets too easily that it necessarily operates inside the technological forms of social intercourse and comes into being only by setting itself off from others.

> The fundamentalism inherent in the notion of community works a ruinous effect on the individual. The "purism" of its system of values tears down the individual's bodily boundaries. Its cult of "genuineness" is a close relation to terror; its demand for "authenticity" appeals to a substance that simply does not exist.

> The cult of "essentialism," which community puts at the center of its concerns, is a phantom; in the light of a code of conduct, it dissolves into nothing.

Plessner often mentions contemporary artistic and literary disputes, especially whenever he senses the presence of the cult of sincerity, which is the immediate target of his code of conduct:

> Industrialism is the exchange form, expressionism the art, and social radicalism the ethic of tactlessness. The cry for physical hygiene, which contents itself with overhead lighting and tiled walls, is the perfect accompaniment to an art that will stop at nothing to get at the essence of things, to a morality of reckless sincerity and the acceptability in principle of causing oneself and others pain. (110)

Plessner does not tolerate the enactment of "naked honesty" or "eruptive authenticity" either in contemporary design, whether the new objectivity interiors of Bauhaus architecture—"with overhead lighting and tiled walls"—or in expressionist stage sets. Hygiene resides for him at the cold pole, "reckless sincerity" at the warm. He takes aim at all forms of unmediated directness, pleading for moderate temperatures and indirect lighting, for art and literature of whatever type as long as they eschew intimate self-revelation in favor of the regulating practice of distance.

Here Plessner not only adopts motifs from Georg Simmel's sociology and takes up Max Weber's opposition to an "ethics of personal conviction." His voice joins that of others, from avant-garde manifestos to vehement communitarian ideology itself, all of them reacting to negative wartime experiences and the old order's decline. The Hungarian aesthetic theorist Ernö Kallai writes in a 1923 manifesto:

> Constructivism is a-ethical. . . . Ultimately there is no wiser humanism than one that takes specific and effective steps to protect us from constantly colliding with the interior lives of others. . . . It is better for us to devote our efforts to securing for each individual the free space necessary to separate him from his nearest and dearest. This means more fresh air for everyone, more mobility, unprejudiced openness, and—fortunately—less monumentality, heroism, and tragic ethos.[59]

Unlike the avant-garde, however, Plessner avoids the anti-heroic bearing that works to such advantage in Kallai's text. Instead, in a move that will assume dangerous form in his 1931 text, *Macht und menschliche Natur,* he finds in his doctrine of distance the underpinnings of an existential pathos.

His earlier manifesto, *Grenzen der Gemeinschaft,* from which the passage quoted above comes, is already a strange and valuable document in the culture of distance. It attacks the "tyranny of intimacy," as the American sociologist Richard Sennett terms it fifty years later in his assault on excessive intimacy.[60] Plessner also shares his aversion for the cult of authenticity with Walter Benjamin, who, glimpsing in the formlessness of pure honesty a "factually and ethically untenable expectation," opposes the "boundless self-revelation" of those who are also often "externally unkempt (the vegetarian type)" to the well-groomed type of the diplomat.[61] In its emphasis on the historical variability of artificial formulas of authenticity, Plessen's text contributes, finally, to a tradition that Lionel Trilling takes up in his *Sincerity and Authenticity* of 1971.[62]

Like Sennett, Plessner argues that the cult of authentic expression generates more suffering than it relieves:

> Sincerity offers no reliable guide to behavior among strangers. . . . A brief collision is necessarily followed by the return of worldly coolness. (107)

Unlike Sennett, however, who mourns the loss of warmth in the public sphere and wants to restore it, Plessner seeks to turn public coolness into a medium that accepts vitalizing boundaries. Sennett looks for orientation to public dialogue in the eighteenth century, while Plessner's theory breathes the air of seventeenth-century French classicism.

Opposed to the overheated images of a closed community and undifferentiated unity, Plessner installs an image of society, which he defines formally as an "open system of traffic forms" populated by unacquainted individuals. What characterizes society in this view is its value neutrality; founded in violence and hostility, it nevertheless has an ever expanding range of possibilities for individual participation. Individuals never appear in Plessner's system in raw form but always in roles; in their interactions with others they define themselves. In the process, people must create a functioning balance for themselves between spheres of trust and mistrust, relying on the instrumentalities of ritual ceremony, prestige, diplomacy, and tact, all of which work to regulate proportions of distance and closeness, objectivity and familiarity. Social interaction, in Plessner's view, requires a virtuoso's ease "with forms that bring people close to one another without meeting, that allow them to distance themselves without causing offense" (80). Plessner aims here at the maintenance of a moderate distance, reminiscent of Schopenhauer's famous parable of the freezing porcupines.[63]

Strong people, according to Plessner, are those who master the rules of the game (society's only "moral law") and surrender to the artificiality of its forms. Any technique that leads from intimacy into distance thus represents relief for the individual. Practicing tact in the private sphere and diplomacy in public, the strong further increase their personal power.

True virtuosos ultimately achieve a kind of aristocratic elegance in their game playing, which was also an aspect of Gracián's cool persona:

> The separation necessarily existing between people is raised to the nobility of distance, in which the forms of courtesy, respect, and attentiveness render ineffective the insulting indifference, coolness, and rawness of people living past each other in a common space. (80)

We return to Plessner's anthropological principles of 1924 only after this reading of *Grenzen* as a code of conduct because, in the light of this reading, the principles appear to reflect a specific habitus. Plessner's directives are not necessarily the result of an anthropology modeled on natural science, although he makes reference to zoology, medicine, and paleontology, presumably in order to represent his code as grounded scientifically in the constitution of the individual. If we are correct in this assumption, then what we have in Plessner's most ambitious work, *Die Stufen des Organischen und der Mensch,* is the naturalization of an eccentric code of conduct.

The principles of his 1924 anthropology may be stated concisely: man is by nature artificial. He is born into the world in an eccentric position and requires the artificiality of a second nature, which is available in the surrounding cultural context, in order to be able to live at all. History becomes a process in which human beings are continually busy developing objective structures to which they submit as the medium and measure of their existence.[64] This recognition of the artificial conditions and forms of human existence will have far-reaching consequences for the development of anthropology; Arnold Gehlen will later erect his theory of institutions on the principle that people are by nature cultural beings.[65] In Plessner's early work, however, we can still separate out the elements of the artificiality axiom, ranging from Nietzschean motifs to the cult of technology, and examine them one by one. We can see how indebted the artificiality axiom is to the polarizing tendencies of vitalism[66]—here the vitalist bogeyman of chilled estrangement abruptly takes on a positive valence. We can understand the switch more readily by taking a brief look at the great mediating figure of Georg Simmel.

Simmel assumes from the outset a fundamental and tragic contradiction in life:

Life in its creativity is constantly producing something which itself is not life, something that is always bringing it to a standstill, something that poses its own legal claims. This something cannot express itself except in forms that are other than it, signifying independent meanings. This contradiction is the real and pervasive tragedy of culture.[67]

Here in Simmel's words we find the intellectual structure of an epoch that constructs tense polar oppositions between internal drives and social compulsion, between the creativity of life and expressive conventions, between unalienated being and reification. Plessner is among those thinkers seeking to transcend a tragic contradiction by giving its polarized expression a surprising turn: only the medium of social compulsion allows drives to develop humanely; conventions alone make humane expression possible. Freedom must thrive within the alienated space of society. The point for Plessner is to accept the developed forms of commercial, convivial, and urban intercourse in their human dignity.[68]

Four years later Plessner reiterates the principle of artificiality, borrowing from the classic formulation in Scheler's major work: "Man therefore lives only when he lives a life." Man realizes himself in social figurations, which make up the natural medium of his existence. Cast out of the nest too quickly, he relies for survival on an environment contrived expressly toward that end:

Existentially needy, internally rent, and naked, man finds in artificiality the perfectly appropriate expression of his nature. Artificiality allows man to travel an eccentric detour to a second fatherland, where he is absolutely rooted in his true homeland. Placeless, timeless, released into nothingness, the eccentric life form creates its own ground. It is his only in that he creates it; only he can carry it. Artificiality in doing, thinking, and dreaming is the internal means by which man comes into harmony with himself as a natural living being.[69]

From such a statement it is possible to derive all the fundamental conditions of the psyche. All psychological expression is subordinate to the systematic lawfulness of artificiality (or, in today's terms, the symbolic order, the public sphere, and institutions); "mediated immediacy" is the lot of man. In order to come to himself, man must first set loose the psychological aspect of his being in a foreign medium.

Joined seamlessly to Plessner's concept of action and embedded in his code of distance, these principles are at the center of his anthropology: the directness and authenticity that the ideology of community demands of the human self is contrary to its nature: "In indirectness is manifest that which is inimitably human." The psyche depends on violent instrumentalities to create a protected zone of distance in which it can unfold. Boundaries expand reflexive latitude. "In nothing is man's freedom demonstrated more purely than in his distance from himself" (106).

Plessner's code is among the more accessible of the documents attesting to the new objectivity of the younger generation that was trying to balance bodily forces that long for community while demanding interpersonal distance. His *Grenzen* is a rare civil and civilizing document of German cultural history, raising a controversial issue, namely, the boundary as the necessary condition of a living body.

As clear as it may seem in retrospect, in 1924 the principle of the boundary had not yet been fully defined. Along with several other intellectuals of the decade—Siegfried Kracauer, Bertolt Brecht, Herbert Jhering, Erich Engels, Walter Benjamin, Ernö Kallai, Paul Tillich, Karl Mannheim—Plessner puts greater emphasis on the anonymity of the public sphere as a necessary medium in which life, in all its shadings of otherness and familiarity, can fluctuate. Remarkably enough—and perhaps thanks to a shared legacy in Kierkegaard, vitalism, or the tradition of cultural criticism—Plessner's description of the public sphere lists characteristics that Heidegger will identify with inauthenticity but assign diametric value to: distantness, lightness of being, restlessness, distraction, uprooting.

In all the phenomena listed, Plessner welcomes the open horizon of potential that characterizes existence. Emphasis on the reflexive aspect of conventional forms frees social exchange among individuals of fundamentalist expectations. The turn away from the complex of "fortified interiority" (Thomas Mann) and the move beyond division into a private sphere of contemplative well-being and public ordeal of deeds open a new chapter in which the horizon of man's ability to do defines his essence. There is no doubt that Plessner is setting out a new formula of authenticity, this one based on the objectivity of the human sciences. It removes the criterion of expressive "genuineness" from the framing conditions in which it had been set previously—impotence, remorse, unconsciousness, and paralysis—binding it instead to the reflection of behavioral effectiveness in reality.

But the deep fissures in Plessner's concept of the person, as well as inadequacies in his arguments and political allusions, remind us that the structure he proposes does not draw on any preexisting cultural tradition, causing it sometimes to appear more the product of high-energy assertion than detailed philosophical elaboration. Notable now and again is the sheer brute force with which Plessner "anchors the reflexive figures of German idealism in the body."[70] Doing so, he reveals fear as an elementary human motivation and installs aesthetic considerations at the basis of anthropological principles, betraying how deeply Plessner's science at its core is yet grounded in the thought of the fathers, continuing the effort to fend off the youth movement's vitalism, which the fathers wanted to forget. It is typical of Plessner's concept of the political in the 1920s that he suddenly sharpens his polarization of the familiar and the strange when he intervenes in ideological disputes (in both texts, from 1924 and 1931). His central concept of the boundary now no longer designates a zone of exchange. Appearing on the scene instead is a highly reflexive individual organized internally around an ego that is strictly demarcated from the unconsciousness of physical being. It appears necessary, in order to act out embodied being correctly, to forget the body. Constantly supervising its borders, the ego exists in a state of permanent alarm.

As others have noted, Plessner's axiom of eccentric positionality rests on the concept of the boundary.[71] The sovereignty of Plessner's persona is beset by the continual challenge of conditions arising out of the natural equipment of every human individual; people constantly find themselves in "border situations," which they can obviously not surmount without the bravura of marking a boundary.[72] Plessner's stage is like a brightly lit fencing hall in which combatants face each other. The hall is closed; there is no opening through which the drives' darker world (or the economy's raw representatives) can gain access. But this image is also skewed. Elementary danger does not threaten from outside or from opponents; the fencers themselves bear it. The more brightly lit the space of reflexive behavior, the sharper will be the shadows cast by a subject's contours. "Wherever a lot of noise is being made about narcissism," remarks Léon Wurmser, "shame is always silently present."[73]

The question is, why must individuals be properly armed to enter the public arena, this patriarchal space? Plessner answers the question with enviable clarity: "Whenever the psyche ventures forth nakedly," he says, "it runs the risk of appearing ridiculous" (70). Here is the one risk that even a man committed to risk must not take. For at stake is dignity, and only armoring can guarantee it. The argument looks suspiciously like a masquerade of virile narcissism. But Plessner welcomes the masquerade as the essence of life in the public sphere; narcissism is a necessary and reciprocal element of the ego's awareness of its reflection in the mirror of others. By marking a boundary between himself and the expressionist youth movement, Plessner augments his virility. And by making these elegant sidesteps, he distances himself from the debacle of the lost war.

There is also a question as to whether any knowledge would be gained by conceding the objections. The tendency at present is to regard exposure as a point of critical superiority; the Freudian theory of neurosis allows us to unmask the dualism of male subjectivity sentence by sentence. It may be more productive, however, to follow the fear of exposure's inner logic. We can get at this logic by considering four different readings of Plessner's central claim that man is by nature artificial.

Plessner elucidates the body-mind dualism, around which his anthropology revolves, by examining the "crisis of ridiculousness." At first glance, it may seem as if the principle, "man is by nature artificial," solves with one ingenious stroke the problem of dualism: the body has no natural aspect, because the instinctive level of human being is bracketed within the cognitive, and sense perception is a thoroughly artificial reflex product; "the senses are themselves structured by mind."[74] But that is not the case in the context of Plessner's code of conduct. Here his principle takes the form of a commandment: man should be artificial by nature! A first careful reading uncovers an imperative in the fundamental statement of his anthropology.

Plessner constructs a subject that is required to balance countervailing psychological impulses, as if walking a tightrope: the tendency to reveal and to expose must constantly counteract the tendency to be ashamed and to conceal. Whenever the maneuver fails, resulting in "unchecked affective expression," the psyche appears "naked" in public (in violation of consensual protective conventions inscribed in the symbolic order). The penalty is others' merciless laughter, which, by offending the dignity of the persona, produces shame. From the failures of an ethics of personal conviction and expressionist politics, Plessner learns that the bourgeois public is not the secularized seat of merciful judgment to which the subject may, in creatural impotence, submit without injury. "Uninhibited self-surrender to spontaneous expression" can in certain conditions be fatal; it is in all situations ridiculous. Plessner seeks the reasons for this along several planes. The lack of inhibition in this sense is necessarily disadvantageous:

> For the subject in the grip of an impulse, spontaneous expression occasions an extreme state of emergency, whereas conventional forms keep a state of appropriate animal perception. Moreover, well-worn verbal conventions are available in the symbolic order for such irresistible expressive impulses (one such impulse leads to "kitsch"). Plessner resolves the disproportion between a subject's claim of uniqueness and cliché according to the embarrassing "tickle" of ridiculousness.

> The fantasies of potency accompanying every passion stand in comic contrast to the absolute defenselessness of the passionate subject.

> Passion of whatever sort requires the discipline of form if its bearer is to cut a good figure in public.

Plessner's prescription of artificiality is intended to ward off embarrassment. In defending against ridiculousness, however, Plessner's anthropology gets drawn back into the shaming theater of the Weimar Republic, which it was trying to get away from in the first place.

Léon Wurmser proposes a phenomenological definition of the fear of shame Plessner's anthropology parades before us as an elementary danger. It is "a fear evoked by sudden exposure, signaling the threat of scornful rejection." "All eyes seem to be fixed on the person who is suffering shame, penetrating him like stab wounds." Reactions range from dim anticipation of the consequences to panic. Shame, in its prophylactic function, is supposed to guard the boundaries of intimacy, and so avoid exposure. And exposure, via the processes of shaming, leads to punishment. In this marginal situation, it has failed. In the final analysis, the fear and dread of being ridiculous represent "the fear of being abandoned."[75]

In this fear of ridicule, two opposed moments in Plessner's anthropology collide. First, a living being needs to defend its core identity against the danger of exposure; at the same time, however, this isolated being must go into the world, become acquainted with the human collective, and preserve itself there under tyrannical conditions. Fear of ridicule is one of the most important stabilizing factors among "primitive peoples";[76] it is what guarantees the durability of institutions.

In the fear of ridicule, therefore, two factors that Plessner had largely removed from *Grenzen* make a powerful reappearance in his argument. Intersubjectivity and institutions did not figure in the concept of "natural artificiality," but now they return: a situation of shamed isolation makes it apparent that the core concept had not anticipated them. All the more dreadful, then, is their effect.

A second reading of the artificiality axiom lays stress on both its backward-looking aspect and its aspect of bold innovation. Plessner's *Grenzen* marks a break with the generation of expressionist youth by going back to retrieve elements of Nietzsche's turn-of-the-century aestheticism.[77] From Nietzsche, Plessner takes the art of drawing distinctions regarded as valid among those who are "noble":

> Care for the most external things, insofar as this care forms a boundary, keeps distance, guards against confusion.
>
> An apparent frivolity in word, dress, bearing, through which a stoic severity and self-constraint protects itself against all immodest inquisitiveness. . . .
>
> [Disguise]: the higher the type, the more a man requires an incognito. If God existed, he would, merely on grounds of decency, be obliged to show himself to the world only as a man. . . .
>
> Pleasure in forms; taking under protection everything formal, the conviction that politeness is one of the greatest virtues; mistrust for letting oneself go in any way, including all freedom of press and thought, because under them the spirit grows comfortable and doltish and relaxes its limbs.[78]

Plessner's sociological discovery of roles as a protective medium is informed by Nietzsche's claim that every profound spirit needs a mask; his anthropology centers on this paradox: "Only masked is a man entirely real."[79] Oscar Wilde's motto—"Man is least of all himself when he speaks in his own name. Give him a mask, and he will tell the truth"— echoes through Plessner's code of distance. The obligation assumed by the dandy, "to be as artificial as possible in life," becomes in Plessner's hands a basic element of anthropology. Thus we may conclude either that aestheticism fundamentally penetrates the existential conditions of modernity or that a major work of philosophical anthropology in the 1920s still unconsciously observes fin-de-siècle convention.

The mask theory expressed in *Grenzen*—like the fear of ridicule— reflects the dilemma at the heart of Plessner's anthropology. On the one hand it assumes at the outset that the essence of man consists by nature in a "mediated immediacy"; on the other, it stresses the constant risk of a relapse into immediacy. As a result, there are two aspects to Plessner's mask theory: it counts masks among the artificial tools responsible for making social life possible in the first place; and the mask protects the individual from exposure, ennobling a select few. The first version of masks will later find a place, under the name of roles, in sociology. The foundation is already present in *Grenzen* in 1924: all social intercourse presupposes an "artificial means" (40) to regulate the distance between people. Masks are part of the gestural language of the public sphere; they are inextricable from ceremony and prestige.

> The individual generalizes and objectifies himself by means of a mask, behind which he, to a certain extent, becomes invisible without that causing him to disappear completely as a person. (82)

Those who would find self-realization in the public sphere "have to play the game," in order to produce the effects that characterize their particular function. The game requires a mask. "The maskedness of the public individual" (94), however, not only exists as a formal technique of social intercourse but shelters a precarious inner substance that must not be delivered up defenseless in the public sphere.

"The armored individual," says Plessner, "wants to fence. A form that renders one unassailable always has two sides: inwardly it protects, while outwardly it generates effects" (82). Inwardly, the form of the mask inhibits the "tendency for self-exposure"; outwardly, it produces the effects of the "official physiognomy" (85). It conceals the expressive elements of "eruptive authenticity," which court the danger of public shaming. And Plessner welcomes the mask's dual role because it offers a chance to breathe the cool air of diplomacy. The mask alone displays man's freedom in the realm of artificiality.

Here we see how the findings of anthropology, the moral precepts of a code of conduct, and elements of turn-of-the-century aestheticism blend in Plessner's argument: "It is part of the fundamental character of the social ethos . . . to desire masks, behind which immediacy disappears" (209). At the same time, Plessner's artificiality axiom frees anthropology from the grip of cultural pessimism, bringing it into the range of new objectivity's obsessive interest in precipitous modernization. The realm of artificiality now shifts to technology and the new media: the dueling subject becomes an engineer, with the cult of technology occupying the site of artificiality, forcing individuals from an exclusive fencing hall into a space pervaded by the hum of the electronic media, the noise of rotation presses, the signals of the modern traffic system, and the machinations of power.

The artificiality axiom leads to bizarre collocations in the image world of the new objectivity. In Brecht's *Fatzer* fragments we read: "we are born a second time in the tank"; in the Hauptmann manuscript of *Mann ist Mann* there appears a character who plans to swim out to a coal freighter one day to get to the big city "because he had no parents"; in Bronnen's *Ostpolzug,* we find a subject "born on the seventh floor, nursed on condensed milk." Aldous Huxley's *Brave New World* makes a precocious appearance.

All the scenes of exposure Plessner plays out are characterized by a failure to adequately protect a boundary. People, reduced to defenseless objectivity, are suddenly subjected to the gaze of others; "impotent," they have nothing to present in public beyond their existence as creatures. But that, according to Plessner, makes no "sense." For "sense" Plessner attributes exclusively to the fortification of the closed self in an agonistic situation. His entire attention is occupied with avoiding situations in which "nonsense"—uninhibited affective expression—takes place. Advertising defenselessness, such expression can only weaken the individual. Plessner concentrates on avoiding exposure; he correctly sees in the discursive rituals of confession, which he identifies among the expressionists, the foil to his code of conduct.

Situations in which appearing armed has an involuntary comic effect —and the military getup becomes an index of nonsensical heroizing— escape Plessner's attention because they do keep making sense. But the fixation on situations in which nothing seems to happen beyond armored egos fleeing ridicule is symptomatic of Weimar's new objectivity intelligentsia (and the point of Plessner's conceptual contact with Schmitt).

The image of the displaced man armed for combat became the material for dadaist experiments with disgrace and the psychoanalytic encyclopedia of shame, *Sittengeschichte des Weltkrieges,* by Magnus Hirschfeld. Occasionally such a comic war hero also appears in the theater. In this latter guise we find a man wholly accustomed to absolute unassailability in a situation in which he wants nothing more fervently than to be gently intruded upon and touched. If a woman does not take the initiative to disarm (as she does in Hofmannsthal's *Der Schwierige*), he is left to brood on the iron code of distance.[80] Whenever the armored ego resolves to be genuine, it inevitably turns sentimental. Precisely that sentimentality becomes the trademark melody of the new objectivity.

The question of what prevents Plessner from adopting a comic perspective on the cool persona leads us to a third reading of his principle. It is surprising that Plessner makes no reference in his work of the 1920s to the philosophical anthropology of Johann Gottfried Herder, even though the essential elements of the artificiality axiom are already present in Herder's treatise on the origin of language. "Regarded as a naked animal lacking in instincts, man is the most miserable of beings," Herder writes in his *Abhandlung über den Ursprung der Sprache* of 1772:

> Even in his very first moments this miserable creature, with no instincts, issuing forsaken from nature's lap, was a freely expressive and rational creature, bound to improve himself, as no other course lay open. All his failings and requirements as an animal set him, with all the powers at his disposal, the more urgently to prove himself as man.[81]

Herder's work anticipates both the theory of the environment, which Jakob von Uexküll elaborates, and the doctrine of the artificial sphere, in which man, by nature, must realize himself as man. "From the midst of his failings" (which appear against the measure of the animal economy), poor "forsaken" man finds his composure in relation to the world, which he creates as a "sphere of reflection."[82]

Arnold Gehlen honors Herder as a predecessor in his most ambitious work, *Der Mensch: Seine Natur und seine Stellung in der Welt* (1940). He comes to the conclusion that philosophical anthropology "since Herder had not advanced a single step." Nor need it do so, Gehlen adds, "for this is the truth."[83] In contrast, Plessner does not mention Herder in the works under discussion here.[84] Whatever the reasons for his omission, substantive reference to Herder might have saved Plessner from some of the more obvious failings, crudities, and dualisms that mar his theory. From the outset the theory's sphere of artificiality both stresses the agonistic character of society—which calls for armoring as a basic requirement in the human sphere—and expresses alarm over the danger of unleashed human drives—which require discipline. These elements move Plessner's theory in the direction of the negative anthropology of the seventeenth century and reflect the broader tendency in the 1920s to underestimate eighteenth-century modernity.

The dramatic literature of the seventeenth century shows us Plessner's type, a man "without any human weakness or inconsistency, constantly vigilant, constantly rational, [who] steadily pursues the coolly premeditated plan which goes with his part."[85] Erich Auerbach points out that this type, in Molière's comedies, is absurd. If Molière is looking for instinctive, uninhibited, and sadistic traits in this character, he does so only for the sake of making them appear ridiculous and unnatural. For the court and polite society in seventeenth-century France, naturalness means being fully and effortlessly at ease within reigning conventions; the ease is a product of "culture and breeding," which regulate social intercourse among individuals, maintain distance, and ensure the persona's invulnerability.[86]

We see this construction of the noble persona in Plessner's duelist. It develops at an extreme remove from popular instincts, which Plessner consigns to ridicule, and an alliance with moral wrong only enhances its nobility. Like the tragic hero, the modern subject remains at all costs bodily intact. Stripped of all trace of physical and creatural frailty, it finds in death an occasion for pathos and a lofty style. Yet where a seventeenth-century audience saw in the noble persona a healthy human understanding and an authentic correspondence between what was natural and probable, the modern critic sees a necessarily eccentric character. This claim, of course, does not rule out its appearance on the scene, like the character of the storm trooper commander in Ernst Jünger's *In Stahlgewittern,* as a member of one of Freud's "artificial groups."

The comedic option is not available to Plessner. His phantasm of the dueling subject remains under the spell of historical models that do not allow for the "feminine" solution. This point leads us to a fourth reading of Plessner's axiom. His idol is Bismarck, whose willingness to take risks he extols, whose amorality at the moment of decision has a Luciferian appeal about it, and whose disdain for the bourgeois vernacular he shares. In Plessner's eyes Bismarck is a decisionist of the first order who—in stark contrast to the type of the democratic politician—never indulges in "the luxury of a rentier's harmonious conscience." Spengler had already celebrated Prince Bismarck as the "last Spanish politician." The prince serves Plessner as a protector against all forms of political indignation: "'Disarmament is not a political concept,' wrote Bismarck to a plaintive civil servant in the margin of the file"—as Plessner remarks in full agreement (78 f.).

It is no surprise, then, that Plessner, as early as this 1924 work, does make reference to Carl Schmitt. From the latter's political theology Plessner borrows the notion of sovereignty, transferring it to the individual (at the cost of "romanticizing" it, from Schmitt's perspective). And Schmitt outfits him with arguments against a conviction-based ethics and fundamentalisms of all kinds. Plessner sends *Grenzen* into the world as a kind of operating manual and code of conduct. But its intended audience is not the urban intellectual nomad and certainly not—as my reading of the book as a new objectivity manifesto might suggest—the masses. Its advice is meant to fortify the "ethos of rulers and leaders." Plessner consigns the rest of the public to the dark schema of oppression: "The majority remain unconscious; that is why they serve" (78 f.).

Plessner's concept does leave open one place beyond reach of the fencing hall and its public treachery. It is a private place, and the calm available here owes nothing to the cool persona or the combatant. Its source is a figure who has made no earlier appearance in Plessner's anthropological arena. The figure is woman. By the "merciful gift" of her love, a man can, exceptionally, let himself go. Except for this glimpse, Plessner allows woman only one more appearance, as a single line in the code. He settles her down outside the sphere of life ruled by power and contents himself with the remark that woman, "as we know from the romantics, [is] nature at home with herself" (76). Banned from the world of artificiality, as in the eighteenth century, woman is still the preserver of first nature (see Figure 4), because she is incapable of realizing an identity in the "second fatherland" of the symbolic order.[87]

This exclusionary clause reminds us of the axiom's fourth reading: man is by nature artificial. In his scholarly memoirs, Plessner simply places the infant boy on the fathers' stage in the form of a little organic bundle, but it also fits the logic of Plessner's principle. His mother does not appear. From the very outset she is absent—barring the possible presence of a woman waiting offstage, to see to the regeneration of the weary warrior.[88] At this point the marked similarity between Plessner's work and Gracián's *Art of Worldly Wisdom* becomes easy to explain. If we compare both documents with French epigrams or English conduct books of the seventeenth century, or even with the elegies of John Donne, what immediately strikes the eye is the German deficit.

The intellectual avant-garde from 1910 to 1930 loved referring to pre- and nonbourgeois cultures. Thus we encounter in Plessner's *Grenzen* the cloak-and-dagger tale of a shame-based culture. There the ego experiences "the collective of others as eagle-eyed inspectors"; a vigilant public has dug itself deeply into the individual's interior. Plessner's persona is constantly beset by rivalry in a theater of its own imagining. It is not conscience but the public, that, as the source of ultimate judgment, metes out punishment.[89] That is why Plessner is fixed on the desire for masks as a "safety factor" for human dignity. Masks are the only way a man can gather his strength on the stage of a culture based on shame.

4. Woman is still the preserver of first nature

(Karl Hubbuch, *Martha mit Bauhaustischchen* [Martha with small Bauhaus table], ca. 1927.
With the permission of Myriam Hubbuch.)

Reading *Grenzen* as a manifesto of the new objectivity seems to confirm a thesis Peter Gay elaborates in his analysis of Weimar culture. He
identifies in the new objectivity the return of the fathers, a finding that
has since been reinforced by some feminist research, which sees in the
cult of objectivity a compensation for fatherlessness.[90] We shall see,
however, that this judgment, though applicable to a number of programmatic statements, misunderstands what several important works have in
mind for the recalled patriarch. The reactivation of the dark side of the

fathers' generation, as well as comparisons between it and the youth movement's call for immediacy, takes place in literary texts, to which we now turn our attention.

ALTERNATIVE IMAGES OF MAN
IN THE NEW OBJECTIVITY DECADE

Do you know what they call the Leidenfrost phenomenon in physics? Alfred Döblin asks Hocke, an idealistically inclined student, in 1931. It has to do with the way a drop of water will dance over the surface of a hot plate. Were the drop of water to think about it, says the materialist, it would consider itself free—as you do. It would sing proudly of its magnificent ability to defeat the law of gravity and dance.[91]

By referring to this minor miracle of physics, Döblin is at once satirizing contemporary materialism and offering a corrective to the wide-eyed naïveté of the student, who had insisted on the autonomy of the will:

> I acknowledge the force of the economy, the existence of class struggles. What I do not concede is that these economic and political phenomena proceed according to physical laws that are beyond the reach of humanity. People are involved in these phenomena, people like us, as actors and, if it can be put this way, when we drive or when we're driven. People don't just take part in them. No, class and class struggle are the living phenomena brought into existence by the social being called man. Perhaps not everyone is able to examine economic theories in their abstraction . . . , but more than a little is known about man, about individual being and about social being. For example: that we operate with values, with judgments, and preconceived notions, that more elemental instincts are right there in the background. Those considerations suddenly put a different face on the economy, and even more on intellectuality, which otherwise always looked something like nice boring literature. It has teeth. It does indeed bite. It is there, and there in a way that is quite like ourselves. The economist juxtaposes "empirical conditions" and "mere will" with great discipline and precision; but he obscures the fact that the will is part of empirical conditions. What happens in the economy may well have a lawlike aspect to it—today it is the crisis cycle, the way the process is driven by crisis—but the way people react, the way they make judgments, their specific social way of having values and applying and practicing them, is involved in the lawlike systematicity of economic processes—it is internal to the economic laws. Such tricks! The vulgar Marxist turns the economy into a fetish, a thing like "fate," and everyone is terrified and starts fainting. What makes people faint—is themselves. We are ourselves the beings whose fates play out here. Images, personifications, and word fetishes serve in this way to cripple people.[92]

Döblin is seeking to balance factors that his contemporaries largely regard as terminally irreconcilable. He combines a theory of class struggle with biology, blends value-free scientific investigation with political decision-making, applies the results of individual positivist disciplines—anatomy, medicine, and animal behavior research, for example—to social projects. In short, he seeks to couple political strategies with the anthropological question, "What sort of thing is man?" What kind of politics can be expected of human beings? On what biological foundation can the modernization project go forward? How does the inertial force of existing mentalities deform desirable undertakings? How are economic mechanisms tied to human drives? In harmony with the findings of the philosophical anthropology of his decade, Döblin recognizes that clarification in these areas can only be achieved by overcoming the reigning mind-body dualism.

Against this foil of contemporary philosophical dualism, it becomes possible to define more precisely the specific weight of the human self-image in the new objectivity, and to cast new light on the artistic figure of the subcomplex subject.

We have so far neglected anthropological currents that identify drives as the essence of human being, obscuring the rise of psychoanalysis to a position of considerable influence in the 1920s. It had no institutional power but was so present in the scandal it stirred up that key terms, such as "complex," "repression," and "Freudian slip," made their way into new objectivity jargon.[93] In the theater, plays such as those by Ferdinand Bruckner, which served up a popularized version of psychoanalysis, found a wide public.

Nevertheless, the majority of new objectivity authors actively resisted psychoanalysis, refusing even the technical descriptions of the psyche offered by the new science. Freudian images of the psyche as a regulatory apparatus that absorbs charges, releases them in dreams and aggression, stores up energy quanta in the manner of steam-engine dynamics, do not appear in the literature. Instead, writers reach back to the older mechanical model of the clockwork—but they combine that image with one borrowed from another of the latest scientific models, the electric field.

"Psychology from outside" dominates new objectivity literature. The distinction between inwardly and outwardly directed explanatory models comes from Max Weber: if we talk about the acquisitiveness of an entrepreneur, we can do so "from inside," identifying a passion or interest or some other psychic force with a particular history. From the out-side, however, acquisitiveness is "the orientation requisite upon anyone striving in conditions of competition to act responsibly in the interests of an economic enterprise."[94]

In the literature of the new objectivity, both of these perspectives are internally rent. Shifting attention to the motor and functional aspects of human action causes authors—if they do not simply resort to a black box explanation—to fall back on notions of instinct, which they legiti-mate in the spirit of Nietzsche's revaluation of the barbaric. The Marx-ist term "character mask," in contrast, emphasizes the economic drive forces that act on the implicated subject.

Döblin shows no pronounced resistance to psychoanalysis. His argu-ment resembles in certain respects the views Max Scheler put forward in 1927 in *Die Stellung des Menschen im Kosmos*.[95] Scheler aims his po-lemic not so much against the materialists (he finds the Marxists among them positively idealistic in their conception of man), as against modern variants of decadence. Scheler's own view is informed by the most recent findings in biology, paleontology, and animal behavior research, and by an acceptance of their "dismal" conclusions: in comparison to the ani-mal world, man is characterized by weak instincts, surplus drives, and primitive organ development. It is on these findings that Scheler and Plessner base their views of man's special status, which consists in his openness to the world.

If research by Jakob von Uexküll had proved experimentally that ani-mals inhabit a necessarily species-specific environment and that they be-have according to innate instinctive schemata activated by environmen-tal signals, Scheler concludes that the human being—having mind at its disposal—can separate itself off from the body schema. Behavior can be independent of environment. At the same time, mind impinges on naked drives by way of ideas, which it dangles as a kind of "bait" for the pur-pose of getting them infused with life and seeing them realized in the world. In opposition to another powerful intellectual current, which re-gards mind as an "adversary of the soul" (Ludwig Klages), Scheler em-phasizes the concept of sublimation. Through a "basic renunciation of drives," the mind can offset all the human failings identified by modern physiology and biology. Man's mind makes him into the social being that he is.

This theoretical sketch points out the extent to which physiological factors condition individual human existence. And, more important, it

shows how man, as a natural thing, is outfitted at the last second with
the power of negation, with the volitional asceticism that Max Weber's
construction had identified as the motor of modernization. Thomas
Mann, taking up this anthropology, lays stress on man's limited powers
of resistance in his depiction of the gentleman from Rome in his novella
Mario und der Zauberer. In an age of mass psychosis, volitional asceticism is worse than impotence; the logic of history is such that whoever
would rely on voluntary negation draws ruin to himself like a magnet.
Is this true? Is Scheler's anthropology also a code of conduct?

Max Scheler died in 1928. And in that year a second major anthropological outline, Helmuth Plessner's *Stufen des Organischen und der
Mensch* (examined above), was published. While Plessner remains to this
day in Scheler's shadow, his work shows greater affinity with the new objectivity's characteristic relationism. Among new objectivity common-
places of the period are statements straight out of Plessner—"man is
an ensemble of functions" or "man is by nature artificial"—and, once
in circulation, they prove themselves as provocatively brazen as they
are untenable. Plessner sets out the anthropological foundation for the
floating construction of the cool persona. He frees the human self-image
both from the prevailing notion of an inner-directed subject operating
within the horizon of humanistic values and from characterizations of a
being fully under the sway of drives. In Plessner's structural analysis, the
eccentric structure of individual life becomes the key to knowledge:

> A basic lack of equilibrium . . . , and not the onward flow of an originally nor-
> mal and once harmonious life system (which could become harmonious
> again) is the "cause" of culture.[96]

Drawing on the results of the same hard scientific research into "man
as a thing of nature" that Scheler cites, Plessner concludes that man
makes himself what he is by taking action: man lives only in that he con-
ducts a life. Plessner's reflections here could not be more consonant with
new objectivity motifs: individual self-realization takes place within
the social configurations that make up the medium of his existence. Forget originary myths of community. Man "civilizes" himself in an obliga-
tory balancing act forced on him from the outset by his "basic lack of
equilibrium."

This new objectivity anthropology not only challenges the originary myths current at the time in the decadence narrative; it also disputes the thesis of *de*sublimation as a means of recapturing vital energies beyond the artificiality of society. In the cool persona's virtuoso bal-

ancing act, and in the radar type's effortless use of media artifice, we see the reflex of new objectivity anthropology. It silently cries out for an accelerated move into the traffic of civilization, rather than an excavation, using old-style cultural criticism, for the phantom of an authentic origin. After all, the mass media themselves artificially disseminate that phantom.

The literature of the new objectivity, in its attentiveness to human action, conduct codes, and positive revaluation of civilization (as opposed to community), presents remarkable correspondences with Plessner's anthropology, which privileges the reflexive type and represses all awareness of man's creatural aspect. Correspondingly, the cool persona and the radar type populate new objectivity writing, as it carries out a positive revaluation of civilization. There are allegories of eccentric existence and bizarre legends that might well derive from the artificiality axiom. Brecht and Benjamin, in harmony with the behaviorist tendencies of Communist pedagogy, cultivate for a time the myth of the "cool child": without the secure wrap of bourgeois family ideology, the proletarian child experiences the cold space of class struggle even before birth. The understanding that even life in the womb lacks security predisposes it to class consciousness. Warmth is available to such a being, if at all, only in the collective. In this legend, too, we glimpse the new objectivity insight that individual human being—not indeed by nature, but by dint of social forces—is eccentric.

The feminist critique of new objectivity anthropology brings into relief the element of the male cult that informs it. To the extent that virile objectivity stresses the moment of necessary separation and self-conscious conduct in post-symbiotic states, the image of the mother risks either sinking into historylessness or being swallowed up by natural creatureliness.

> Forgetfulness is good!
> How else is
> The son to leave the mother who nursed him?

as Bertolt Brecht put it, in his *Lob der Vergesslichkeit*.

People who experience themselves as sovereign beings only within the artificiality of the second fatherland, as Plessner's code of conduct demands, are obliged to forget their real origins. Only when institutional crisis threatens to destroy the second fatherland will they long for reassurance in the phantom of maternal origins. Hence new objectivity novels toward the end of the republic show us once secure men, their lives now ruled by the systemic logic of the object world, returning to women who, for their part, lapse into the ahistoricity of nature.[97] It remains for the women writers of the new objectivity to show us female characters who themselves, for the sake of their own survival, tend toward eccentricity. Problematizing the compensatory projections of the new objectivity male—reflections of the second fatherland's image of woman—women's literature stimulated considerable animosity. Marieluise Fleißer shows us this scenario.

EXPRESSION, LOSING FACE, AND A RETURN TO THE BODY'S RHETORIC

Rodin, as we know, one day made a man with no head:
a man in his stride. . . . The simplest thing we can say
about this is that Rodin was unable to imagine a head
that went with the body, that would stride along with
it. Simplicity, in any case, can be carried no further than
this. Nor will any expression come from the strider. . . .
We need only think of men who took part in the war:
their motives were as various and changeable as the
clouds in the sky; but no matter; their bodies were
already under way.

                    Alain, *Spielregeln der Kunst*, 1921

The shift of attention to the observation of behavior has far-reaching consequences for psychology in the 1920s.[98] The category of expression, as a form of inner experience, undergoes a dramatic devaluation. In a positive revaluation of scientific procedures, the eyes of the other acquire the power to secure and validate the self's identity: only that which is subject to simultaneous registration by at least two observers—ultimately suggesting phenomena that can be captured on film—can be accepted as "fact." The decline of expression as the signifying counterpart to an interior psychological event ends the ideal of authenticity that had dominated German culture since the eighteenth century. The decade of the new objectivity turns to a rhetoric of visible behavior, of physiognomy and pathognomy.[99]

Among the behavioral sciences, ethology and social psychology arrive reluctantly on the scene in Germany, often under the banner of American behaviorism or Russian-Soviet reflexology (Pavlov and Bekhterev). Here, and in sociological theories of action stemming from Max

Weber, a field of facts subject to empirical confirmation excludes the hidden motives of social actors or whatever else is available only to introspection. Even Scheler picks up on the concept of behavioral research, although, to be sure, not without distancing himself from physiological reductionism of behaviorism. He takes over behavior as a "psychophysiologically neutral concept" that defines the intermediate field of observation on which the social sciences are now to base their work.[100] By making this move, according to Scheler, social scientists escape the restrictions of subjective introspection and avoid the reduction of the field of action to stimulus-response schema.

If subjective motivation is to be inferred only from observable behavior, phenomena identified as "expression" must be either bracketed off from scientific analysis or redefined as a form of behavior. And in a variety of scientific disciplines, we accordingly see expression being integrated into the field of action and gesture, for example, in the theory of expression formulated by psychologists and the linguistic theorist Karl Bühler.[101] In anthropologies exclusively geared to action, such as Arnold Gehlen's, there is no longer any place for "pure" expressive gestures.[102] The banishment of expression also does away with attempts to overcome ambivalence. With the rise of the traffic topos, every expression becomes a signal.

BÜHLER'S ACTION THEORY OF EXPRESSION

Who knows what would be left to express were it possible to wean man of the need for fiction, masks, and role playing in every form.

Karl Bühler, *Ausdruckstheorie*

Plessner's *Grenzen* involved a shock for those accustomed to the bourgeois concept of culture based on interiority. A comparison of his 1924 leap into the science of behavior with Bühler's *Ausdruckstheorie: Das System an der Geschichte aufgezeigt,* published in 1933, works to sharpen the contours of Plessner's polemic against the cult of expression.

Karl Bühler's book is part of a rhetoric of the body; it begins with observations on the gestural language of the cinema and ends by reproducing Quintilian's discussion of the rhetorical functions of miming and gesture. In his look back into history, Bühler lays out a panorama of lexicographic and physiological explanations of expressive movements from the eighteenth and nineteenth centuries, from the physiognomy

and pathognomy of Lavater, Goethe, and Lichtenberg to the psycho-
physics of Wilhelm Wundt. At the forefront in Bühler's survey are those
theoretical elements that aid him in the task of uncovering the grammar
in the theory of expression.

His point of departure is a principle that has meanwhile emerged as
a commonplace of the new objectivity decade:

> It is necessary for us to have a living organism present before us in the space
> in which it acts, if we are to discern from its movements in what way and to-
> ward what end it acts. . . . A behaviorist can do this by observing the re-
> actions of an animal or a child in a given experimental situation, and we can
> also do it in natural life situations, in which we follow animals and our fel-
> lows with an understanding gaze. There is only one type of observation for
> which it is impossible, or at least very difficult, to fix what is seen neatly and
> simply in its own scientific language, and that is introspection, when the at-
> tempt is made to discern from experience as such what can at bottom be seen
> only with outwardly directed (physical) eyes. (163)

From the perspective of action, the theatrical doctrine of Johann Jakob
Engel, published in 1785–86 under the title *Ideen zur einer Mimik*,
moves to the center of Bühler's historical investigation, because this text
understands every expression as the "action impulse" and elaborates it
in the form of self-enactment.

Amazingly enough, Bühler devotes the most extensive chapter of his
book to the image of the introspective observer; when it comes to ana-
lyzing experience, he has high regard for Ludwig Klages, the representative of this scientifically suspect procedure, and praises him as a grapho-
logist. Bühler's focus on Klages also gives an opportunity to articulate
both his own critique of behaviorist reductionism and his elementary
objections to the psychophysiology of Wundt. In contrast to tendencies
in experimental psychology ("Expression becomes consumptive in the
laboratory, when one attempts to produce it in experimental subjects
outfitted with pulse and respiration meters"), Bühler emphasizes, Klages
never loses sight of the whole. Bühler calls on others, who disdain
Klages's work as "obscurantist" from the standpoint of the "exact" sciences, to take his challenge seriously; he names Klages the "first consistent relativity theorist of expression" (137), because the latter explains
even the most inconspicuous expressive gesture in relation to the whole.

Bühler's objections to Klages's theory of expression are nevertheless
so fundamental that his praise pales in comparison. The problem is that
Klages assumes the existence of unfalsified expression as "pure emotional outpouring," which can take place independently of such physio-

logical processes as exogenous stimuli: anger is the expression of an urge to annihilate; fear is the expression of flight; wonder expresses the need for orientation. While action occurs always in the context of a singular goal, bodily movements associated with affective expression are possessed of a general goal. "I can, for example, wish to destroy an enemy, a fly on the wall, or an institution; but inherent in rage is also the general inclination for destruction as such" (153).

In order to lay bare pure expression, Klages has to free it of three extraneous elements:

> Whatever has passed through consciousness, becoming through reflection the means to an intended end, Klages excludes from the sphere of pure expression.
>
> Expressive movements bound up in historical or culturally determined conventions, which are therefore variable, cannot be regarded as genuine outpourings.
>
> "Spontaneous" movements that are in fact the product of a learning process or take place merely as a reflex response to an external stimulus have no more claim to the status of expression than gestures that serve to accomplish intentional communication.

Will represents for Klages a "universal inhibitor" that must be excised from expressive motion if expression's origin is to be recognized; the will can never dictate genuine expression. Klages illustrates the point with the following example:

> When the destructive urge is discharged in the pounding of a fist, it is directed neither against the table nor against any other things but aims instead at the impression of resistance, because only in palpable resistance can breaking, destroying, or overcoming be *experienced*. The condition of anger, the destructive drive, is fulfilled in the breaking of resistance, and the self that falls prey to it executes the movement as if driven to do so, thus entirely without consideration of what occasioned it. Expressive movement is always goalless, in most cases even inappropriate, as indeed the example of pounding on the table, which results also in the inkwell falling to the floor, reveals. If we regard this as a reason for calling the urge to emotional expression *blind*, still we may not overlook the fact that it is no less *sensible* for being so. Given this qualification, we may formulate as follows: arbitrary movement completes a prior intention; expressive movement follows the stimulus of an impression.[103]

Ludwig Klages separates will from expression with a "pure cut." In his terms, all arbitrary movements are movements that have been constrained by the will: "What is the aiming of a marksman but the constraining of arm and body movements, as the most precise stopping of a motion already under way?" All expressive movements, as conceived by objectivity, take on the character of arbitrary movements; what characterizes them is the inhibition of a general "outpouring," because what predominates in them is the intentionality of action. We might compare this with the pure expressive movement of a toddler indulging countless detours on the way to the bakery—its path to the goal has not yet been "channeled"—or the actions of a dog off the leash—it runs all over the landscape, while its master sticks to an accustomed path. Is the animal not "drowned in its expressive movement"? asks Klages. And therefore, Bühler concludes, pure expressive movement for Klages consists in "goalless fluctuation," and adds mockingly: "when the fluctuating is done, nothing has been achieved; everything remains as it was" (166, 179).

The contrast to Plessner's attitude toward expression, as we shall see, is considerable. But, while a comparison with Ludwig Klages's theory of expression makes us aware of the dimensions of noninstrumental playfulness Plessner leaves out, Klages's ousting of the theatrical, masks, and all elements of self-enactment reminds us that unfalsified feeling and pure expression remain part of his relentlessly exclusivist fundamentalism, that he subjects it all the same to an extreme formal discipline.

Bühler's critique of Klages's theory of expression is coolly composed and informed equally by the latest results of animal behavior research and the insights of the Russian and Soviet reflexologists. Regarding anger, he remarks dryly:

> A man who is burning with anger sometimes pounds on the table purely for purposes of discharge; that is true. It may be that something analogous sometimes occurs in the animal world; but it is a mistake to regard the substance of animal behavior as parallel to the sort of human outburst that results in the inkwell tipping over. For, first of all, it seems dubious to me that inkwells in animal habitats would be located as regularly as they are among humans in precisely the spot most inconvenient to the angered being. And, second, an accumulation of serious impairments wrought of such affairs would necessarily critically impair survivability for any living being. Our first and second reason here are inherently related, and research into animal life has shown how they are related, how animals learn to avoid subjecting themselves to serious impairments. Klages indeed adopted the old formula, already put forward by the stoics, whereby animal behavior subsequent to such outbursts is blind, but "no less sensible"; but he has left it entirely up to us to guess how he really imagines the harmony between what is subjectively sensible and the objective requirements of life. (175)

Bühler's criterion of objective requirements recalls the perspective that guided science and the arts more generally in the new objectivity decade. In contrast to Klages, he emphasizes expression's inextricability from verbal conventions, its contingence on physiology, and its dependence on factors of socialization, but Bühler does not do away with the latitude left over for creativity in human expression. As a former physician, he is eager to refer back to findings in physiology, anatomy, and reflexology to undercut the theory that pure expression is not learned behavior. Klages may assert that genuine expression takes place in a manner just as unmediated as changes in physical digestive processes, given a change in food; but Bühler notes that Pavlovian experiments with trained animals had demonstrated the extent to which physiological secretions and digestion are conditioned:

> Saliva and glandular excretions are both subject to conditioning. According to the comparison Klages himself puts forward, so presumably, to a degree that must be established, is imitative expression. (158)

In the future, Bühler hopes, the empirical sciences will achieve greater clarity concerning neurohormonal regulation of the affects. A climate of disillusioned realism forms the modern context for his treatment of Klages's theory of expression as a relic of the human sciences: Klages ignores the discoveries of the natural sciences in order to avoid obfuscating physiologically the notion of a pure outpouring. The theory may indeed represent an awareness of the whole; still it is archaic.

Bühler, however, goes on to note that in film and theater, as well as in the lifestyle of his contemporary sophisticates, pathetic expressive movements were giving way to restrained gestures, indirect signs, and broken voices. He claims that the contemporary lifestyle—which a trip to America had doubtless helped him study—eschews all types of gestural displays "carried out for purely expressive purposes and therefore removed from objective action and objectively representative speech." In this way, he foregrounds the social function of mimic movements as a means of communication. Gestures—rather than being (recall Karl Jaspers's claim about the masses' existential form)—have come to affect all sectors of culture. Bühler directs his attention to the function of expressive movements in social traffic; his "semiotics of the affects" investigates the intersubjective "game" of mimic movements, of reciprocal processes of address and response (50, 22, 136). Even the most fleeting of expressive phenomena in the most everyday situation contain a "dramatic moment," in which they remain bound to the mimic "organs of the contact partner."

In contrast to the theorists of expression from the fields of medicine or psychophysiology, to which the theater remained suspect, the grammar of "illusory gestures" is of great scientific interest to Bühler. He values the moment of self-enactment in communication and studies actors at work to analyze it. The ubiquity of masks in early human history not only indicates a magical mind-set; it also prompts him to inquire into "the meaning of the motionless mask, as a staple in the inventory of an actor's properties, what it has to offer and what it leaves out."

> What it offered must have been valuable at the time and what it left out must not have been worth pursuing; for it is a priori unlikely that the mask is nothing but a historical relic and that that which it excluded was entirely unknown. (16)

Bühler's positive assessment of mask coincides entirely with Plessner's code of conduct, even if it remains true that, in contrast to Plessner, Bühler emphasizes the intersubjective function.

Bühler also addresses a problematic that we discuss later in the context of Ernst Jünger's theory of perception. It has to do with the rise of the new technological media, and the way they are put to work in an experimental psychology of expression. Bühler believes that Philipp Lersch makes exemplary use of film in experiments he reports in his 1932 book, *Gesicht der Seele.* Lersch filmed unwitting subjects taking personality tests and analyzed their eye behavior, including eyelid coordinates, angle of vision, and eye movement. Photograms—shadowlike images on light-sensitive paper—allowed Lersch to make precise measurements of the "position of the eyeball in the coordinate system of the eye socket" and compare the "expressive valences of the eyelid movement" with the subject's overall habitus. The procedure suffers, however, from the problem usually associated with the use of the new media: it isolates the phenomena. Isolation, as Bühler himself points out, is among the accepted procedures in the "house of science." At the same time, however, science threatens to mistake its object in favor of methods designed to ensure scientific precision. Lersch makes great use of scissors: from strips of film he cuts out particularly suggestive frames and uses the scissors again to separate the eyes and surrounding area from the nose and mouth. In this case, Bühler considers the isolating procedure a success, because the selection includes the "fruitful moments" of facial play, which, in addition, represent the "successive forms" of expressive movement (81).

Thus did it seem possible in certain situations to classify physiologically based narrowing of the eyelids with basic expressive valences (of active coping, for example).

The physical rhetoric gets lost in a technologized space, which no longer corresponds to what Quintilian had in mind in his treatment of the uses of gestures and facial expressions. In the writings of Walter Serner and Ernst Jünger, the use of technological apparatuses designed to record expressive movements begins in fact to condition them.

PLESSNER'S EXCLUSION OF EXPRESSION

We have already seen that in 1924 Plessner feels obliged to combat expressionism. What he means by the term is, variously, the fundamentalism of the radical movements, with their cult of authenticity and ethics of conviction, which Max Weber had criticized, or the unconventional manners of the youth movement. He takes these diffuse variations of the concept for signs of an inner experience of impotence, perplexity, and frenzy stemming from the memory of defeat. Expressionism is its symptom.

Plessner is not alone in this estimation. "At bottom the reaction of expressionism was more pathological than critical," we read in Walter Benjamin. "It sought to overcome the times that gave rise to it by making itself the expression of those times."[104] In all the expressionisms identified by Plessner he discovers phenomena that, by virtue of a self-disarming gesture, range dangerously near a zone of "ridiculousness," in which the body is delivered up defenseless to its attacker and the price levied for expression is abandonment. Consequently, the urge for unbroken expression cannot in Plessner's anthropology indicate an attempt at meaningfulness; rather, Plessner uses this category to mark off the animal kingdom from the world of human being:

> Animals are ultimately direct and genuine in expression as well. If it all came down to expression, nature would have remained at the level of the most elementary beings, sparing itself the indirection of man. (106)

Those, therefore—so runs the logic—who would elevate "genuine expression" to cult status blur the boundaries between the animal and the human, rob themselves of the defensive protection of distance, and soon fall victim to ridiculousness.

In Plessner's new objectivity anthropology of 1924, he cries out for a militant front against "everything expressive, all forms of eruptive genuineness" (107). His code of conduct proclaims that untruth that protects is better than truth that injures. If man is inseparable from his dependence on artificiality, if every externalization of a psychological state is necessarily formed by the medium of the symbolic order, then everything psychological requires cultural mediation "in order to realize itself." The ideology of community calls for psychological immediacy on the part of its members, but for Plessner, community is precisely *not* the place where authenticity could possibly be realized: "The soul cannot endure the directness of expression demanded by community" (26). Even the heart longs for distance, Plessner decrees in the manner of a courtly code, carrying Nietzsche's thoughts about the actor a step further: the inner being cannot breathe "without the cold air of diplomacy, with the logic of the public sphere" (112).

Plessner's call for a civilized "hygiene of the soul" (87) presupposes the use of violent means to channel the raw energy of drives. But if man is "by nature artificial," why use force to prevent the "raw" psyche from following the path of least resistance to expression? Via the risk of spontaneity, the dualism between mind and physical drives sneaks back into Plessner's anthropology. Scheler, on the other hand, registering the same set of facts, derives the need for sublimation.

The violent means with which Plessner diverts the urge for direct expression are as follows: tactical maneuvering; conventional masks; diplomatic balance—a series of stratagems that he summarizes all together as *Verhaltenheit*.* The term itself suggests that behavioral self-reflection can be a guide to psychological externalization. Among its extended meanings are a range of techniques for slowing things down, for deferring gratification, or even for a self-destructive holding (*Verhalten*) of the breath (Diogenes supposedly used this technique to exit life voluntarily). From putting a damper on "eruptive" emotion all the way to suffocation, *Verhaltenheit* suggests an act of mental awareness, which is what Plessner demands of his "practical occasionalists." The mime of *Verhaltenheit* is the smile; it avoids "the extreme of the affectively charged grimace."[105] The effect is pleasant: inside Plessner's fencing hall sounds are subdued (and the hordes roar from farther away).

The concept of *Verhaltenheit* introduces a remarkable fissure in Plessner's thought, which once again bears on the special status he accords to woman. "It is not good," he repeats once more, "to disappear totally in expression," illustrating the dictum with a comparison that would re-

---

* "Restraint," though the best rendering here may be "mannered behavior," to preserve the root meaning of *Verhalten* as behavior.

cant his entire theory of artificiality—yet now in the spirit of the eighteenth century, he offers it in reference to the youth movement:

> The cry for a corsetless form of dress deserves an echo only in the case of very good figures. Why should it be otherwise in the psychological sphere? [106]

That there could be such a thing as a naturally "good figure" in psychology, supposedly bound exclusively to artificiality, Plessner had categorically denied in his code of male conduct.

Just a year after the publication of *Grenzen* we find a more moderate attitude in Plessner's short essay, "Deutung des mimischen Ausdrucks," which nevertheless will have far-reaching consequences for the further development of the theory of expression.[107] The dualism is obscured, the pathos absent from his delineation of the dangers of expressionism. Perhaps he owes this pragmatic turn to the Dutch zoologist Buytendijk (identified as a coauthor). Buytendijk's experiments with toads supply a broad range of new considerations, reaching ultimately to Klages's theory of expression. At issue for Plessner now is an image of movement in its entirety: in expression he recognizes the relationship between changing internal states and the external environment understood as a structured field. He discovers the "intermediate sphere" of the "social world" as an expressive space in which the "play of functions" in interpersonal relations becomes visible. This behavioral stratum, the sphere of the "reciprocal mutuality of bodies," is where the formal language of the psyche develops. It neither originates in a "mimetic ur-alphabet," as Klages maintains, nor slots into categories of instrumental activity. Rather, it is an element of intersubjective coexistence. Plessner's emphasis in this text falls more radically on the turn outward than it had in *Grenzen* but eschews dramatization in any form. The "internal localization of the psychological in the body," he remarks laconically, "is understood as nonsense." Expressive movements are part of the formal language of behavior; knowledge of the situation in which they occur makes them understandable. While the civil war atmosphere remains evident in *Grenzen,* the new essay concentrates on a third sphere, the sphere of relaxed interpersonal behavior.

Scheler's 1928 *Stellung des Menschen im Kosmos,* in contrast, displays a generalized upgrading of natural expression. Against Darwin, who saw in expression an "epitome of atavistic instrumental actions," the rudiment of a practical gesture that had lost its communicative meaning, Scheler accords expression the status of an urphenomenon of life.[108] It is present even in plant life but acquires the function of understanding only among animals and humans. Human expression has nothing instinctive about it; physical schemata do not dictate it. Though drives may energize expression, from the outset expression links an intellectual element to the body, while simultaneously documenting the human capability to achieve distance from the world. As a result, there is no simple connection between expression originating in drives and physiological conditions. Just as action resulting from drives is for Scheler the absolute opposite of instinctive behavior—since drives can often be senselessly excessive—the pleasure principle is in no sense original, but the result of "associative intelligence," an indication of the way drives can be isolated from instinctive survival behavior. Scheler thus arrives at the conclusion that the state termed "Dionysian" (following Nietzsche) has nothing to do with elemental wildness but draws on a complex volitional technique of desublimation. Wrapped up in human expression are moments of an ability to overrule drives. In expression the "corridor of consciousness" intersects with the "corridor of external stimulus"; energy from the drives powers this switch point.[109]

In Scheler's understanding, the question of the "genuineness" of expression—in the sense of its immediacy—therefore does not arise. Nor does he consent to Plessner's rigid behavioral admonition, that letting oneself go in expression courts the "catastrophe of ridiculousness." Scheler's advice is to tolerate the risk of being ridiculous. He wagers on the doctrine of nonresistance to evil, recommended by Spinoza in his ethics, because drives are malleable only as they come to expression. He knows that the militant negation of drives leads only to the opposite of what one intended; in his view, it would thus not merely be unreasonable but directly counterproductive to attempt, as Plessner does, to prohibit "eruptive" expression. Reason is not capable of regulating passion, unless—thanks to sublimation—it becomes a passion itself.[110]

CONVENTIONS OF PAIN

It is impossible for a man, with his arms all akimbo in
strenuous defence, simultaneously to open his mouth
to scream out loud, for the simple reason that the arm
movements presuppose a chest taut with the pressure
of expiration.
                    Charles Bell on the puzzle of Laocoön, 1806

The critique of expression reflects not only the influence of behaviorism, the concentration on observable behavior, and the general struggle against psychologism but an idea found in Nietzsche as well. The critique's target is almost exclusively the expression of pain. The experience of war had unleashed extreme and contradictory expressive movements focused on pain: the cultivation of cool armoring to achieve honor and hardness; the metaphysical interpretation of the meaning of suffering; and unmediated "naive expressions of pain and suffering," in which pain simply remained pain.[111]

Suddenly abandoning his own cool armoring in 1916, Scheler found a human way out of the situation. Now, directly alongside the armored ego, the figure of the defenseless creature achieves currency: "The scream of the creature, restrained so long, once again echoes freely, bitterly through the universe."[112] Plessner would rescind the distinction between the icon of the warrior and the icon of the creature by elevating once again to ideal status the discipline of *Verhaltenheit* that Scheler had dropped; Plessner draws a veil over the icon of the creature, thereby withdrawing from the public gaze.

Under the banner of the new objectivity, writers in the 1920s explore the convention of pained expression and its social function. Nietzsche's idea comes in for an update. "Every sufferer searches instinctively for the cause of his suffering; more precisely, he seeks a perpetrator," writes Nietzsche in his *Genealogy of Morals*. The search begins, in any event, not within the body but in the world outside it. From an evolutionary perspective, this search is "rational" behavior: ultimately the species that understands its pains primarily as indicators of external sources of suffering, only turning later to possible internal causes, will gain a survival advantage.[113]

New objectivity writers focus their attention on the social constellation in which pain makes its appearance. That suffering in the form of "pure outburst" might be able to find an adequate literary form for itself is an idea that inspires Brecht to mockery:

> People also say that this or that writer has had some bad experience, but he has lent fine expression to his suffering and so can be grateful for it: something came of the sorrows; they expressed the man. Besides, in being formulated, they have been ameliorated in part. The suffering passes, the poem remains, they say, smartly rubbing their hands. But how is it when the suffering has not passed? When it remains there just the same—if not for the singer of verses, then for those who cannot sing?[114]

Pain always comes to expression within the frame of convention, so that it is difficult to say in what form pain finds its genuine expression. Karl Bühler compares two attitudes toward pain, without deciding which of the two deserves the seal of genuineness:

> The so-called primitive man suffering pain and sadness breaks out in loud plaintive tones, rips his clothes, and injures himself by his own hand; all of this in essentially the same situations in which man today remains silent, wraps black crepe around his arm, and goes neatly about his business. (166)

Programmatic literary statements that bluntly repudiate the cult of expression offer three general arguments. The first is that the creature's scream always counts on being heard in some seat of judgment, whether in the universe or the republic. In 1920, the expressionist Rudolf Leonhard offered the following to his readers:

> For the word is not a means of conveying information, but rather a means of expression, is expression itself. . . . It is a sound issuing from the depths of isolation, and the miracle of communication lies not in the mouth but in the ear. The most sacred mystery is that we are heard and understood.[115]

The expression of pain has the quality of an appeal and therefore does convey information; it is not the act of solipsism that it pretends to be. Embedded in the convention of the "penitential pilgrimage," it anticipates grace in heaven or a merciful audience on earth.

At issue in the expressionist topos of the creature's scream was the medium of writing itself. Since the conventions of writing could not replicate the scream unchanged, the expressionists pursued the detour of the form, in order, on the one hand, to forge a way for the primal utterance and, on the other, to reflect the inappropriateness of artificial signs.

The decade of the new objectivity held out the possibility of calling on the techniques of the physiognomic gaze to get beyond the dilemma inherent in writing, as the older expressive medium. The medium of photography, the camera's eye, meant that immediacy had finally found its neutral medium in technology. The physiognomy of the screamer could be photographed; the unwritten scream came out of the radio, without mediation—like music.

A second argument for the critique of the cult of expression insists on the performative aspect in every expression:

> When bankers express themselves to each other, or politicians, then we know that they are acting at the same time; even when a sick person expresses his pain, he also signals with his finger to the doctor or others gathered around,

and he also acts. But about poets people believe that they produce only pure expression, so that their action consists solely in expression and their intention can only be to express themselves.[116]

In the epic theater, Brecht replaces the category of expression with that of the gesture and—as Plessner does—defines it as "expression in the light of an action." The gesture reconnects the abstract signs of communication to the body. If the sign exists within the exclusion of the body, the gesture returns the body to center stage; the gesture brings the sign back to the site and moment of its production (Carrie Asman). The danger of this reconnection, however, is that the supremacy of the sign will overwhelm the body, leaving nothing but a ruin with an allegorical meaning attached to it.

A third argument for the repudiation of the cult of expression has to do with the way the repercussions of prescribed, ritualized expressive conventions on the emotions become the focus of attention. The earlier psychological finding, that physiological movements produce emotion, that crying not only is rooted in sadness but can also occasion it, acquires a new currency under the influence of behaviorism.[117] The technique of producing affects mechanically travels from the theater to the marketplace, and from advertising back to theater. A new field of philosophical and sociological reflection opens up; research begins to describe the conventions of symbolic interaction as a medium of expression in order to uncover the historically variable core of expression. The criticism of expression combines the critique of ideology with a search for the hidden center of power behind the expression. Benjamin discovers in the poetic signs of allegory not only the convention of expression but also the expression of convention, which is, "therefore, the expression of authority, secret as befits the dignity of its origins and public in accord with its sphere of validity," as he formulated it for the baroque period.[118] For the modern period, of course, no authority can claim the dignity of an "origin."

The new objectivity subjects expression to the functionalist gaze and makes a corresponding reduction in its existential weight. If man is conceived as "a being poised for action" (Plessner), it is the pragmatic aspect of expressive gestures that captures all the attention. To those who fear that the result will be a "flattening" of expression, the functionalism of the new objectivity points to a gain in the spatial breadth of action. The idea of psychological depth comes in for a hearing as to whether it necessarily makes the field of action smaller. The mobile subject upon which the new objectivity focuses may appear flat from a traditional perspective but opens up the depths of the space of action in such a way as to eliminate what causes the expressive world of pain's depth. Lurking inconspicuously in even the "barbaric" campaign against expression is a humane subversive element, though it is not easy to trace.

The critique of expression opens up a new space of sociological reflection focused on symbolic forms. Expression is no longer an unfiltered manifestation of a stimulus center, as Klages had claimed. Scheler emphasizes the intellectual element in the spontaneous; Plessner notes that every expression, as soon as it appears, becomes subject to the regularities of the symbolic order. Karl Bühler describes expression in terms of its conditionality, between physiological states and external stimuli in the field of communicative action. Kracauer stresses the camera's ability to undermine the conventions of the expressive arts, in order to make visible the natural foundation that exists unconsciously in the frozen gesture. Brecht recognizes the intersubjective significatory character of self-expression, drawing far-reaching consequences from it. Communicative signs depend on conventions, and these conventions underlay the regularities of class, the public sphere, the media, and the market. The conventions represent the anonymous dark side of the expressive intentional mirror—its reified nature and commodity character—but do not mean disaster. The arts and sciences of the new objectivity decade have confidence in their ability to bring some light into the darkness of reification. This sense of self-confidence makes them part of a historical process that will soon be demanding new formulas for the authenticity of pain. In the 1930s, attention will turn to the natural history of the expressive mirror's other side.

PLESSNER—SCHMITT:
ASSOCIATION AND DISSOCIATION

In the end phase of the republic, Helmuth Plessner radicalizes the political elements of his theory.[119] The inclination toward *Verhaltenheit*, which tempered the advice he was giving in 1924, is gone. Now an emphasis on decisions gives his anthropology a practical edge. If he once considered it "a crime to employ brute force, instead of the logic of play," now his code of conduct leads into the realm of political anthropology, which (for the sake of conceptual clarity as regards the "political") includes, provisionally, the physical killing of the other.

In his 1931 book *Macht und menschliche Natur,* in any case, Plessner has no reservations about relying on *Der Begriff des Politischen* (1927), by Carl Schmitt, who in turn refers to Plessner's work in *Begriff*'s second edition (1932), as an adequate anthropological foundation for his theory.[120] The affinities of Plessner's 1931 text—which sets aside or drops the central concepts of 1924, such as balance, compensation, play, tact, *Verhaltenheit,* and diplomacy—and Schmitt's study of politics are little short of astounding. Plessner has meanwhile gone over to the idea that, "in an epoch in which dictatorship is a living power," it has become impossible to continue reflecting naively about politics within the categories of classical liberalism. Politics, says Plessner now, means a struggle for power, and the task of the anthropologist is to discover the extent to which this will to power is part of man's essence.

Plessner now realizes that the agonistic political sphere is not some contingent physical existential state external to man, but that the "originary relation of friend to enemy" is to be counted among his fundamental anthropological conditions.[121] In opposition to Max Scheler and Martin Heidegger, whom he reproaches for contriving images of a "genuine" human being, Plessner strives in his anthropology to understand the individual as an "accountable subject" (*Zurechnungssubjekt*) in the violent world. Those, like these two rivals, who stretch philosophical anthropology between the poles of the leap into genuineness, on the one hand, and the forgetfulness of *Man,* on the other, manage only to update Luther's split between a private sphere of salvation and a public sphere of violence.[122] In contrast, Plessner insists that the individual, as a being consigned to artificiality from the moment of birth, can realize himself only in the sphere of "man." He voices the suspicion that these existential doctrines, obsessed with genuineness, actually underwrite political indifference and are the real sponsors of violence. Therefore he demands the politicization of anthropology, which he supposes will keep politics from setting an ambush for anthropology.

The theoretical alliance between Plessner and Schmitt, their exchange of arguments and approving references, went on for a decade—after 1933 Plessner allowed the episode to sink out of sight; and in the decades following 1945, the issue of the liaison, which might have occasioned deeper insights into the fate of the Weimar intelligentsia, was simply not taken up. While the correspondences between Walter Benjamin and Carl Schmitt have meanwhile become the focus of extensive research, the investigation of affinities between Plessner's early works and Schmitt's theory of the state have remained the preserve of younger scholars working on the margins.

It is remarkable and telling that all three, Plessner, Benjamin, and Schmitt, felt themselves drawn to the baroque period. The "stage and theatrical feel of those engaged in political action in the seventeenth century" obviously confronted them with an extreme example of representation, and it fascinated them.[123] Equally conspicuous is their combination of the new objectivity concept of action with the aestheticizing of evil. "You must give the Devil his due,"* writes Plessner, as a motto above the introduction to his *Grenzen* of 1924. In an incidental note, he registers the "Luciferian" appeal emanating from decisive men. The motif of gambling with the devil leads directly to a principle the new objectivity shares with the seventeenth century's political codes of conduct. As soon as the hope for religious redemption disappears, the political subject tries to intervene in the machinery of violence. The cult of evil is an inversion of the salvation narrative.[124] We read already as early as 1649: "For he / who would live among the foxes and wolves / must also howl with them."[125]

Max Weber, distancing himself from the youth movement's passionate impatience, put the principle in terms of the saying: "Mind you, the devil is old; grow old to understand him."[126] He points out the need to immerse oneself in an enemy's assumptions and empirical characteristics, study and assess them, rather than increasing the enemy's power by disarming or taking flight. Plessner seconds the idea in *Grenzen,* coining the new objectivity slogan: "Dealing with reality means dealing with the devil" (126). Benjamin lays stress on the way a patient study of fascinating evil can also bring its weaknesses to light: "Lucifer is beautiful. . . . The beautiful brings to expression the fact that what he lacks is an ultimate totality."[127] Schmitt, Plessner, and Benjamin—along with the contemporary avant-garde—dream of amoral mobility, which searches for spaces of lawlessness in which to indulge itself, turns against security-mindedness of neutrality, and cultivates the consciousness of danger. Readings of Kierkegaard and Sorel, Nietzsche and Lenin, Schopenhauer and Hobbes blend strangely in their minds. Remarkable correspondences run straight through the various political camps.

Lucifer may have been their identifying sign—the angel who fell from heaven like a lightning bolt and claims, as prince of darkness, to be the bringer of light.[128] While coming to some arrangement with the idea

---

* The phrase is in English in the original.

of power, thinkers like Plessner and Schmitt want to remain part of the enlightenment. The concept has few precedents in the German cultural tradition.

In 1932 Schmitt acknowledges that Plessner's anthropology, through its "venturesome" realism in the construction of man as a risky being and its "positive reference to danger," may well come "closer to 'evil' than to goodness."[129] Everything depends for both thinkers on the moment of decision "out of nothing." Lacking a solid basis in nature or a sheltering metaphysics, an individual makes an unending series of decisions in order to lead an active life and, in doing so, secure his identity. Schmitt, admittedly, has very stable moorings. His metaphysical shelter is Catholicism, and his decisions rest on the pillars of a "healthy economy inside the strong state." Like Max Weber, he continues to adhere to the liberal age's uncontested dogma of separate spheres for production and consumption, price-setting and the market, with no guidance from ethics or a specific worldview, and most certainly not from politics.[130]

Plessner's *Grenzen* already has conceptual figures that blend easily with Schmitt's friend-enemy formula of 1927. In *Macht und menschliche Natur,* Plessner elaborates his thesis of the individual's eccentric position, taking it in the direction of a political anthropology. Yet Plessner's individual, in contrast to Schmitt's, has to see to his own needs, so that institutions can take nothing away from him; he must continually reconstitute his native spheres, which were not his at birth, as he endlessly makes and remakes his "open foreignness." Thus he takes over an area between the native zone and the "uncanny reality" of hostile foreignness.[131] In the psychophysiological dynamic of drawing boundaries between the familiar circle and unfamiliar otherness—the line traced with a duelist's foil—Plessner glimpses the original constitution of man's essence.

Since the sphere of familiarity has no natural boundaries, uncanny forces threaten every moment to colonize it. According to Plessner, no humanitarian concept offers to protect it. But what then? Plessner's reference to Schmitt means in this context that the two agree on the necessity of violence, which in turn necessitates the drawing of boundaries. In certain concretely existing circumstances, otherness can imply the negation of "one's own form of existence," and in that case, Schmitt writes, "the real possibility of physical killing" becomes part of the meaning of the friend-enemy concept.[132]

This extreme, which marks the borderline case in Schmitt's 1927 text, may seem to be the point where the two theories coincide but can also be taken as the point where the two once again drift apart. The relativism of the spheres of familiarity emphasized by Plessner, his desire to break through cultural ethnocentrism, and his aversion to the stylization of community into a natural sphere of familiarity, make it easy to recognize in retrospect the possibility of collision. (We would like to know more than his lecture series on the "belated nation" [*verspätete Nation*] tells us about Plessner's reaction during the dictatorship's first stage, when he was forced to recognize how smoothly—crudely but effectively—Schmitt's decisionism, to which he had himself adhered so long, could blend with the ideology of community.) Leaving out of consideration, however, the extreme case, it is possible to recognize the dynamic mix of affinities on the more abstract level of Schmitt's definition: "The distinction between friend and enemy," writes Schmitt in 1927, "implies the most extreme degree of intensity achieved by a union or separation, an association or dissociation." The political enemy is not to be conceived negatively, in moral, aesthetic, or economic terms. "He is simply other, the stranger, and it suffices in regard to his being that he is, in an especially intensified sense, something other and foreign."[133] This level of abstraction echoes in Plessner's anthropology.

Degrees of intensity in separation had an aesthetic appeal for the Weimar intelligentsia equal to that of coolness. Plessner's persona constantly draws from the mirror of the other as potential enemy an image of a self that would be adequate in that reality (a figure in the mirror stage of identity formation is always in flux). Schmitt's theory opens up the possibility of escape from the spell of isolation, of leaving the area of that which has been distinguished, in order to enter the terrain of political relevance on the level of the state. Now, before a broader public, Plessner wants to frame the necessary decisions anthropologically.

That Plessner, in contrast to Schmitt, failed in the endeavor is not merely the consequence of external conditions. To this day, the single extensive work devoted to the case comes to the conclusion that Schmitt's theory of the state is the "congenial complement" of Plessner's anthropology. It calls Schmitt's theory of the political the "operationalization of Plessner's anthropological analysis of the present."[134] This judgment obscures other possibilities and I cannot agree with it. Yet if we read the two works in their political context as a single text, we can use the putative identity to rescue both thinkers from the intellectual taboo hovering about their temporary connection. And we can more easily reconstruct the contours of the individual theories and chart their divergence.

For while Plessner's theory hinges on the myth of the individual, Schmitt's concepts put the state at the center of attention.

Perhaps in 1932 both thinkers would have energetically denied the possibility that their theories would clash on the stage of the historical process. They probably read each other's work extremely selectively. The seed of conflict was already there in 1931, in Plessner's orientation toward Dilthey's historicism and his penetrating understanding of aspects of psychoanalysis. Referring to Freud, Plessner defines the "other as that which is familiar and surreptitiously one's own externalized, and therefore uncanny."[135] Schmitt approaches this definition only after the Second World War, recalling Theodor Däubler's formula, "The enemy is the form assumed by our own question." Schmitt's empty matrix of the friend-enemy relation arbitrarily brings in substances at any time, whereas Plessner's definition of the other categorically excludes biological determinacy. He takes over the relativity of all boundary markings from historicism:

> Cultural history manifests the unremitting displacement of the horizon of the uncanny and, correlatively, of the sphere of friendly familiarity, so that the figural transformation of the friend-enemy relation can only be investigated historically.[136]

Was it Dilthey's relativism that prevented Plessner from constituting as absolute the familiar sphere of a people (*Volk*)? Was it his aversion to community, which the legal theorists of the state sought to instrumentalize? Since Plessner's initial point of departure was not an ontologically determined marking of boundaries but rather one variably informed by the play of power, he was unable for theoretical reasons to follow Schmitt when, in 1933, the latter definitively introduced racial identity into his matrix, as the criterion for friend. An anti-Semitic turn—in "hatred of the concept of law" (Raphael Gross) as the defining characteristic of Judaism—marks all of Schmitt's commentaries on constitutional doctrine in the 1920s.[137] Racial identity now irrevocably becomes the substance, enriched by power, of Schmitt's sphere of familiarity; as a result of racial politics, the sphere necessarily became for Plessner one of mistrust.

A further indication of both like-mindedness and differentiation is apparent as early as 1924 in the agreement of Plessner and Schmitt in their admiration of the figure of the Grand Inquisitor in *The Brothers Karamazov*.[138] Even in the nineteenth century, Dostoyevsky's character

was regarded as the quintessence of Machiavellianism and thus of a "jesuitical politics." Gradually, however, the connotation of Jesuit in political semantics shifts to the Jew.[139] Here the cool persona's path splits in
a way that the play of definitions had not foreseen. For a while Schmitt
—the "crown jurist of the Third Reich"—remains jesuitical. But because the dictatorship's racial politics now uses biology to mark its
boundaries, Plessner falls into the sphere of the enemy. He is forced to
emigrate, via Turkey, to the Netherlands. Since the course of their lives
diverges so sharply, it obscures their early affinities.

When Plessner published a new edition of his book *Die verspätete
Nation* in 1959, he lumped together Schmitt's decisionism and Heidegger's anthropology, ascribing to both the "aestheticizing of politics,"
which, in Benjamin's formulation, gave impetus to fascism.[140] Plessner's
student Christian Graf von Krockow had a year earlier published the
first conclusive work on decisionism in Schmitt, Heidegger, and Jünger.
Von Krockow, who quotes the critique of communitarian radicalism
from *Grenzen* (1924) and the "principle of the indecipherability" of the
historical from *Macht und menschliche Natur* (1931), does not mention
the interconnections between Plessner's and Schmitt's conceptualiza-
tions. We infer indirectly from the introduction what he regards as the
differences between the two. In the aftermath of Nietzsche, according to
von Krockow, it was not only conceivable but consistent to imagine an
individual who throws off all transcendental norms in order to run the
risk of his own decisions. Throwing them off, he elevates the burden of
existence to the extreme. "For, having renounced all authoritative ties,
the individual would find himself surrounded, in normative terms, by
'nothingness.'" Von Krockow recapitulates the intellectual situation
Plessner experienced in 1924 in order to supplement it with an idea that
leaves open the possibility of rescuing decisionism in humanistic terms:

> Insofar as the humanity of the individual is indicated by his being in the midst
> of decision, the outermost step would perhaps produce something like hu-
> manity as a life form—but it remains a difficult question, whether such a life
> form is tolerable or even at all possible.[141]

If at this point a free exchange of arguments among Plessner, Heidegger,
and Schmitt even remains possible within a humanistic frame, the next
step is to separate out their respective positions. Von Krockow's invoca-
tion of the burden of existence has already suggested that the individual,
constitutionally overburdened by the permanent pressure of making de-

cisions, seeks relief. Schmitt and Heidegger explore this possibility by requiring of themselves a decision that was imposed on them, thus escaping the burden of having to decide "out of nothing."

Helmuth Plessner decides on the hazards of exile, although of course it was really not a decision.

A HISTORICAL CONTEXT
FOR THE CODES OF CONDUCT

Plessner's code of conduct aims at achieving the participation of the single individual in existing structures of power. He depicts an individual who, with a high degree of reflexive alertness, is supposed to find his identity in a balance between the demarcation of his physicality, the bracketing of his longing for community, and dissociation from the enemy sphere. Where in the Weimar Republic do we find a social carrier for such a concept? Within recognized political camps, certainly, it would be hard to locate.

Literary examples come spontaneously to mind—the character of the confidence man in Walter Serner's *Handbrevier für Hochstapler,* for example, or the image of the storm troop commander, conceived by Ernst Jünger. In Jünger's construction, we find the tense alertness demanded by Plessner. Here is the image of a metallic subject whose intellectual awareness never lapses, as if he "had an electric bell going off nonstop inside" him. In this figure of the *maschino* are elements of aestheticism, self-demarcation from the horde, the pathos of decision-making out of nothing, the defense against or colonization of the other under "cool" skies—all of these blended together in their military variants.

Jünger's figure also dispenses with the orienting mechanisms of social institutions and minimizes integration into social collectives. Economic motives, on Jünger's stage, as on Plessner's, flash brightly in their absence. The spotlight shines on a rare example: the sovereign subject acting alone, putting its awareness to the test in an unending series of duels—yet betraying no consciousness of imperative drives or other determinants that mediate its identity. This fabulous figure of the individual was obviously a key figure of the imaginary that held the Weimar public in its spell. Where, however, were its institutional moorings? In what uniform did it enter the arena of politics? The communitarian ideologies of the left as well as the right formed the warm spheres that hatched the cool idol with its armor intact.

By publishing his anthropological treatise on the subject of power in the *Fachshriften zur Politik und staatsbürgerlichen Erziehung*, Plessner was seeking to gain a hearing for his ideas inside state institutions, but Carl Schmitt, who incorporated them into his theory of power, was probably the only one who understood the ramifications of the complicated text. Once it becomes clear that there is no social carrier for the boundary subject's code of conduct, however, there remains nothing much to it—outside characterology! In the final analysis, the code thus amounts to a lifestyle conceived as a style of power.

The courtly codes of distance as the Weimar period updated them do not end with this deadly trajectory into decisionism. We follow their remarkable transformation in a different social stratum in a later chapter about the radar type. The modernization of the codes in heroic form, however, seems to have run its course at the close of the 1920s.

In the 1930s, politically cut off from the actual developmental space in which the modernization took place, exiled intellectuals begin to reconstruct a historical context for the courtly code of conduct. Norbert Elias, escaping to Switzerland, France, and England, undertakes his cultural historical studies in a search for another type of subject. He identifies a "rational type," set aside in favor of its successors, the professional bourgeois *ratio* and the inner-directed subject of the Protestant ethic. Elias finds this example of "existence at a distance" in court society, beneath the rubble of the nineteenth-century cult of psychologizing.[142]

In a world lacking in security, the prebourgeois rational type finds orientation in a set of behavioral rules that teach him to gauge degrees of intimacy and distance. He is required to move about on terrain in which "free-wheeling emotion" of any sort is penalized with social decline or degradation. Conspicuous in Elias's reconstruction of courtly behavior is an anti-expressionist impulse, reminiscent of Plessner:

> The dosage of an affective discharge is hard to calculate. Unmeasured, it exposes the true feelings of the person in question to such a degree that it can be damaging; it can mean giving up trump cards to a rival in the struggle for favor or prestige. It is ultimately and above all a sign of inferiority; and that is precisely the condition that a member of court fears most of all. The competitive struggle of court life thus forces the restraint of affects in favor of a precisely calculated and thoroughly nuanced bearing in social intercourse.[143]

The constraints on historical reconstruction of the 1930s inflect its critique. A self-critical concession that reality had pulled the rational type off balance, leaving it only the option of resistance, sets off a search for traces of the type's humane possibilites, wiped out by its development. Elias signals his approval of civilization—the Weimar intelligentsia's defining characteristic—but details the civilizing process's psychosocial costs: "In the course of this process," he warns, "consciousness becomes less subject to the drives and the drives less subject to consciousness."[144] As the other side of the civilizing process, he observes (and David Riesman later describes) chronic psychosocial anxiety.[145] A contrasting argument in Max Horkheimer and Theodor Adorno's *Dialectic of Enlightenment* stresses the necessary structural interconnection of civilization and barbarism.

Removed from the dramatic decisions of the republic's end phase, and outside the compelling forces of mobilization, Werner Krauss, Norbert Elias, Erich Auerbach, Ernst Kantorowicz, and other scholars of court society lay bare the repressed dimension of the behavioral codes. They discover the horizons of humanism that, in Gracián's *Art of Worldly Wisdom,* allowed an admixture of goodness and virtue in moderation that was absent from the preceding decades of the avant-garde. Unable to find a political landscape in Germany for the rational type's development, they uncover a textual space in history bearing witness to just that possibility.[146]

One of the macabre aspects of German intellectual history is that the avant-garde thinkers began to excavate humanism's buried potential at a time when exile largely deprived them of any possibility for action. During the 1920s and 1930s they failed, to their own disadvantage, to recognize the modernity of the eighteenth century. Historicism, the phantom enemy, the great adversary of that passionately impatient period, was once again in demand as a medium for the recall of humanistic principles. Now readers could enjoy Gracián in all his dimensions, celebrating his attentiveness to the friendly gentility and magnanimity of the soul, the virtue of timely introspection, and the value of faithfulness. In Plötzensee and Torgau, Krauss retrieved these aspects of the Jesuit's thought.

Erich Auerbach, reacting in October 1947 to *Graciáns Lebenslehre,* which Krauss had sent him just after its publication in Frankfurt, refers to a merit we have not yet discussed:

> I have just come across a page of notes that I made, at the very beginning of my ocean voyage [to America], reading your works. And if I'm not mistaken, I've not yet written to you anything about it. In my memory . . . everything pales in comparison to the Gracián book, the density and richness of which

is never far from my thoughts. Not only the figure of Gracián himself, but all
the relations and connections that you uncover and pull together, concerning, for example, the court sphere or the concept of moderation; they are extremely interesting to me and will prove fruitful also for my own work.[147]

The atmosphere of the 1930s humanist turn is particularly evident in the
chapter on Gracián's concept of moderation. Here Krauss stresses the
worth of the middling virtue. This median value is not an average or a
compromise. It is an "extraordinary accomplishment of combined intellectual capacities" that mediates extremes rather than eliminating them.
Krauss demands achievements that may appear paradoxical: "discreet
audacity" and "prudent daring" (149). Risky acts of balance transpire
in the middle space. Only exceptional natures can achieve the art of balance, he concedes; they realize they must neither annihilate extreme affects with "stoic asceticism" (108) nor act them out without reserve but
instead neutralize them by means of another passion. They do not tame
the affects' wildness but turn their force in another direction. This balancing of affects creates a passion for balance in the service of a special
interest, which is subject to political, economic, and moral definition.[148]

Ernst Jünger's diaries during the Second World War have a comparable treatment of the logic of extremes, turning it to the service of
the virtue of moderation. Enforced contemplation weakens the spell
of the philosophy of history in which his mobilization fantasy originated
and increases his interest in what is humanly possible. An approach to
the tradition of the French moralists recalls to Jünger's mind some
durable humane insights, at a time in which they are being consciously
called into question.[149] In his *Kaukasische Aufzeichnungen,* on 1 January 1943—shortly after he witnessed the involvement of regular army
units in carrying out the genocide on the eastern front—he notes three
resolutions:

> First, "Live moderately," for nearly all the difficulties in my life have stemmed
> from violations of moderation [see Figure 5].
>   Second, "Always have an eye out for the unfortunate." Man has an inborn
> tendency not to perceive genuine misfortune; indeed more than that: he turns
> his eye away from it. Compassion lags behind.
>   I want finally to do away with thinking about individual salvation in the
> maelstrom of possible catastrophes. It is more important that one behave
> with dignity. We cling to the surface points of a whole that remains hidden
> from us, and it is precisely the escape we devise that can kill us.[150]

Krauss also compares Gracián's worldly arts with the French moralists, elucidating Gracián's circumscriptions. They distance him from the

5. Live moderately

(Ernst Jünger with Lieutenant von Krienitz, at Regniéville, 1917. With the permission of Schiller-Nationalmuseum, Deutsches Literarchiv, Marbach a.N.)

Volk, which Gracián would regard as an enemy and approach only fully armed, in the "male-bonded" encapsulation of the persona. But gender psychology is not one of his themes; he eliminates "incidents of passion" from his considerations—and in this issue Krauss finds the sharpest contrast to a male model derived from the French moralists, which "takes shape in constant consideration of the female partner role" (157).

Nevertheless, Krauss stresses the benefits of the virtue of moderation in Gracián's code, in contrast to the fanatic attitudes of his own time. He knew the risky brilliance of the cool persona, which he could juxtapose to Gracián's counsel no. 266:

> Not to be bad from an excess of goodness: that is the lot of someone who never gets angry. These insensitive sorts scarcely deserve to be called people (personas). Their condition does not always stem from indolence, but often from incompetence. Sensitivity, given an appropriate occasion, is an act of personality: birds often make fun of a scarecrow.

The Cool Persona in New Objectivity Literature; or, Figures Devoured by the Shadows They Cast

UNDERMINING THE SOVEREIGN

The era of the first republic set the pain of separation and the desire for fusion—two sources of aesthetic fascination—at opposing extremes.[1] A bourgeois culture of shadings and mixed temperatures gives way to aesthetic segregation, the polarization of life spheres, and a fascination with distinct boundaries and clear contours. The phenomenon of fluid boundaries becomes as suspect in politics as in aesthetics. The art of terrible simplification grows attractive, not only because it offers relief, but primarily because it is terrible. In the hothouse climate resulting from rampant status inconsistencies, variations on cool make it possible to register distinctions;[2] the cult of separation operates to demarcate cool spaces of mobility in the overheated agglomeration centers of the metropolis. The record turns up high praise for nomadism, positive assessments of the social "ice age" that has descended, resigned acceptance of estrangement, a taste for statistical demystification, a rhetoric of forgetting, and the behaviorism of perception. Cool conduct's ritual, actions, and lifestyle inscribe themselves as traces of separation within the world of fusion's imaginary spaces: birth memories, faith in the completeness of the life cycle, longing for spheres of trust, praise for warm zones, a weakness for myths of origin.

The split into extremes of pain and fusion from what would otherwise be collective experience sounds an ominous note. Political camps take form around the two poles, consolidating their opposition. The separation experts move to the left, proving that myths of separation can be just as potent as myths of origins. The proponents of fusion gather in the right wing. Only a few prominent intellectual figures, such as modernist writers of the older generation—Thomas Mann and Robert Musil (who are attacked by the avant-garde)—admit their mixed motivations. It is as rare in the republic to come across the relaxed feel of relativism, accepting a degree of separation that operates as a corrective, as it is to find a recovered awareness of origins or a wish for wholeness, qualifying the sense of estrangement. Instead, the logic of extremes dominates the literature of the avant-garde.

A look at the political implications of polarization reveals the one-dimensional images of the individual it sets up. At the same time, the split into opposed spheres obscures their reciprocal conditionality; both separation scenario and fusion drama draw energy from mutual negation and find in the other a horizon of uncanniness that keeps the universe intact.

One-dimensional figures of naïve pathos are singularly attractive as crystallization points of the Weimar imaginary. Institutions, in contrast, seem to some to offer a chance to repeal the separation, combining the desire for separation with the longing for fusion. Carl Schmitt, in his friend-enemy construction, formulates an ingenious key to the combination of familiarity and otherness. The pathos of *distinguo, ergo sum* he discovers here maintains the myth of the isolated individual intact, even while the formulaic consistency of the slogan preserves his shelter among the state-sponsored collective of friends. Paul Tillich, writing in 1932, captures the uncanny dynamic whereby separation wishes and fusion desires interpenetrate, flowing together in the stream of the National Socialist movement. "Contained in the call for community," Tillich remarks in *Die sozialistische Entscheidung,* "is simultaneously a demand for the mother to be created from the son and the father to be recalled out of nothing."[3]

Our examination of the theoretical constructions of the cool persona acquaints us with numerous variations on the attempt to recall the father out of nothing. If the writers held strictly to the slogan, we might expect to find literature populated by one-dimensional characters, but the scarcely concealed wish for the mother to be created as well lends a certain plasticity to the form. The program, announced with pathos, is threatened with destruction by the shadows its figures cast.

While Plessner transposes the idea of sovereignty from Schmitt's *Politische Theologie* onto the individual, constructing his dueling subject, Walter Benjamin uses the landscape of baroque tragedy to expose presumptions of omnipotence, turning the stage's harsh spotlight on the prince to show "his status as a poor human being."[4] Alongside his creatureliness, Benjamin notes the "decision-making incompetence" of the tyrant, who may indeed tirelessly emphasize his sovereignty "in stoic turns of phrase" but, subject to "the sudden caprice of emotional winds that can shift at any time," unwittingly rediscovers himself in the role of the martyr.[5] The effect is the "dismantling of the sovereign, who is split into an ultimately ineffective, if bloody, tyrant, and a no more productive martyr."

The introduction of the idea of sovereignty into the world of the tragedy does not lead solely to this disappointment, which seems to follow the logic of the imprisoned Mercier in Büchner's *Dantons Tod*: "For once, follow your phrases until you find the point where they are embodied." Benjamin's point is a more terrible one. He dissects a character in baroque tragedy who, outfitted with all the attributes of the cool persona—"full understanding and an intact will"—holds the key to fate in his hands. Decision is his métier: he is the intriguer making strategic calculations to seize the mechanisms of the passions controlling others, which are in principle uncontrollable.

Following the trajectory of Schmitt's concept of sovereignty into Benjamin's book on baroque tragedy, we watch it dismantle the decisionists' glory, so that what remains in the end is a schemer. Benjamin registers the extremism of his contemporaries' political anthropology, but he locates their self-confidence on his tragedy's crooked plane.[6] Deprived of the illusion of a solid footing, they suffer vertigo, rushing—along with other insignias of domination—headlong into ruin.

The role of the body in Plessner's construction allows us to follow his isolated duelist into the aesthetic imagination.[7] Plessner's reflexive individual delights, as we have seen, in his possession of a self that exists in sharp distinction to the unconsciousness of physical being. In order to make an elegant presentation in society in physical form, the self must forget the body. Careful watch over the internal boundary by which the self secures its identity delivers it up to a state of chronic anxiety. If surveillance fails, blame threatens. Benjamin's aesthetic is not vulnerable to this threat. The culture of shame, and its self-evident concern for matters of distance and honor, appeals to him as well, but his writings reveal a countervailing effort "to relax the strictness of the self in intoxication."[8] Benjamin searches the literature for glimpses of zones in which the sovereign self wants, in vain, to surrender to forgetfulness.

> Because, however, the most forgotten other is the body—our own body—we understand how Kafka called the cough erupting from his insides "the animal." It was the most advanced outpost of the great herd.[9]

Schmitt's and Plessner's doctrines of sovereignty are ultimately inextricable from the world of the fathers. Both look for examples of decisions in the sanctioned space of the ancestors. Plessner admires Bismarck, brandishing him in opposition to the youth movement. Schmitt sighs over the "absence of the father." "Legal positivism," Schmitt still enjoys complaining after the Second World War, "kills its father and devours its children."[10] Reading Freud's study of Moses prompts the thought that the "Yahweh religion" includes "a mythology of eating up the father" (311). Wherever he sees the figure of the father under attack, wherever he finds the father's place vacant, he senses the proximity of anarchism.

There is no place of honor for decisionist fathers in Benjamin's writings. From the early essay "Metaphysik der Jugend" to his Kafka studies there rings a craving for the destruction of the fathers' world. If it appears in the first as follows,

> Daily we expend unmeasured powers, like a sleeper. What we do and think is filled with the being of our fathers and ancestors. An ungrasped symbolism enslaves us without ceremony.

we find it again in reference to Kafka's figuration of the powerful:

> They are nowhere more dreadful than where they rise up out of the deepest ruin: out of the fathers.[11]

The armored figures that attract Benjamin's interest are not Plessner's or Schmitt's idols, men basking in the glory of sovereignty, but those who, subject to "the sudden caprice of emotional winds that can shift at any time, . . . rise like tattered, fluttering flags," because their guide is not intellectual self-confidence but "physical impulses."[12] On Benjamin's stage, the cool persona walks the crooked plane.

A variety of images of the cool persona surfaces in new objectivity literature, operating under the spell of total mobilization. The artists' favored self-enactment is in that pose. They stand in self-portraits in the posture of Nietzsche's North Pole voyager, casting a mercilessly distinguishing gaze back from the canvas. Otto Dix, a reader of Nietzsche, appears in that pose; George Grosz celebrates his own "pack-ice character." Others proclaim the necessity of putting moral criteria "on ice," if perception is to be precise; knowledge must be "cool" so as not, as Gottfried Benn put it, to become "familiar." Such maxims give an impression of the appeal emanating from the habitus of the cool persona.

The realism of disillusion characteristic of the time, however, means that even the heroic habitus of coolness is infiltrated by the body, its ambivalence exposed. Karl Bühler's *Ausdruckstheorie* analyzes the underlying physiology of coolness, isolating it for experimental examination. Philipp Lersch describes the physiology of the cool gaze—the vertical crease in the forehead, the fixed angle of vision, the narrowed eyes. After capturing the gaze in countless photographs, he subjects it to phenomenological interpretation.[13]

Vertical lines in the forehead had occupied theorists of expression since the time of Greek antiquity, Bühler writes, because they can be understood variously as symptoms of anger, antagonism, or concentration.[14] Lersch, in pursuit of greater descriptive precision, offers a primary explanation of forehead creases in a Darwinist mode, referring to the function of protecting the eyes from bright light, tracing them to alterations of blood pressure in the brain. Only then does he proceed to psychology, deeming them the result of an "actively antagonistic tension in which the musculature around the eye" is activated:

> This concentration of psychological energy on the processing of some sort of sensory or mental object, in the sense of an adaptation to the vital intentions of the individual, is what we must always assume as given from a phenomenological perspective, wherever we observe either the mimic act itself by which a vertical crease is made in the forehead or the lasting mimic traces of such an act.[15]

It seems plausible to Bühler to conclude that wherever we come across a vertical forehead crease, a concentration of psychological energy must be present.

Angle of vision and eyelid behavior are also part of the totality of expression. For the eyeball, depending on its direction one way or the other beneath the forehead crease, requires a specific adjustment of the eyelids and presupposes certain behavior on the part of the eyebrows. In the case of the cool gaze, what guides the focusing motion of the eye musculature is an interest. The impulse to squint is transmitted simultaneously to the muscles that lower the upper lids and raise the lower ones, and again to the muscles that open the eyes. A more or less narrow slit remains open, resulting in the familiar image of eyes peering between nearly closed lids. Bühler, following Lersch, attributes a "basic expressive valence" to this physiological impulse:

> Now, as concerns the psychological interpretation of the nearly covered eye, it is reasonable to conclude without further argumentation that, in the tendency to activate the lid-lifting musculature, a will to maintain apperceptive contact with the environment is at work.[16]

In situations where two people stand face to face, in which eye-to-eye contact occurs, a slight narrowing of the eyelids serves to prevent the penetration of the other's gaze. If concentrated vision through narrowed lids occurs in the absence of a human other, the assumption is that the gazer desires to master the object of the gaze. Situations calling for optical concentration place the person, like an animal in behaviorist experiments, in the mode of attack. Bühler finds the appropriate metaphor: "The gaze patrol either rushes ahead or turns back; the head first, only then the troops, the 'torso,' follows after."[17]

The sharp gaze signals preparedness for action. It probes the environment intentionally, measuring and calculating what it strives to master, at the same time warding off intersubjective interference. In contrast to the habitus of contemplation, whereby eyes "rest on things," letting them appreciate the vagueness of their contours, the sharp gaze of the attack habitus scans the environment, preparing the perceived object, as it were, for consumption. The cool gaze thus belongs to the habitus of a conqueror, the man who tackles something and, at the same time, shields himself from contact.

If it is easy to discover the traces of the cool persona in the artists' self-portraits, in their theories of perceptual acuity and characterology, it appears more rarely in the third person in their works. The causes of this disproportion reflect the Weimar Republic's absence of social structures in which such a figure could develop. Within the marginal spaces of artistic and literary production, the cool persona does thrive as an expressive figure. But here on the margins—at a remove from the machinations of power—it remains an aesthetic phenomenon, mocking the artist's ambition to penetrate to the centers of power. Somewhat frantically, therefore, artists search for points of connection with society's "cool apparatus," finding them in the Communist Party, in the military, in the Freikorps. The situation is similar in the Catholic Church: the Fathers take their stand in the name of the mother church. They do not have to be called up out of nothing; for they have already besieged the republic.

The Marxists assume from the outset anyway that the individual traits of bourgeois heroes (the cool persona included) merely represent masks over the economic drive forces of society, which remain hidden even to the heroes. Insofar as such character masks appear on the stage or in literature, what interests Marxists is their class coding, the underlying guide to dynamic processes on the surface. Yet when the cool persona appears in the type of the party functionary, it is taken to be a figure with a direct line to the party command center.

If we search literature for the type in which Plessner's dual personality, his negative anthropology, and the conduct code of distance coalesce, we find figures of quite various provenance. We shall note that this wish projection blends an aristocratic resentment against the citizen-patriot with a plebeian hatred for the bourgeoisie. Thus does the cool persona appear in a variety of mixtures.

Whether the habitus of the cool persona resonates today depends on our view of aesthetics. From the perspective of the 1970s and 1980s, which attributed therapeutic claims to literature, all the variations on the armored subject fell to annihilating critique. There can be no doubt —the habitus of the cool persona still has a repellent and even unhealthy aspect, even if its adherents, such as Ernst Jünger, live to be over a hundred years old.

Since the plea of this book is for a culture that encourages interrelation—of ego strength and productive regression, of arts of distinction and stopgap forms of fusion, of temporary armoring and its surrender, of clear and blurred boundaries alike—a culture that marks difference and has tolerance for diffusion, we bring a measure of its friendly skepticism to the following eight portraits.

The passage from self-confident cool persona to abandoned creature calls for a degree of personal participation but need not plunge us into a "catastrophe of ridiculousness" (in Plessner's terms). If history has not cast our figures in a comic light, they can nevertheless, as grotesques, be instructive.

FRAMING STORIES

Concepts such as type, icon, and character mask direct attention to a portrait's static contours. Literature nonetheless conceives its human images in the context of experiments that, in the style of the time, were designated as montage or *démontage,* and, in contrast to the following example, are only rarely comic:

Don't talk about danger!
You can't drive a tank through a manhole:
You'll have to get out.
Better abandon your primus
You've got to see that you yourself come through.
Of course you need money
I'm not asking where you get it from
But unless you've got money you needn't bother to go.
And you can't stay here, man.
Here they know you.
If I've got you right
You want to eat a steak or two
Before you give up the race.
Leave the woman where she is.
She has two arms of her own
And two legs for that matter
(Which, sir, are no longer any affair of yours).
See that you yourself come through.
If you've got anything more to say
Say it to me, I'll forget it.
You needn't keep up appearances any longer:
There's no one here any longer to observe you.
If you come through
You'll have done more
Than anyone's obliged to.
Don't mention it.[18]

The armor donned by the subject in order to survive can, in the next moment, become a dangerous burden. The advice that we find in Brecht's *Reader for Those Who Live in Cities* seems paradoxical; but everything depends—this is the text's logic—on not allowing the paradox to paralyze us. The slogan calls, not for single-mindedness, but for agility, and the radar type Brecht presupposes is prepared to relinquish any "appearances," including the militant one.

The *Reader*'s world destroys the social conditions that were supposed to make inner-directed orientation possible: contractual systems are no longer valid; violence is not waiting on the periphery of the communal order but sets the tone of daily life; there can be no talk of fair competition; there is not enough money to go around; there are no peer groups in sight. Reduced to the lowest common denominator, not even the wish for existence as a creature survives. At the end of the successive reductions there is nothing but the body that slips through all the typologies. It appears momentarily, as in the poem "Cover Your Tracks," as an abstract principle of movement, an energy quantum of negation, that does not feed into any dialectic; at most what remains is an object of animal behavior research. But once all its substance is gone, Brecht gives this leftover something a historical charge. Before it takes the stage as proletarian, it amuses us as slapstick.

The literature of this period plays through stages of existential atrophy as a way of dealing with the alarm an older character type feels at being overrun by civilization's sudden advance. The process does not go forward in secret. New objectivity slogans shine over the spectacle like neon lights:

> The process leads straight through the mass ornament, not back from it (Kracauer).
> The individual does not retrieve his humanity by getting out of the masses, but by going into them (Brecht).

As things unfold in the world of the body—in stories of ruin and of being flattened, of imposed conformity or isolation—they generate fear. Joseph Roth comments,

> The future world will be such a triangular track of powerful dimensions. The earth has gone through several transformations—in accord with natural laws. It is going through a new one, according to constructive, conscious, but no less elemental laws. Mourning for the old forms that are passing—that is comparable to the pain of an antediluvian being over the disappearance of prehistoric conditions.[19]

Against this backdrop it would seem wise to present the process of montage without anxiety, as Brecht tried to do in *Mann ist Mann*. The history of the play's revisions, however, betrays a frantic attempt on the part of the author to supply his new hero with ties to the correct collective.

Storytellers in the new objectivity decade encounter a series of framing stories about modernization, which make themselves available as crude but nonetheless helpful procedural forms. One such is Max Weber's narrative of disenchantment, in which the idea of increasing rational feasibility in the world is linked to the feeling of increasing impotence. Novel stories are ones that declare their acceptance of the irreversible process of alienation, that argue in favor of accelerating modernization, exploring the question of whether the individual is able to endure the process at all. Such stories, spectacular as they are, belong to the category of marginal phenomena in the republic. We may expect to hear them from dadaists, the Brecht circle, Bauhaus architects, *Asphaltliteraten* (or, in right-wing terminology, *Kulturbolschewisten*), Bronnen and Jünger.

Much more influential in this decade is the decadence narrative, which finds in the gradual disenchantment of community the "successive stages of a fatal inexorability,"[20] from the "warm" landscapes of originary scenes to the "glacier" of civilization. Civilizing innovations appear from this perspective as signs of the loss of vitality.

In the mid-1920s, Max Scheler notes, in contrast, the epochal process of "*de*sublimation,"[21] signaled by the elevation of sports to cult status, by drive psychology, the revalorization of childhood, and the "desire for a primitive mythological mentality." Scheler registers a "retrograde ethical movement" on the part of peoples who had at one time been the beneficiaries of European culture, a "countercolonization" resulting in the valorization of "barbarisms." The youth movement, in "revolt against the earlier sublimation," had struck back at the fathers' ascetic ethic of work and acquisition; World War I had also represented such an uprising.

Scheler is a skeptical observer. As long as the decadence movement goes on rejecting reason, he expects that desublimation will remain a critical aspect of it. Wherever it appears and no matter what ideas and valuations may contain it, desublimation — like the longing for the primitive, the childlike, a lost naïveté — remains in itself a sign of the age and of "wearying of vitality." The revocation of sublimation is for Scheler a process that spans the period from Jugendstil to the fascist movement. The culture industry of the new objectivity he understands as an integral element of the revolt against techniques of sublimation that had been developed in an age of inner-direction.

Disenchantment and decadence and desublimation: three names for narratives of social development, to which *progress* must be added as a fourth. Progress narratives found their secure foothold in the political organizations of the working class.

These four names stand for models available to narrators for their stories. New objectivity narratives elide disenchantment and desublimation. Ethical retrogression heralds the possibility of progress. "Street people," written off in the decadence narrative as "deserters from life," acquire value as nomads. The revaluation does not come off painlessly —even the comedy of these years (*Mann ist Mann*) cannot do without war. The legend of demystification as a "fatal inexorability" accompanies even the comedic restructuring of the new objectivity type. War, the lime pit, assassination, suicide, social degradation, commodification— all of these are inseparable from the scenario in which the modernization of the German subject plays itself out. Horváth begins one of his popular plays with a woman sacrificing her body to anatomy. She is admitted into the circulation of goods and bodies only as a corpse. Sally Bowles, Christopher Isherwood's new objectivity character, disappears as a foreign Anglo-Saxon body into the German shadows of death.

Disenchantment, decadence, desublimation, progress—not even the sum of these narratives yields the historical process that appears to us in retrospect. For none of these narratives construct a future that coincides with what came in the 1930s and 1940s. Their narrative future was blind to the reality that developed, and it is no wonder that new objectivity intellectuals ultimately felt deceived. The resulting bitterness explains the appeal of the "dialectic of enlightenment," which, at the end of the 1930s, combines the narratives of disenchantment and decadence, desublimation and progress, into the conceptual figure of the paradox.

PORTRAITS

TALLEYRAND ODER DER ZYNISMUS

That Franz Blei dedicates his 1932 novel, *Talleyrand oder der Zynismus*, to his Catholic friend from the bohemian days of his youth might appear simply a historical curiosity if the friend had not gone on to become the renowned constitutional lawyer who (also in 1932) formulated the legal justification for the chancellor to banish the Social Democratic government. Blei's dedication reads, "For Carl Schmitt, in friendship and respect."[22]

Yet the dedication has more than a hint of irony, for Blei's novel about cynicism works to expose the shortcomings of the future Prussian state official. Taking Talleyrand as the "exemplary model of the consummate politician" (345), the novel illuminates the failings of the new Machiavelli: the French statesman did not "rise through the ranks but was born to his position" (15), his aristocratic resentment against the citizen-patriot intact. The passions and drives Schmitt had repressed in his political subject as a decision-making apparatus return in Blei's Talleyrand. "He is not exactly of a criminal disposition," Blei repeatedly quotes the American envoy, "though certainly indifferent between virtue and vice" (12 [English wording in the original]).

A first glance at the novel displays the correspondences between the novel and certain of the slogans popularized by 1920s political anthropology. Axioms from Hobbes's *Leviathan* hang like signboards over the scene (using the new objectivity language of Bertrand Russell): "People do good to the extent that they are forced to do good, and bad to the ex-

tent that no power prevents them doing it" (344). Talleyrand knows that
the success of political action depends on the "clever channeling of
drives and vices" (10). The idea of "inborn goodness" he dismisses with
a laugh as no more than an element of political romanticism that Blei,
following Schmitt, ascribes to the "discussing class," the bourgeoisie.
Parliament may indeed be a fitting institution for endless bourgeois palaver, but liberal indecision cannot but fray the nerves of a true politician, who is instinctively drawn to dictatorial measures. "As soon as
discussion exceeds the time allotted to it," the genuine man of power
"withdraws" (12)—thus Blei in the spirit of Schmitt's critique of par-
liamentarism. While most of the programmatic Schmittisms reproduced
in the novel are confined to the introduction, we shall see that Blei's hero
scarcely deviates from Schmitt's overall political design.

Blei's hero also betrays personal characteristics drawn wholly in
Schmitt's spirit: Talleyrand's impassive exclusion of moral judgment
from political considerations; his aversion for all forms of fundamentalism, in which Schmitt suspects a marriage of humanism and terror. The
"political," for Blei as well, has "no substance" to it; it takes place in
the realm of the "conditional," permanently split off from the realm
of the "actual" (7). "The ethical concept of truth and lies is relativized
wherever it enters into the fictional construction of the political." The
author cites, approvingly, the characteristics Balzac had given the prince
in *Père Goriot:* "There are no principles, only results; there are no laws,
only circumstances" (330).

When politics cannot be derived from substantive values, when all
that orients action is effect and principles become nothing more than
functional values—when there is no "ground" beneath a man's feet—
stability comes to depend on explicit codes of conduct. So, too, in the
case of Talleyrand. His life trajectory arches over a landscape rocked by
social historical earthquakes, wherein only the practice of an astounding degree of flexibility ensures stability within the relatively rigid behavioral codex to which Bishop Talleyrand—not contradicting his flexibility in the slightest—adheres even in risky situations.

Maxims from Talleyrand's manual are sprinkled throughout the
book. Blei speaks of Talleyrand's "general apparatus of behavior" (34),
which eliminates the need for spontaneity, even while it secures certain
pleasures. The regulatory system is not original; Talleyrand holds with
such as Machiavelli and models of *il cortigiano;* he is familiar with the
French moralists and has absorbed his precepts from Gracián:

> Avoid demanding anything that you know will subject you to unnecessary demands.
> Show no sign of haste, although it were needed, but do occasion it in others.
> In critical moments, assume an air of indifference. (34)

Talleyrand uses these rules to negotiate relations with Louis XVI, the Directorate, Napoleon, the Vienna Congress, and Louis XVIII. The apparatus supplied by his code of conduct effectively replaces the conscience, proving itself every bit as reliable a compass amid the temblors of revolution and restoration as it would, for example, following the lead of the finance bourgeoisie. To this point, the resonance between Schmitt's polemic against political romanticism and Plessner's code of distance and Blei's image of Bishop Talleyrand is still audible but stops as soon as Blei is required to explain what drives his hero. The motivations that a decisionist construction obscures are "lust after women" and an exceptional measure of monetary greed. What Schmitt tries to filter out of his theory of the decision-making machine—the economy and all greed—suddenly reappear center stage. Woman, in Blei's representation, is not only Talleyrand's vital elixir but also the secret of his diplomatic successes. That Talleyrand's friend Madame de Staël portrays him in a novel as a woman causes no offense to the bishop. The boundaries between diplomacy and amorous adventures are fluid; the "feminism of his being" (287) favorably influences his career, and his particular brand of wit makes even his crippled foot irrelevant.

Such a turn is little short of miraculous from the 1920s perspective of the armored self. We see here a political subject that is not afraid to seem undignified the moment it lays down its arms, a subject that shrugs off charges of cowardice, in the knowledge, shared with Gracián, that "a finely executed retreat is also worth something" (123). In Blei's novel, in other words, we encounter a character that is impossible in the political understanding of the decisionists. German culture had no place for the man of politics as gallant; the protean figure of the politician also fell victim to the fear of ridiculousness, leaving him interesting only in one of several "iron" variants. On paper, Plessner's duelist and Schmitt's decision maker are beings devoid of economic interest, while Blei's Talleyrand, for whom money is a "spiritual power," surrenders to "unrestrained monetary greed" (175). He takes pleasure in the stock exchange and the market, a pleasure just as fundamental as that he finds in his amorous play. Considering that Blei's Talleyrand is outrageously deficient in secondary virtues—he was famous for his laziness, accustomed to his *levée* around noon, and regarded slowness as a cardinal political virtue—we see emerging beneath his characterological surface the stereotypical image of another political subject, one cast in the image of the Jewish politician on the model of Disraeli, toward whom Schmitt harbored a love-hate relationship.[23]

If we compare this figure with the political subject imagined by Jünger, or Plessner—which never escapes the pathos of the solitary combatant even while serving the collective—what we notice is Talleyrand's lack of an essential element of the militant subject. "Attitude," in the sense of a decision kept in effect over time, not only is essential to the militant construction but becomes a magic word more generally toward the end of the republic. Talleyrand's cynicism teaches that it takes more than attitude to survive.

In the historical period traversed by Talleyrand, what was the fate of "faster" politicians, those who were able to make split-second decisions, who suddenly emerge out of the nothing of the moment? Franz Blei's sideswipe at the future "crown jurist of the Third Reich" is unmistakable: Napoleon is described as a man who sought "to overcome the debacle of revolutionary achievements through the form of a total state" (235). Blei links Schmitt's terminology to the fast-moving Napoleon: the concept might perhaps serve its purpose for a time, but its days are always numbered.

On the eve of the Third Reich, Blei couples the idea of the total state with the fiasco of a fast-paced temperament. On his stage an extra wears the character mask from behind which he will enact the future terror. The "tactless Fouché" turns ups only on the margins of the action, where he demonstrates that ethical rigidity and cruelty are the inevitable elements of a petit-bourgeois blend. Still, this type is characterized by a greater affinity with the "ghostly abstraction of political officialdom, which is called reason of state" (137); the services it offers therefore fit the modern bureaucracy.

Fouché may indeed be lacking in the glamour of a cool persona on the model of a Talleyrand—he represents much more the banality of evil, which can be more easily institutionalized—but it is to him that the future belongs. In 1929 Stefan Zweig sketched Fouché's physiognomy in a gaslight, bleaching all the color from his skin, confirming the reputation of the police chief as "reptilian" in nature. In Zweig's likeness of the political man drilled in the school of Loyola, the dreadful features of the cool persona are harshly revealed:

> He is neither ruled by his nerves nor seduced by his senses; his entire passion charges and discharges behind the impenetrable wall of his forehead. He puts his forces in play, always on the lookout for others' mistakes; he lets others be consumed by their passions, waiting patiently until they are exhausted or their lack of self-control exposes them: and then he strikes. Terrible is the superiority of this nerveless patience; a man who can wait like that in hiding can fool even the ablest. . . . Thus the coldness of his blood is Fouché's real genius. His body neither restrains him nor carries him away.[24]

Not long after Franz Blei's novel appeared there arose a political constellation in which Schmitt, the object of Blei's dedication, would become a legal philosophical prompter for a rival Fouché.

SERNER'S *HANDBREVIER FÜR HOCHSTAPLER*

The counterbalance to the cool persona's aristocratic type is the confidence man. The social claims he makes do not coincide with his origins; should his actual heritage be discovered, his social existence is lost. Hence he moves on a terrain littered with traps set by the reality of his past. He moves in a world where the only mortal sin is to allow his attentiveness to lapse. The con man's life is the "as-if" existence par excellence, in which success depends on the virtuoso application of the behavioral codex of an alien class. "Appear civilized," Gracián had counseled. The swindler makes this his creed: appearance is profitable. In line with courtly codes of conduct, Walter Serner declares: "Whoever you may be, say this to yourself: ALL THAT TRANSPIRES AROUND ME CAN ALSO BE FEIGNED. Then you will remain healthy and things will go well for you on earth" (maxim no. 422). And maxim no. 325 makes it clear that in truth Serner's *Handbrevier* is a manifesto against the cult of sincerity:

> The distinction between virtuoso dissimulation and genuineness is too small to be measured. The former can be acquired only through intensive practice, whereby you also develop the ability to recognize genuineness. If occasionally, however, it continues to exceed your capabilities, then forgo dissimulation (the great ruiner!) and say what you may not act out.

The "devilish" transgression of the line separating authenticity from artificiality is the characteristic movement of Serner's writing. What he prescribes in his *Handbrevier* he puts into practice in his crime stories: not even elemental feeling eliminates the possibility of being a "useful fiction."[25] Theodor Lessing, in his 1925 review of Serner's crime stories, stresses the point that the author's accomplishment is to represent passions in such a way that the reader cannot finally distinguish whether the characters are deceiving themselves or "actually experiencing each other." Lessing locates the acuity of Serner's diagnostic gaze in his concealment, in impenetrable darkness, of the "crossing of genuine emotional flows and leaps with manufactured and feigned sensations." The presumption of a clear distinction between unconscious "primitive" outpourings and "willed" actions fails in the face of Serner's gangsters and their molls.

> [It is impossible to keep track of] where the truth of affective life lapses and where the performance of it begins. If something natural does manage to break through, ice-cold games of life immediately interpret and exploit it. Often the characters' excesses are cold hypocrisy; but they nevertheless remain under the pressure of real unconscious excess; at other times something ultimate does break out through a cocaine-paralysis of the soul.[26]

It is as if Serner sought to illustrate Plessner's anthropology with the example of the confidence man: there is no core self; the various masks have not only the function of adapting a substantial self opportunistically to a situation but also offer the possibility "of being the other to the respective roles."[27]

> Indeed, maintaining an insistence on being who one is, while certainly desirable, would be all but fatal if it were to congeal into a *single* role, and not only on account of the limitation entailed, but primarily because it eliminates the possibility of changing roles.[28]

It is easy to understand how the confidence man, as a type, can be fascinating in a situation broadly experienced as bottomless; con men appear everywhere, in the theater and film, in detective novels and the mass press. This eccentric character reveals how fragile are the strategies of distinction in a society in which money operates as the great leveler and what the market honors above all else is the pliability of one's attitude. In the con man, the ideal of personal autonomy appears only in the form of virtuosity in the changing of masks. He wants to be what he appears to be to others, but if he allows himself to become that, he loses the remainder of his autonomy, which exists solely in that latitude of difference.

In certain of his traits, the confidence man resembles the autodidact as described in sociology: he possesses little cultural capital of his own, learns from models, and is filled with anxiety over being discovered.[29] The broad public delights in the techniques with which he succeeds in confounding the distinction practiced by the distinguished class. What he also calls to mind, however, is the danger of falling from one day to the next to the bottom of the social heap.

The practical part of the *Handbrevier für Hochstapler* appeared in 1927.[30] In it are blended the dada cult of indifference and Nietzsche's theory of masks with an ironic reference to the new objectivity imperative of action. The form is borrowed from Gracián's *Art of Worldly Wisdom,* as contemporary critics were already aware.[31] Serner's handbook contains 591 rules, divided into thirteen chapters. Rule no. 338 concerns intonation:

> It is better to speak conventionally, rather than in principle, if you want to gain time, and better in a chatty, rather than informational, manner, if you want to gain power.

The maxims are delivered deadpan, in a manner reminiscent of Buster Keaton; the book offers guidance to those who are already ruined. "People tolerate you, because you cannot be ruined" is the consoling advice of no. 116. In the tradition of dada, the *Handbrevier* is a handbook for "the balancing act over the abyss of murder, violence, and theft" (Raoul Hausmann).[32]

The habitus recommended in the *Handbrevier* draws our attention to the figure of the dandy, an important link in the tradition of the cool persona. This nineteenth-century type extolled alienation as an art of living. Unscrupulousness and discretion were present alongside the fetishism of affective control, the treatment of nature and drives as mechanical systems, and the meticulous avoidance of the traps of relationship.[33] The exclusive figure of the dandy looked anachronistic to twentieth-century observers, but certain features of its habitus showed up, remarkably, in an artists' group as early as World War I. Dadaism, a laboratory of shaming and disgrace, practiced attitudes of indifference—"American Buddhism"—and its proponents tried, through a cult of meticulous exposure, to make themselves immune to power exercised to shame the subject. Even in advance of the Berlin dadaists, Serner extended the rite of self-shaming into language as such ("Every word is a *Blamage*"); he saw only one chance for self-consciousness: it must already have blamed itself. "Severely blamed. Outrageously blamed. Blamed entirely without measure. Blamed so horrifically, that everything else is drawn into the blame."[34]

Conditions, however, are precarious for the modern dandy. Assimilation into the aristocracy's higher social standing does not facilitate his behavior. The disciplining of the affects requires uninterrupted "train-ing," to which Serner devotes a chapter of its own. The persona prac-tices strategies of distancing. Its habitus consists in remaining, as we would say today, "cool." The law followed by the persona reads—in English, the favorite language of the new objectivity: "First one must master all those elements of self and situation whose unmastered pres-ence constitutes the condition of embarrassment. These include spaces, props, equipment, clothing, and body."[35]

Thus declare the rules of balance:

> From time to time, excesses are necessary [see Figure 6]. After two months of uninterrupted regularity, the body is sick of it. Allow it a brief, but furi-ous storm. (no. 320)
>
> Never show your hatred. (Hidden hate is a source of strength.) If the num-ber of your enemies grows too large, show contempt; that will cause those whose hate actually consists in envy to assume that it would be dangerous to arouse your hatred. But where you must show it, follow it with the cor-responding deed. (no. 337)
>
> However complete your anesthesia against praise and criticism may have become, the danger of a relapse is always present. (no. 349)
>
> If suddenly you find yourself lacking the strength to lie, then at least be cruel. (no. 344)

In the *Handbrevier*'s world no formula of authenticity is valid. The point in this hall of mirrors is "impression management" (Erving Goff-man); that is, the goal is to leave behind in others' eyes the impression of authenticity. As disconcerting and unscrupulous as this idea might be to a member of a guilt culture, for the inhabitants of a shame culture it has become a necessity. "In the case of shame," we read from Agnes Hel-ler, "the authority is social custom—ritual, habits, codes or rosters of behavior—represented by the eye of the other."[36]

Serner's confidence man exploits precisely this circumstance, that he is the object of the other's gaze, playing out the various possibilities open to him. The point at which the ego-ideal of autonomy fears fiasco is where he begins the drama of his self-enactment. As a precaution he keeps with him at all times a small hand mirror so he can test his facial expressions before he puts them to use. Now and then it is advisable to make quickly for the rest room "to practice an expression" (no. 328). Since the distinction between dissimulation and genuineness is too small to measure on this ground of sheer mobility, the foreseeable effect of an expression is what decides whether it counts as authentic.

6. From time to time, excesses are necessary

(Christian Schad, *Der Pfiff um die Ecke* [A whistle around the corner], 1927. With the permission of Christian Schad, G. A. Richter, Rottach-Egern.)

> Above all, practice the effect of your eyes every day by standing in front
> of a mirror. Your gaze must learn to rest still and heavy on another, to veil
> itself quickly, to sting, to indict. Or to emanate enough experience and
> knowledge to shock your counterpart into offering his hand (no. 323).

The mirror serves the actor in the study of the self. The type of self-
perception required is that which we have already found in the baroque
duelist's conduct code: "The gaze directed at its own physiognomy in
the mirror has assumed within itself the gaze of the others."[37] The mirror of conscience, on the other hand, which a guilt culture demands that
its members use offstage, is of no use to the actor. Serner's subject de-
spises psychoanalysis, as befits the cool persona. Instead there are die-
tary rules: "Eat little meat (never fatty), but a lot of fruit salads and
green vegetables. Take frequent deep breaths; bathe only twice a week
(ten minutes, lukewarm)" (no. 316).

For melancholy moods, Serner recommends such tongue twisters
as *teremtete*—the word games of the dadaists seem to be migrating to
the ground of the soul. Unarmed, lacking a soldierly physiognomy, the
dandy persona transplanted to the world of the new objectivity must not
show its true face in public: "If you could appear visually as the mon-
ster of indifference you really are, a ten-minute stroll would leave you
dead. No one could endure you for even a second, without falling upon
you with both fists flying" (no. 108).

Werner Krauss discovers, as he reconstructs Gracián's code of conduct
in the "enormous realm on which the Habsburgs' sun set," that the
"con-man morality" often occurs as a kind of "maintenance morality,"
a survival technique.[38] Guided by Serner's *Handbrevier,* the persona
moves about in a tertiary sector. It is ready to take on situations in ho-
tels, train stations, post and telegraph offices, in vehicles of public trans-
portation, and in private interchanges. In all these settings there is one
fundamental rule: "If you stumble into a false appearance, combat it
by maneuvering yourself into another false appearance" (no. 245). Gracián had already offered a roundabout version of the same advice: "One
would not wish to be taken for a man of dissimulation, although it is
not possible to live these days without it." Serner's 591 tips take up the
Spanish Jesuit's agonistic image—outfitted with modern requisites for
moving successfully in the world of the new media:

> Do not imagine that telephone conversations conducted in a hotel room
> or in the hall are not being overheard (no. 132).

Learn to telegraph in such a way that it appears to be encoded, without being so. And vice versa (no. 558).

Refuse banknotes bearing private signs and change them immediately (no. 576).

Do not go to masseuses, unless you want to be massaged. Otherwise it can happen that you will be seen and photographed (no. 433).

Regard every ear within earshot as an enemy ear (no. 444).—In hotel rooms, undertake important activities very quietly and only with the curtains drawn (no. 452).

Make a habit of standing in front of shop mirrors. In this way you can conveniently observe what is going on behind you (no. 478).

Serner's *Handbrevier* and Brecht's *Reader for Those Who Live in Cities* open a new chapter in the literature of the city. Urban decor, local color, facades, squares, building complexes or sounds appear before us only in an orienting function. The city is much more a specific terrain of behavior.[39] The eye assesses possible obstacles; it is a tactical organ and a trained physiognomist. The ear functions as an alarm, with the special task of supervising the voice's volume (and, when necessary, reducing it to a whisper). The focus of perception is entirely outward: it listens, probes, scents. The new media, such as the telephone, telegraph, and tickertape, convey the necessary information to Serner's character. Language acquires the function of an advance scout in enemy territory, identifying possibilities for movement by the person who remains undercover.

Obviously, Serner's gentleman is a virtuoso in the art of separation. Symbiotic relationships of whatever sort, even provisional ones, represent a trap. The ultimate in obligation is a "free marriage," which Serner, borrowing from colloquial slang, terms a "mixed bag." Here as well he advises distance: "Never live together with your lover. At most in the same building" (no. 213). The family is not only disqualified as a form of sociability and reproduction but also eliminated, in tip no. 359, as the locus of origins: "Blood ties are an invention. Not simply because only the mother can ever be sure. Once the cord is cut, it is over."

Although Serner's con man is incomparably more flexible than Plessner's man of decision, the *Handbrevier* advises him to calculate carefully the danger of appearing ridiculous. He may surrender to mockery only in a single place, with a single person:

Everything can be ridiculed. Indulge this pleasure, however, only with your lover; it will increase her passion for you. (Every woman is a closet anar-

chist.) Forbid it among men: it will paralyze your creatures; and your associates will quickly find you ridiculous. (no. 102)

While Plessner sought out a site of "mercy," where the self worn out
from fencing could recuperate, Serner is comfortable in the company of
the female anarchist (a frightful image in the duelist's universe)—and
she, of course, represents much more than an anarchist.

Serner's exercises give us no help examining our conscience, but
he does offer tips on tactical skills aimed at the optimal exploitation of
opportunities. The discursive ritual of confession, a favorite in late expressionism, is recommended only when it is sure to win territory; guilt
feelings are dispensed with altogether. Self-knowledge can inadvertently
come about, but it never results from plumbing the depths of the individual soul or cracking the family vault for secrets; it arises only in the
mirror of the other's assessing perception. The individual sees himself
surrounded by many gazes and uses all the vantages of surveillance to
learn about his own identity in the focal point of hostile perception.
Naturally, the practice demands a degree of mental awareness that can
quickly lead to exhaustion, which threatens even a confidence man with
melancholy. In such cases, however, the reader is referred to commandment no. 357: "If you take ill, take cover. That will make you well more
quickly."

Although many of the directives in the *Handbrevier* correspond to
Plessner's behavioral doctrine of distance—not least because both
derive from motifs of aestheticism—worlds separate the two. More
precisely, what distinguishes the two texts is Serner's exploration of the
underworld.

Serner bathes his unscrupulous persona in a comedic light; he teaches
the armored ego dances that it can only perform awkwardly in combat
boots, and, above all, a matter of life and death permits his character to
be cowardly (no. 33). The attitude demanded by Plessner and Schmitt is
for Serner so much ballast. Still, the comedic light is intermittent: in the
end, the individual flitting through Serner's *Handbrevier* is as anxious as
the others, as if pursued by invisible agents of surveillance. He, too, is in
a chronic state of alarm: "It is easier give a pursuer the slip than it is to
escape being pursued" (no. 470).

The only available shelter is the code itself, and even here conditions
are precarious, for it is in the nature of language to undermine appearances. Rather than give the reader a false sense of security, Serner puts
his practical manual of behavior at the beginning of the revised version

of *Letzte Lockerung,* the first part of his 1920 dadaist manifesto. As introductory material, the *Handbrevier* warns that even the view of the world from the standpoint of the conduct code is no more than a "combination of words."[40]

> Every word is a *Blamage,* be it well noted. There is nothing to do beyond spewing out verbiage, performing circus tricks on suspension bridges (or over plants, canyons, beds).[41]

Serner's *Handbrevier* does not forget for a moment that the comedy of dissimulation it recommends is itself only a manner of speech, serving "to manufacture a redemptive heaven over this chaos of rubbish and puzzles."[42] But, since the persona always acts only from within the awareness that unfeigned authenticity is not to be had—where language itself is already elementary dissimulation—the point becomes to deploy signifying conventions in the consciousness of their artificiality and expression in the knowledge of its schematic nature. The commandments of the conduct code thus propose the possibility of living "inside appearances" (Nietzsche).[43]

Yet the question arises of whether Serner manages to do entirely without authenticity. The crime stories that he collected in the books *Der elfte Finger, Zum blauen Affen, Der Pfiff um die Ecke,* and *Die Tigerin* lead us to locations where, he hopes, authenticity does in fact exist, in the cool version of the criminal underworld. There he comes upon an astonishingly rational codex, a high degree of self-reflection on the model of Gracián and Plessner, not nourished by interiority but dictated by the presence of mind of a chess master playing several games at once. Here he finds long-lost genuineness in a deceitfulness that has become first nature. Here too he finds the artful concentration on dissimulation that every one of his actors seeks to achieve, without forgetting about "the dissimulating, deceitful surveillance of the other," which was one of the cardinal points of the code of courtly behavior.[44] Hope for a language of the heart runs through the criminal underworld.

In one of the stories from the volume *Der Pfiff um die Ecke* an international check forger wants to make a deal with the Scotland Yard specialist that has been put on the case. They share a brief moment of consensus: "Among high-level experts like ourselves, the only place to explore matters of trust with any security is at the dizzying edge of a cliff."[45] Trust nevertheless remains a tactical move, subject, like all communication, to cynical calculation. The story of the "Ermordung der Marchese de Brignole-Sale" reports on the contact established by a male gangster with a female bandit. Here as well the antagonists are momentarily of one heart and mind:

> "It's especially hard, practically impossible, to reach an understanding if at least a tiny little bit of trust isn't—given up. The way a better player gives up something to a weaker one."
>
> "But I'm always surprised when I pull it off. That's one of the clearest sources of mistrust."
>
> She fell silent. Sorhul thought he caught the hint of a smile.
>
> "It's probably altogether impossible to talk, except as a wild gamble."
>
> "I'm not sure. Sometimes all you have to do is talk to recognize the opponent's aim. What actually gets said is entirely beside the point."[46]

And then both walk right into the traps they have set for each other.

No other access to interiority seems to be available to Serner, and it is not surprising that later on he would also condemn this type: in the intellectual space of prefascism he identifies it as "cool romanticism," alternating between iron hardness and suicidal tendencies. To this day, Serner's *Handbrevier* stands as a "cynical spectacle on the eve of the dictatorship."[47] The judgment stems from the disarming quality of an amoral character about whose creatural substance nothing can be determined with confidence.

Annoyance with the type also stems from the difficulty involved in establishing anything definite about the person of its creator, beyond the evidence of his texts. By calling his crime stories memoirs, Serner cultivated a legendary identity even during his lifetime. Thomas Milch compares the author to one story's mysterious analyst of a "memorable conversation" in Florence. Responding to the question, "Who are you?" the character pisses his name in the sand, illegibly, and then disappears into the darkness. His identity has the substance of a dadaist artwork, written in chalk on a blackboard and then wiped out after the performance.[48] Serner cultivated the mask of the gentleman criminal, or the "baron among the soldiers of dada" (Hans Richter), the brilliant cosmopolitan regardless of circumstances, or the pimp.[49] For information about the "genuine" existence of the writer Walter Serner, we have to rely on the few documents that have been gathered over the course of many years' research: official records, birth certificate, university files, police reports, and hotel registrations—and deportation lists for the Theresienstadt concentration camp.[50]

The cult of sincerity does not come to an end until the inevitable anger of disillusion fastens on those who discover that even the unconscious, seemingly the last residue of spontaneity, is "entangled in inauthenticity."[51] The discovery itself is a form of cynicism that appears simply to accept—not without a certain eagerness—the loss of emotional genuineness. The prognosis for the cynical personality is as ominous as we can imagine:

> If an actor rejects from the outset the attitude of sincere communication, then manipulation of the outer world, rather than the expression of his inner world, takes over his dramaturgic orientation.[52]

Those who squander the opportunity for "genuine expression" (and the assumption that the symbolic order in which it could take place offers a transparent, undisguisable glimpse into the inner world) need not wonder if what they suffer in exchange is defeat.

In his critique of American researchers such as Erving Goffman, who stresses the necessity of a dramaturgy of self-enactment, Sighard Neckel maintains that such "artificial" behavior inevitably goes wrong:

> Wherever Goffman's "impression management" has become a social norm, the situative dilemma immediately comes up. It represents a particular serious latent danger where public exchange among individuals has a ceremonial coloration.[53]

Attempts to manipulate the codes of ceremonial communication always produce bad results:

> The more powerfully . . . the protagonists of ceremonial behavior are driven . . . to maintain at all costs the "illusion of their own noninvolvement," the greater may be the corresponding fear of losing their aesthetic distance from events, of bungling the performance, of suffering a minor interpersonal catastrophe. Fear as a rule only heightens one's vulnerability to embarrassment, which is precisely what coolness is supposed to reduce.[54]

Avoiding catastrophe was already the point for Plessner. The danger, for both him and his descendants, would be half as great if only they would give up the either-or attitude, combining the art of ceremonial behavior, when the situation calls for it, with the reflection that formlessness does not make a situation that has nothing to do with public formality any more authentic.

It is a macabre fact of German cultural history that the "end-to-sincerity" problematic had to be addressed through the medium of the *Handbrevier*—a handbook for confidence men, that relegates the possibility of humane nonliteral exchange to the criminal demimonde. Serner's *Handbrevier* focuses on this sad circumstance through the genre of comedy, which is how a shame culture puts its humanity on display. As he formulates it in maxim no. 47, "The world is ruled by comedy, and VICTORIES ARE TO BE HAD ONLY UNDER THIS SIGN. Therefore, never fight for anything. PLAY for it."

Serner's fate after 1927 demonstrates that the German cultural tradition—unlike the French or Anglo-American—had no experimental space for his intellectual figures to operate in. Having had his small oeuvre published by Paul Steegemann, he withdrew from sight, prompting legends at the time that he had vanished into the milieu of his stories. Today his disappearance suggests "the cliché . . . that the great cynic, after 1927, stepped down from the pedestal and lived out the lapidary bourgeois life of a married man."[55] Thomas Milch, pointing out that Serner continued his restless life unchanged but simply avoided Germany after 1933, attempts to refute this tale of exhaustion. In 1938 Serner rented an apartment in Prague and married his longtime companion, Dorothea Herz. Their attempt, following the Nazi invasion, to get a visa for Shanghai failed:

> Official documents of the time list Walter Eduard Israel Serner as a language teacher, and Dorothea Sara Serner as a housewife; they are registered in the Prague Jewish community under numbers 36213 and 36212. On 10 August 1942 they were relocated in Transport Ba (as numbers 253 and 1338, among a total of 1,460 people) to the Theresienstadt ghetto, and deported from there on 20 August in Transport Bb to the so-called east. The destination of their final journey is not known.[56]

What is it that prevents us from using the telescope of our research to peer "all the way through the bloody fog at a mirage" of the 1920s, in order to recognize the humanity of that time in the refractions that, as Benjamin put it, would show it "in a future state of the world emancipated from magic?"[57] Reconstructions these days tend to raise the dictatorship and its horrors to a telos, which lends all the processes and intellectual motifs an objective function leading toward a wrong end. But in Serner's obscure case we can glimpse the mirages, which ultimately took on more concrete form far from Germany and innocent of the fear. This perception itself is practically taboo, for the faraway land was America and the place was Hollywood.

In Ernst Lubitsch's films, which he made as an emigrant in the 1930s, con men, seducers, betrayers, and liars abound. Required of them as well is the mental awareness of the chess master, but the demand does not put them in the chronic state of alarm suffered by their German forbears in the 1920s. In Lubitsch's films we see the slogan "Appearance civilizes" (see Figure 7) cast in the light of uninterrupted comedy. There

7. Appearance civilizes

(Ernst Lubitsch. With the permission of Süddeutscher
Verlag, Munich.)

is no trace of the cult of authenticity; unmasking is not the issue.[58] Lubitsch shows us how well masks can go with a face, if they are part of
the economy of a relaxed life, hazy intentions, and an avoidance of self-
torment. The masks allow possibilities to come to light, possibilities that
are not hidden within the individual but brought to him or her from
without.[59]

These possibilities are lost to German development because they arise
in a place that suffers excommunication by German cultural criticism.

INFANTRY DOGS IN A BAUHAUS APARTMENT

In 1926 Bertolt Brecht tells a story of two male types who, having shared
the narrow confines of the trenches during the war, meet again in the republic, in a Bauhaus apartment. There would be no story to tell were the
apartment not the site of a catastrophe of ridiculousness, which, as we
know, it is the aim of every code of conduct to avoid.

It has long since become an established fact that in November and December
1918 a very large number of men, whose manners had suffered somewhat,
returned home with their habits and got on the nerves of the people they had
fought for.[60]

Brecht begins the story with this sentence, deriving the appeal of the
Bauhaus aesthetic from the experience of infantry dogs in the trenches.
At the same time, however, it quickly becomes apparent that any such
rational enclosure as a Bauhaus apartment also produces an "unfathomable desire" for chaos. An engineer by the name of Müller is of the sort
whose manners got a bit wild. His counterpart is Kampert, another
engineer, whose sole desire, having survived the mud and slime of Arras
and Ypres, is to live exclusively in a tiled bathroom (see Figure 8). Ernst
Bloch also remarks that functionalist dwellings had something of the
"charm of a sanitary facility," and the opening paragraph of the story
explains—quasi psychoanalytically (which we would least expect from
Brecht)—the longing of returning soldiers for hygienic rituals:

There's nothing you can say to these sorts that will entice them out of their
tiled bathrooms, after they've had to spend a few years of their lives lying
around in muddy trenches.

The drama begins when comrade Müller, along with the laconic narrator, yet another engineer from the trenches, is invited to Kampert's
apartment. Its appointments follow all the rules of new objectivity design: black lacquered hooks in the wardrobe; American recliners in the
simple white-walled living room; a Japanese straw mat hung like an
awning in front of the oblique atelier window; a red mahogany cabinet
for counterpoint; an iron spiral staircase leading up to the simple bedroom, with iron bedsteads and simple enamel sink; and, separated from
it only by a chintz curtain, the spartan study with shelves and a pine
table and a hard, low chaise longue.

Müller, having been conducted through the new objectivity quarters,
mumbles guiltily: "Well, it's actually living just like a pig." Where nothing is left to chance, an accident always occasions a minor catastrophe.
The drama that now gets under way displays the return of the trench
warriors to the scene of objectivity; or, vice versa, it reveals that the stylistic rigor of the apartment and its inhabitants represents a return of the
heroic, which all three protagonists, in the mulch of Arras, had dis-
dained. Kampert's retreat into the cool interior of Bauhaus design is a
kind of civilian reassimilation of heroic armoring.

8. His sole desire is to live exclusively in a tiled bathroom

(Soldiers killed in the trenches at the Western Front, 1917. Photo by Ernest Brook. With the permission of Imperial War Museum, London.)

The satirical element of the story can be more easily understood against the backdrop of Bruno Taut's defense of the new dwelling. Taut's book, *Die neue Wohnung,* went through five printings between 1924 and 1928, reaching a circulation of 26,000 copies by that time. Readers learned from Taut to expect from the new interior the effect of a "refreshing bath." Paintings hanging on the wall are outfitted, as they are in Kampert's apartment, with curtains: art works should not be witnesses to such banal necessities as eating and digestion. "Bodily hygiene must now be joined by mental hygiene," Taut demanded. Contrarily, "there is no need to shut off conversation in a tidy environment," justifying glass walls surrounding the dining room.[61]

Taut's leitmotif is the "elimination of atavisms," which he suspects not only in the remnants of the "sumptuous Orient" of *Gründerzeit* apartments, but in all concavities and dysfunctional elements that upset the aim of being "indisputable master in one's own home." Taut is building Plessner's fencing hall! Quite logically he also covers the chaise longue in his cool interior with polar bear fur, adding with satisfaction: "The fur is used as pure material, without any of the barbarism of gaping mouths and claws."[62] Ornamentation, in the Wilhelmian era, still admitted barbarism; now it is gone.

"But I don't think," Brecht's narrator continues the story, "Müller could have endured this deliberate harmony and reformist utility any longer." In this ominous way the reader is prepared for the coming disaster. Müller develops a "battle plan," and it is he who at the end reigns over the demolished furnishings.

The variants of warm-cool polarity play out in this story. At the warm pole camp the egalitarian "hordes," with their anti-heroic tendencies, their spontaneity, and need for asymmetries. At the cool pole we find the disciplining of affects, the desire for transparency, the law of discretion and symmetry.

Reading the story as a satire of Bauhaus ideology admittedly simplifies it. Yet irritatingly, even an "inappropriate" piece of furniture has a delicately contrived place in the overall decorative scheme of the apartment; the visitors also dislike the way cool industrial functionalism is presented in the form of pieces wrought by individual artisans. The story takes place at a time in which industrial Bauhaus production was making its first inroads against the reform movement's commitment to the crafts. But, in all of Brecht's dramas, we can identify the Dionysian infantry dog who runs amok inside rational constructions. In the world he represents battles are being fought over the remnants of chaos, and these remnants contain the last of humanity. But chaotic natures in this same world are fond of setting traps. When Brecht announces that "man is the mistake," he is breathing the same distressed sigh as the new construction architects when they see what has become of their new dwellings a few months after the people have moved in.

Brecht's 1926 story is also a disdainful postwar echo of the blending of aestheticism and the reform movement among the architects of the prewar period, who still entertained the illusion that architecture could be the means to educate the individual. The creed of modern architecture expected reform dwellings to enforce its salutary moral effects on character—representing a code of conduct in three dimensions. Brecht's story confronts architecture's claim with the rather unwieldy nature of foot soldiers and mongers of chaos.

His narrative recalls a painful episode experienced by one of the pioneers of the reform movement and modern architecture. Influenced by Ruskin and Morris, in 1894 Henri van de Velde had built a model complex, Bloemenwerf, in Belgium.[63] The reformer narrates in his memoirs —not without a hint of satisfaction—a delicate situation that arose in this building. It nearly led to catastrophe and, in his mind, would have done so without the tasteful structure's "ethical" influence. Harmony in the van de Velde home went so far as the delicate integration of clothing worn by Maria Sèthe, the mistress of the house, into the color scheme. For special occasions, interior colors were even allowed to dictate what color food would be served.

So they did on one day in February 1896, when Toulouse-Lautrec was a guest at Bloemenwerf. Wearing a strawberry-colored gown, the blonde-haired Maria served the food: yellow eggs with red beans on plates that matched the violet and green dahlia design of the wallpaper in the vestibule. The excess of harmony activated a sarcastic streak in the guest from Paris. Mildly intoxicated, he leapt up onto the table and launched into a speech that, to the disgust of the host, threatened to degenerate into "obscenities." "But," writes van de Velde in his memoirs, "it did not go that far. The atmosphere of our house did not fail to have its effect, and Toulouse-Lautrec's remarks ended in words of gratitude. The singular nature of our house, normal and extraordinary at once, did not leave him untouched."

Brecht's story lacks such a good ending. The moralism of the modernist credo remains powerful enough to trigger a small sense of guilt in engineer Müller but not to alter his behavior. Put in the form of a crude aphorism: modernism here lets down its postmodern hair, whereby the "post-" serves only to indicate the return of the repressed. The foot soldier's shame has become an object of comedy. Four years later Brecht will compose learning plays in which—under the enormous pressure of the last phase of the republic to declare one's commitments—no one gets to laugh at the same collisions between spontaneity and cool construction. Now he follows the rules of discipline to their fatal consequences. As a means of behavioral correction in the Communist Party schoolhouse, engineer Müller, former infantry dog, is killed, his body tossed into the lime pit.

The avant-garde discovered in prebourgeois cultures a type characterized by affective discipline, constant alertness, and an ability to bracket considerations of morality. But in fact there was no need to go elsewhere in search of such a type, since a storehouse of images of the armored subject, acting without the benefit of an inner compass, lay ready to hand.[64] The military comprised a cool culture subsystem within contemporary Weimar society and, like out-of-the-way cultures in distant times, functioned mechanically like clockwork and froze historical change.[65] The new objectivity decade elevates the image of the soldier to the status of an icon: the army helmet crowning the soldier's strong profile, penetrating gaze, and forceful chin. It fosters images of the mobile type who refuses to succumb, from the new objectivity dandy to the Bolshevik functionary, from the engineer to the veristic painter.

The army was for millions a site in which behavior was shaped under the pressure of mortal danger; in Brecht's *Mann ist Mann,* it is called "Mama"; in the *Fatzer* fragment we are born "in the tank."[66] In the army, the need for an internal regulation of the conscience falls away; the external voice of orders takes over. The cardinal virtues are the ability to discharge a duty and react quickly. The rapid change of persona, from affective control to blackout, from etiquette to aggressive frenzy, is the order of the day at the front.

The soldierly icon is hard to separate from the typology of the new objectivity. Neither the cool persona nor the radar type exists without a military shadow: in the "gray army" of white-collar employees (Theodor Geiger), sociology finds it in the midst of the consumer sphere. Even the creature (type 3) is often only the other side of the coin. Jünger's construction of the worker blends the persona type with the iron figure of the soldier. This amalgam was part of a tradition that regarded the industrial worker as a metallized body.

Even a writer as opposite to Jünger's sensibility as Joseph Roth, observing the worker against the iron landscape of the railway system, outfits him with soldierly qualities:

> There a man in uniform saunters amid the bewildering systems of tracks, tiny; the individual in this context is important only as a mechanism. His significance is no greater than that of a lever; his effectiveness no more portentous than that of a switch. In this world all the potential of human expressiveness is reduced to the mechanical communication of an instrument. More important here than an arm is a lever, more than a wink, a signal. Here the eye is of no use, rather the lantern; not the cry, but the whistle of an open vent. Here it is not passion that rules, but regulations, the law.[67]

In the workers' literature of this decade, we rediscover the type of the cool persona in the person of the Communist cadre: Leninism is his *Art of Worldly Wisdom.* Existence from a distance defines his pathos, and morality comes to expression in the tactical rules of survival in the midst of a generalized threat. Coolness is the quality that marks him off from the warm zones of the tradition-minded Social Democratic communities. There is a role already there for him in the code of conduct that Brecht sets forth in 1925 and 1926 in the poems of his *Reader for Those Who Live in Cities*.

BRECHT'S HAND ORACLE FOR CITY DWELLERS

Toward the end of the republic, attitude—a decision made for the long run—comes to occupy a central place in political ethics. "Attitude"— sighs Benjamin, in a review of *Krieg und Krieger,* an anthology edited by Ernst Jünger—"'attitude' is the third word in all their speeches."[68] Those who have in fact surrendered to the direction of powerful institutions seek to demonstrate through an attitude of decisiveness that they have determined their course themselves.

Whenever attitude becomes a fundamental value, it spawns invulnerable-looking monsters. As a rule, however, keeping up the requisite steely appearance taps all available resources, so that the monsters are exhausted before they have ever undertaken a truly risky step. Fear of disgrace undoes them. Making the most of an aesthetic of disgrace, dadaism refined the acceptance of indignity. In Serner's new objectivity *Handbrevier,* "cowardice," Gracián's notion of a "finely executed retreat," and the art of minimalist survival still center on character. In contrast, Brecht's tips for city dwellers abandon the anchor in character.

The character that specializes in a steely attitude, as we have already seen, encounters a dilemma:

> Don't talk about danger!
> You can't drive a tank through a manhole:
> You'll have to get out.
> Better abandon your primus
> You've got to see that you yourself come through.[69]

The topos of an earthquake landscape appears in an advanced stage in Brecht's *Reader for Those Who Live in Cities*. No landmarks of collective memory are left—even their ruins are gone. We saw this social space in Gracián, Plessner, Blei, and Serner: a space shot through with agonistic tension, peopled by compassless navigators who must therefore rely on external voices. And these voices urge: seek distance; regard shelter as provisional; separate yourself from your cohort; cut family ties; avoid exaggerated individuation; pull your hat low on your brow; retreat from all sources of warmth. But Brecht's *Reader* does not stop with these tips for the existential nomad. Total mobilization defines the

space Brecht propels his subjects through and ultimately demands that
names too vanish:

> Part from your friends at the station
> Enter the city in the morning with your coat buttoned up
> Look for a room, and when your friend knocks:
> Do not, o do not, open the door
> But
> Cover your tracks!
> If you meet your parents in Hamburg or elsewhere
> Pass them like strangers, turn the corner, don't recognize them
> Pull the hat they gave you over your face, and
> Do not, o do not, show your face
> But
> Cover your tracks.
> Eat the meat that's there. Don't stint yourself.
> Go into any house when it rains and sit on any chair that's in it
> But don't sit long. And don't forget your hat.
> I tell you:
> Cover your tracks.
> Whatever you say, don't say it twice
> If you find your ideas in anyone else, disown them.
> The man who hasn't signed anything, who has left no picture
> Who was not there, who said nothing:
> How can they catch him?
> Cover your tracks.
> See when you come to think of dying
> That no gravestone stands and betrays where you lie
> With a clear inscription to denounce you
> And the year of your death to give you away.
> Once again:
> Cover your tracks.
> (That is what they taught me.)[70]

This code of conduct, like the others we have examined, requires its
adherents to specialize in separation. What they must separate from is
clear, but not why or to what end. The question we find posed in Brecht,
therefore, is what his hand oracle could possibly promise, when the behavioral commandments of an anonymous voice offer no provisional
guarantee of a place to rest beyond the chronic state of alarm.

The person who follows Brecht's injunctions gets nothing back, beyond the certainty that his gravestone will bear no inscription that could
refer to an identity. Thus new objectivity conduct codes finally arrive
at zero, which indeed guarantees a maximum of mobility but leaves

no more in the way of an epitaph than a trace of the velocity of one's disappearance.[71]

To be sure, the imperative "Cover your tracks!" remains very puzzling. It has become standard to see in it an order delivered by "reality itself." Gratefully following the tip Brecht offers in the tenth poem of the cycle,

When I speak to you
Coldly and impersonally
. . . .
I speak to you merely
Like reality itself . . .[72]

we find in this self-denunciation the solution to the puzzle. The subject speaking here, as Heidegger put it, was the "they" as the "subject of dailiness." The anonymous voice recommends the rhetorical simulation of alienation in order to demonstrate that its logic leads to self-dissolution. What remains awkward, however—as Rudolf Arnheim remarked—is that "reality" never "speaks" coldly and in general but always individually and with promises of warmth.[73] And the process by which the personal becomes anonymous proceeds apace, without anyone having to force it. In the logic of escalation that Brecht demands from his persona, what we see at work here is not so much a mimicry of negation but an assumption of the individual's ability to cover his tracks. What therefore appears as the null point of the disappearance of the subject can be read as the fulcrum of subjective empowerment; neither social institutions nor obscure historical processes cause the city dweller to disappear—the ego itself flees into the future, where death is waiting.

Gracián's persona comes back into view; Plessner's dueling subject and Serner's confidence man resume their roles, avoiding the hordes and gambling with the enemy . . . But for what purpose? under which magical eye? for what reward? Here the Hungarian Marxist Béla Balázs offers an instructive intervention, revealing that poems like this one document an especially perverse form of the "Dionysian frenzy of self-denial."[74] From behind the Marxist mask of the artist comes the voice of Nietzsche. What does this interpretation add to our understanding of the subject?

Brecht's poem of self-dissolution itself bears an ineffaceable signature, which has prompted an entire series of analyses. The poem about covering one's tracks has come to appear to us as nothing but tracks. Reactions to Brecht's poem over the long run reinscribe sharp subjective contours in a text that is itself supposed to blur them. Critics find characters in the poem ranging from the "cheerful barbarian" to the "robot."[75] As soon as the poem appeared, Benjamin saw in it the traces of a "destructive character," not without mentioning, for the sake of clarity, the director of the national credit bank as a man devoted to building upon nothing. A little later, though from a great distance (after 1933), Arnold Zweig finds in the poem instructions for immigrants seeking to lose themselves in foreign cities, while Benjamin returns to the text to perceive in it, with stubborn acuity, the Communist cadres operating illegally in the underground of the bygone republic.[76]

The poem remained Benjamin's obsession: he inscribes every possible political turn in the text, to which he denies all personal memory. "The destructive character," Benjamin concludes in 1930, "is a signal. As a trigonometric sign is subject to the wind from all sides, so is the destructive character vulnerable from all sides to talk."[77] In a journal entry of 1940, he registers the appearance in the poem of the spirit and figure of the GPU.[78] Later yet, Franco Buono discovers the "urban guerrilla" in the poem ("rules of behavior for underground fighters in occupied cities").[79] The psychoanalytic climate of the 1970s brings its sadomasochistic elements to the fore; in favor in the 1980s are its implications for communications theory.[80] And in the 1990s readers discover in it a little forgetfulness machine, apt for reuse in deconstruction theories.

The list is not a random assortment. Analysis alternates between the extremes of the armored ego and the unbounded self. The value neutrality of the poem facilitates extension to various notions of the self-empowered subject; its conceptual development toward destruction makes it possible at the same time to retract the empowerment. Of what use, we may ask, is the updating of the venerable tradition of Gracián's code, when this external voice sends the persona in all possible directions? When the moral vacuity of the code in its terminal stages spurs desires to melt into communities promising to combine strict behavioral directives with meaning? "And when death brings at last the desired forgetfulness," says Nietzsche, it "sets the seal on the knowledge that 'being' is merely a continual 'has been,' a thing that lives by denying and destroying and contradicting itself."[81]

While Nietzsche, however, registers the human inability to "learn to forget,"[82] Brecht puts forgetting before the subject as a daily lesson. Does it make any sense to see the poem as an aquarium in which Nietzschean motifs and fragments of court maxims swim like colorful fish? We could easily add other swimmers, like the slapstick figures of American silent films or ones from Walter Serner's *Handbrevier*. We might determine that the poem alludes to the tradition of behavioral primers, which narrow into paradoxes, combining strict rules of behavior with the horror of identity dissolution. Or we might discover that it sets the Nietzschean motif of the subject awash in joyful denial into the sturdy housing of a conduct code. Reactions to the poem have cut through these knots. The pedagogical solution above all refuses to allow paradox to hamper it. It discovers in the tenth poem of the cycle its Archimedean point; for in this last poem, we read in one interpretation, "the poet comes out of his hiding place" to "expose" sham behavior.[83]

Here the poem slips into a tradition of rhetorical irony that we encountered first in Gracián's code of conduct. There and elsewhere *dissimulatio* attracts suspicions. It lies in the negative act of concealing what the speaker actually means; the defining characteristic of rhetorical irony's other mode of speech, *simulatio*, is to present positively what is not actual.

"Simulational irony accordingly consists in the transparent feigning of a contrary standpoint, and dissimulational in the discernible concealment of one's own conviction," we read in a discussion of the fundamentals of rhetoric. Presupposed here is a sovereign self in control of its boundaries that raises itself out of the sameness of communication through its special capacity for double negation. In a complex process of simulation, an unmistakable "authentic personal style" comes into being through the conspicuous use of the double negation and the blandness of laconic language. Thus we can deduce the presence of an individual exploiting the scenarios of separation that allow the poem to form a versatile self playing out—in its black-colored *mundus rhetoricus*—images of "alternative possible being" to the point of self-dissolution.[84]

Repetition is the medium for the practice of rhetoric, and memory is its reservoir. What, therefore, is to be done if storage in memory, along with rhetoric itself as the vehicle of oral transmission, is to be extinguished? The poem provokes an image of the clever pedagogical salvation of the self-empowered subject, only to drive it into paradox. For where is the site of speech concealed and what is the fate of the self in the entire cycle of the *Reader*? In Brecht's intention, the site of speech was a phonograph; he conceived the cycle's ten poems as recorded texts. Between the poems, readers see an injunction "(This record needs to be played more than once.)"[85]

The search for the speaker's location draws attention to a complication that, fully in line with the reception history, we cannot avoid. The

parentheses in the final line of this first poem—in the manner of a philo-
logical source reference to the origin of the voice that prescribes the possibilities for action—might lead readers to the site from which the
speech came. They perceive the written text's parentheses in an instant,
along with the behavioral rules, yet the recorded voice puts off revelation
of the "simulation" all the way to the final line. And what do the parentheses enclosing "That is what they said" (1926)/taught me (1938)" reveal? Is it a voice from offstage, which has so assimilated itself to its ad-
dressee that it announces its origin only in the poem's last line for the
sake of decency? Since the hints contain a series of authorial motives—
the praise of separation and forgetfulness, the disqualification of expression, and the image of the "iron jaws eating the world out of house and
home" (Benjamin)—it is tempting to identify the parenthetically speaking self as the medium of the author's voice. Nevertheless, it is not clear
that the self of the parentheses, which had already absented itself from
the behavioral rules' self, can mount any resistance at all to the voice
from outside.

Speaking in the second poem of the cycle is an imperial "we," a collective instance that threatens exclusion and at the same time juxtaposes
to the commandment "Part from your friends" a "staying"—the cohort
strikes back; the relation between the external voice and the subject is
agonistic. In the third, the prodigal son simulates the voice of the fathers
who would have the former "vanish like smoke." The voice of the fathers is suspiciously resonant with the voice in the first poem. In the
fourth, we encounter to a particular degree the presumption of a subject: "I" occurs thirteen times. A young woman strives to find her identity through reflection in a hostile environment, and at the same time to
relax—just as Gracián's *Art of Worldly Wisdom* recommends; she over-
exerts herself—in vain. The fifth poem marks the strangeness of the other
person ("That's something I've heard a woman say."). Here woman, tra-
ditionally the object of virile codes of conduct, is reduced to sheer matter. On this level of reduction, she acquires a historical philosophical
charge: "the wind / Fills my sail." The principle of "rising from the ruins" is played through the first time on a woman's body. The sixth offers
a report ("That's something I've heard people say before now") of the
embarrassing spectacle of expressionist sons who, ignoring the new
objectivity conduct code, proclaim deeds in the old manner of youthful
indignation, tactlessness, and penitential pilgrimages, without realizing
that they are thereby condemned to decline. With no exterior voice, the
seventh poem presents us with a distinguished, armored subject as a

slapstick figure. Following the two parodies of disarming and armoring, the eighth paints a landscape removed from all bourgeois codes of conduct: the lawless space of a "trench community" (Marc Bloch) for which the new objectivity behavioral rules are designed: "(Not that anyone should be discouraged by that.)" The "Four Invitations to a Man from Different Quarters" (the ninth poem) repeat the reduction schema from the first one, teaching us to accept friendliness as a stopgap (with no parentheses). And then, in the cycle's tenth poem, the author finally emerges from hiding. But what sort of voice is it?

Throughout the cycle the authorial voice wanders restlessly, splitting itself among different instances that threaten to absorb it. Boundaries between an authentic "I" and the impersonal "one" are lost; the sixth poem delivers the tone of the complaint and its disarming in the bygone manner of parody. Authenticity has nowhere to hide for the winter. The foundation of the ironic rhetoric is undermined.

"Cover your tracks" deprives an ironic rhetoric of its basis in a secure subject. Gracián's *Art of Worldly Wisdom* displaces it into paradox. Nietzsche's concept, whereby the subject is put into vigorous play, which informed Brecht's early poetry, falls under the influence of institutions dangling the prospect of relief or threatening extinction. What continues to appear here as an uninscribed gravestone will quickly turn into the drafting table for engineers plotting measures. Their voices are already intervening in the world of the city dwellers. The "I" begins to dissolve into the "they," so that action becomes possible by way of participation in this subject of the world of daily existence—toward what goal, remains unknown. As in Heidegger's *Being and Time* the "it" of the unconscious has shifted into the external world of the "they";[86] in systems of action, the "I" fancies itself a subject, although the "they" has long since destroyed the humane horizon that the subject once constructed.

This general "they," into which the persona threatens to dissolve, is no neutral medium. It exists under the law of the fathers. One unprepossessing thing in Brecht's text draws attention to this fatal circumstance. It is the only object that the scenarios of forgetting do not forget: the hat.[87]

Twice it comes into play. The first time, pulled down over the eyes, it serves to hide the face, so that the parents are unable to recognize the son. It returns then in the third verse, which instructs the nomadic reader not to forget his hat. Whatever is tied to the figure by a possessive pronoun—"your parents/face/ideas/death"—is delivered up programmatically to the procedures of forgetting, except "your hat." This object accompanies the figure through all the stages of its reduction.

In the mid-1920s, the hat concealing the face is a conspicuous trademark of new objectivity portraits: it is a characteristic feature of new objectivity paintings by Anton Räderscheidt, George Grosz, and Christian Schad; Hans Richter sets hats to dancing in his film *Vormittagsspuk*. Faces in expressionist painting remained expressive surfaces open to internal stimulation; now the head's contours close it off. The interior of characters becomes opaque; the hat pulled down over the face prevents expression from coming into view at all. The sixth poem in Brecht's cycle presents us with one final anachronistic expression of outrage. The habitus of proper rage here requires that the hat be "tipped back" so that attention can be drawn to the individual signs of private rebellion (Brecht associates them with hesitation over making a practical decision). This is rebellion in the manner of the expressionist "sons," who never learned the ABCs of violence, which is the property of the fathers.

Up to this point, the origin of the hat has not been mentioned; the poem says, "the hat (*Hut*) they gave you." The injunction is never to forget the parents' gift (perhaps the souvenir of a *behütetes* [sheltered] upbringing?). Anyone who follows all the instructions remains tied, through the gift of the hat, to those from whom he wanted to separate.

A radical separation from the parents (cf. Serner's precept no. 358) is one of the initiation rites of the city dweller. In an early draft of *Mann ist Mann* we read:

> he will advance   one day (he) will float on one of these steamships up to
> the big city   he is the man for it   he has no parents.[88]

The man on the steamship, to return to the image of the *Reader,* floats off with the hat from his parents on his head.

Is this inseparability from the hat an indication of the desire for the "continuation of parental care" that Jürgen Manthey finds at work everywhere in Brecht's writings?[89] Or does the hat instead signal why the persona finds itself in a chronic state of alarm? Does it lead the reader, as Susanne Winnacker ventures, to the idea of the potlatch, a gift designed to destroy rivals in the next generation? Or, as Hans-Thies Lehmann supposes, does it suggest the ineradicable burden of a debt—for example, the debt incurred by the son's mere existence—so that only death could occasion the desired forgetfulness?

Those who follow instructions so strictly that they wind up accepting absurdities never pull free of the spell of the paternal law, which they wanted to escape. When we pull our hats over our faces, "we speak to our fathers," as the third poem declares. Speaking with our fathers is among the fundamental acts by which the generation of the new objectivity marked itself off from the generation of the shamed, expressionist sons.[90] But whoever echoes the fathers' words only repeats the fathers' dictum: *You cannot have been.* In this logic of the third poem, Walter Benjamin, in a late diary entry, will register sadism: the dynamic of youth enforces the law of the fathers.

Is this reference to the law of the fathers the secret revealed in the avant-garde act of forgetting? Is it indeed the case that "the more radical the rejection of anything that came before, the greater the dependence on the past"?[91] Brecht's poem puts these ominous readings of the avant-garde act into play by means of a curious thing—a hat. It brings the paternal law onto the crooked plane of the text and relativizes the fathers' revenge in the light of comedy.[92]

Thus a memory of the paternal law appears in texts in which we would least expect it. Just how explosive the appearance can be is expressed perhaps in Paul Tillich's formula cited above: that the call for community contains the demand "to create the mother from the son and to summon the father out of nothing."[93] The father is supposed to appear with the authority of the state, in order to sublate the world of civilized separation in favor of symbiosis, to reconstruct the mother and in doing so conceal the "origin." This "superfather" is clearly in a position to recreate, by means of his ice-cold measures, the maternal warmth of "community" and keep her constantly under watch—a paradoxical procedure, which is hard to bring off. "Political romanticism thus suffers its most severe disillusion at this point," remarks Tillich; "nowhere is the contradiction between desire and reality felt more painfully than here."

Brecht's poem reminds us of the desire to call the father out of nothing, in order to enact disappointment by means of a curious object. With a touch of humor, it haunts the *Reader for Those Who Live in Cities.* Soon, however, the law of the fathers will appear in the learning plays, no longer playfully, but with relentless insistence, in the name of a collective.

DIE MEHLREISENDE FRIEDA GEIER

If the new objectivity served the "function of social and compensation for a generation of men who had lost their identity," the appearance of a woman armed with Gracián's *Art of Worldly Wisdom* seems inconceivable.[94] Marieluise Fleißer, in her novel *Die Mehlreisende Frieda Geier,* puts the example to the test.[95] For Frieda Geier—relatively mobile in an automobile and equipped with a leather jacket or man's overcoat (and then again in mixed garb, in order to appeal simultaneously to urban and rural customers)—new objectivity norms are not rules for a game you make up but dictates inscribed on the body.

> The supreme commandment of someone doing business with someone else is that the former must never step into the latter's shoes. Compassion cripples.[96]

Acknowledging the other's right to existence unavoidably diminishes your own substance. Whatever you've not gotten your own hands on will be stashed away by someone else.

> People are only too eager, for anyone they take to be an outsider, to hang the breadbasket a little higher. That means you end up with nothing but the table in your teeth.[97]

Business trips and sex are like a gauntlet for Frieda Geier; she endures them with mixed feelings because others are always intent on curtailing her mobility. Her lover, a sports idol (selected from the "breeding material" of the provinces) cannot cope with this "double being": he cannot merge symbiotically with a figure who is at once "sensuous female" and "ascetic with short hair."

> This restless creature, you have to hold it down with every fiber, hold on to it with all your might.[98]

To the small town she ultimately seems to be a vampire, undermining the businessman's livelihood, draining the athlete's vitality. Surrounded by a pack of men, the heroine is forced to disappear so that her lover can overcome his crisis, in both his athletics and his business. She reappears one final time, but the idol's comrades lie in wait for an ambush—at the Jewish cemetery.

> Individuals must stand up, experience ostracism firsthand, and with their slender selves stomp through the thicket of reigning opinion.[99]

If the cool persona in the figure of a woman cannot be instrumentalized as a prostitute, she is hunted as a "witch."

Marieluise Fleißer's novel is a medium that exposes the self-destructive aspects of new objectivity leitmotivs. The transfer of themes of winning mobility through anonymity, incognito, or minimalist survival—woven through a soldier's mentality or a dandy's attitude—to a woman evokes a (thrilling) note of *Angst.* In the handbooks—whether composed from the perspective of court society or the new objectivity—woman was an object, to be (mis)treated according to all the rules of the art. As the epitome of symbiotic warmth or as an instance of mercy, she occupied a central place in the imagination of the coolness freaks; because she threatened to restrict man's mobility, she had to be consigned to the imaginary. The advocates of cool distance also experienced an immense need for sources of warmth, which, however—as Plessner's *Grenzen* demonstrated—they excluded from the arena of struggle itself. *Die Mehlreisende Frieda Geier* represents an attempt to materialize autonomy and sexual desire on a terrain littered with economic aspects neither Plessner nor the community fanatics had foreseen.

Fleißer had already put into words a woman's experience with men of the sort of Plessner's duelist in her collection of stories, *Ein Pfund Orangen*, which appeared in 1929. "She got to know men," says one of her characters, "and one was like the other, having a system for women, but no mercy."[100] We encountered this system in the conduct codes of distance; Fleißer directs her outsider's gaze at it, registering its unshakable rule: "The man determines the distance."[101] And the system assigns a place to the other sex: "she was warmth, and not a person."[102] As a lesson for women, it prescribes the code of virile distance:

> These were the frosts of freedom [see Figure 9]; she had to learn to freeze. No one depends on anyone.[103]

But the female characters in Fleißer's texts get a lesson in a decisionism of their own. The author sends them into the system of the conduct codes, where they learn to their horror that "the natural enemy is them."[104]

Perhaps what we see here is the shadow that Schmitt's *Begriff des Politischen* throws over the battle between the sexes. Or perhaps it is the deeper ground from which the theory developed. We recall Schmitt's definition:

> The distinction of friend and enemy denotes the utmost degree of intensity in union or separation, in association or dissociation.[105]

The "enemy" in this conceptual system is always "the other," and it suffices for "his nature that he is, in a specially intense way, existentially something different and alien." This kind of knowledge, which the female characters learn firsthand, offers them neither a standpoint from which they can deal with the other sex nor a feeling of self-determination that would enable them to draw boundaries. The lesson is imposed on them. For a time they seem to assimilate the principles of boundary drawing in

9. These were the frosts of freedom

(Karl Hubbuch, *Improvisiertes Frühstück* [Improvised breakfast]. With the permission of Myriam Hubbuch.)

an initiation rite granting them access to the combatants' fencing hall: "Maturation meant that a light had gone on about the enmity prevailing among people."[106] But since women have to represent the estrangement of first nature inside the sphere of trust, their claim to their own subjective artificiality suddenly ends up in the sphere of dissociation, where the intensity of the separation they embody is too much even for separation specialists. Those who sermonize on the "frosts of freedom," says Brecht, eventually shy away from the effects.

Operating in the sphere of mistrust, Frieda Geier learns the enemy rules of behavior:

> "Men must be destroyed, or else they destroy you," a woman friend had said. Suddenly a thought came to mind—knowledge cuts to the quick.[107]

The point is that it cuts her. Describing these techniques, the female author clearly has need of a certain masochism to set her heroine down in enemy terrain—allowing her to "swim free," I might have said, were swimming not the domain of the sports hero she is trying to thwart.

Béla Balázs, in a polemical remark aimed at the coolness doctrine in *Reader for Those Who Live in Cities*, notes Brecht's effort "to howl with the wolves" as a way of deceiving the pack; Balázs clearly fails to recognize the usefulness of the pack. Fleißer's heroine experiments with her enemy's code of conduct. In the social structure inhabited by her heroine, the maneuver comes at the cost of real-life substance. "She cannot howl with the wolves."

Plessner, Schmitt, Serner, Brecht, and Jünger present variants on the cool persona. "Watchdog," Fleißer will later term this avant-garde type; it watches over the boundary drawn by the dueling subject.[108] A paradox develops from its simultaneous resistance to and desire for decentering, whereby what Musil termed the "dis-armoring of the ego" (a genuinely modernist impulse) undermines the will to be a "subject in armor" (a motif of the decisionist avant-garde). Marieluise Fleißer's novels show us that the woman who allows herself to be pulled into this melee of virile narcissism gets cut to the quick. That pleasure can be gotten from the act is testimony to the uncanny dimension of Fleißer's texts.

GINSTER—A SWAN SONG

In 1928, Siegfried Kracauer's novel *Ginster: Von ihm selbst geschrieben* appears, throwing a comedic light on the dilemma of the self-assured subject.[109] In Kracauer's hands the fetishes of objectivity become the stumbling blocks of conformity. Ginster, the hero, a new objectivity egoless phenomenon, stumbles in the general mobilization of 1914–18. Like the other characters under discussion here, he loves the anonymous life, seems even to have halfway internalized the precepts of Serner's *Handbrevier* when, having escaped the unpleasantries of the war and revolution, he sighs, "So nice, a proper hotel. He was sorry that, as of tomorrow, he would have to go back to sleeping in private quarters." This attitude, along with all the others drawn from the spirit of objectivity, fails him, though he takes great pains to adapt them to circumstances. Thus Ginster knows the utilitarian value of Brecht's new objectivity minimalism. Faced with a threatened call-up to the front, he tries to increase his chances of survival by eating as little as possible: "The skinnier he got, the smaller he was as a target."[110] Nor did Ginster have anything against failing to be on hand for important historical moments. He cultivated a talent for missing them:

Ginster always had bad luck at public events. He either came too late or, to his surprise, got an excellent seat, which, however, as he soon found out, was free only because it faced the wrong direction.[111]

For a time Ginster is a gunner with the Cologne infantry, and he strives to adapt mimetically to the heroic discourse. But, as Inka Mülder-Bach puts it, "he always misses the right tone by a decisive nuance":

> The daily reports are also so nicely stylized, Ginster noted, aware of his desire to slip in an appreciative statement of some kind.[112]

In the hero's inability to make the discourse of militant objectivity his own, Joseph Roth saw one of the brighter aspects of the republic, distinguishing Ginster—"the civilian pure and simple"—from the more general run of the army. In 1928, at the beginning of the boom in war literature, Ginster's appearance, though easily overlooked, was a minor sensation. Among the martial figures of gray marauders, the impossible civilian seemed born of American slapstick; Kracauer's hero was greeted by contemporary critics as a "sociological Chaplin."

Ginster, always eager, like Serner's characters, to hit the road, is innocent of their compulsively melancholy rituals. Rather than take flight, he merely stumbles along. Since nothing connects him to the popular mass, he differs from the good soldier Schwejk; where everyone else reacts quickly, his sluggish reflection works a subversive effect. He contemplates the "grammar" of the barracks talk, which reveals to him the thinglike character of the man in uniform but does not exempt him from the category of thing.[113] The military hierarchy brings him face to face with other problems that semiotics tempers:

> In the barracks, in the hallways, on the street, superiors loomed before him, with the impenetrability of a hedge in a fairy tale. To get the hedge to yield, he had to make a special sign to it. He suddenly stiffened up like a wall, the vegetation dying out, his eyes two holes. . . .
> Ginster . . . , for his part, had to direct his eyes at the subordinate officer without, strictly speaking, looking at him or letting the sight of him prompt any thoughts; so that his eyes became openings into which the officer could pour orders. Like cemetery urns, suitable for anyone's ashes.[114]

What makes the awkward hero stand out against contemporary attitudes of heroism is his essential other-directedness. As Mülder-Bach notes, Ginster does not act—"he behaves." His resistance consists not in protest but in "his kind of receptivity." Ginster suggests a type that appears only in vague outlines in the scanty civilian literature of the republic, which we shall describe in more detail in the chapter on the radar type.

JÜNGER'S FALL INTO THE CRYSTAL

Silhouettes   The habitus of the cool persona is determined by the claim it stakes on perceptual acuity. Ernst Jünger, in the foreword to *Der Arbeiter,* maintains that an understanding of the new reality depends entirely upon "the precision of the description, which presupposes eyes with complete and unbiased powers of vision."[115] Desires for perceptual acuity become powerful whenever a traditional interpretive frame is in collapse. Such situations generate calls for a retrieval of "pure" perception of "sheer facts." Perception, exhausted by the drone of prescribed discourse, regenerates itself by focusing on meaningless things.

Programs aimed at the restoration of perception, however, do more than prompt a passive registration of objects and events. Aggression sets the effort's fundamental tenor; its tone is not without a hint of sadism. The sharp-eyed persona is fond of comparing itself with the surgeon, while the habitus of perceptual acuity requires that the subject transgress moral boundaries. The precision of a moral norm's negation not only lends expression to a new objectivity habitus but also reinforces its claims to the empirical sciences' exactness. Stripping perception of moral judgment necessarily *de*psychologizes the observed object, reducing it to its basis in physiological or economic data and assimilating it to the rules of natural scientific discourse. The intrusive gaze thus becomes an instrument of pure perception.

It is a commonplace among avant-garde artists that the precondition for seeing an object "sharply" is removing it from all moral entanglement in its environment.[116] By excising the object from its moral, pragmatic, and atmospheric integuments, the artistic gaze isolates it in its razor-sharp contours. If people are its object of observation, the sharp gaze works by changing them into physical objects in the sway of mechanical laws. The emotional effect of coolness stems from this act of transformation. "Coolness as a tendency," remarked Osip Mandelstam in 1930, "stems from the incursion of physics into the moral idea."[117] We read in Benjamin, writing at the same time, that precise observation becomes possible only when "the moral personality has been put on ice."[118]

In the early 1930s essay "Über den Schmerz," Jünger suggests a view of human beings as alien objects, without regard for their pain, their passion, or complaints.[119] The discourses of the sciences facilitate this cooling off of perception, according to Jünger, and, carried over into literature, are capable of producing "subzero temperatures."

"At such temperatures," Jünger repeats later in *Strahlungen* (1949), "flesh and erotic contact also lose their luster; their physical condition comes to the fore."[120] Perceptual acuity calls for an anthropology that understands people as physical objects, making a retrieval of seventeenth-century modes of anthropological understanding the next obvious step. Likewise attractive is the incorporation into literary writing of the new scientific discourses of animal behavior research, psychotechnics, and sociometry.

Having identified these areas of overlap with scientific styles of thought, however, we need to stress the value placed by advocates of the cool gaze on the "cult of evil" taken over from the nineteenth-century dandy. The dandy juxtaposes his perceptual acuity, as an "apparatus of disinfection and isolation," to bourgeois moral conventions.[121] The dandy's descendant finds himself in a world transformed by the technical media's progress. As technological devices, still and moving picture cameras appear to possess the prized characteristic of perceptual sharpness. Jünger attributes to the camera the same quality of impassiveness he expects of the cool persona:

> The photograph exists outside the sphere of the emotional [see Figure 10], which lends it a telescopic character; one notes that what happened has been seen by an unemotional and invulnerable eye. It can just as easily capture a ball in midflight as a human being in the moment he is being ripped apart by an explosion.[122]

The transposition of "horrific vision" to the world of the apparatus lends it the value-neutrality of a technical norm; the transfer of this mechanical competence back to human perception frees it from the demands of morality.

By the end of the 1920s the trenchant critique of the conceptual realists counters the ideology of the camera's eye, disdaining the "romanticizing" attitude of "pure" perception. Brecht's famous line from the *Dreigroschenprozeß* documents the change: "A photograph of the Krupp Works or A.E.G. yields next to no information about these institutions. The real reality has moved into the functional."[123] Kracauer's polemical remark in the first chapter of his study of white-collar workers argues similarly: "A hundred reports from a factory do not add up to the reality of the factory but remain for all eternity a hundred views of the factory. The reality is a construction."[124] Both authors emphatically distance themselves at the beginning of the 1930s from the pathos of perceptual acuity, to which both had earlier appealed.

10. The photograph exists outside the sphere of the emotional

(Publicity still for *At the Rim of the Sahara Desert*. With the permission of VG Bild-Kunst, Bonn.)

Musil calls on the results of cognitive psychology and phenomenology in his formulation a few years earlier:

> It is known that we see what we know: ciphers, signs, abbreviations, attributes of the concept; permeated and carried merely by isolated dominant sensuous impressions in a vague plenitude of the rest.[125]

Musil is convinced that seeing in ciphers corresponds to the "necessity of the practical orientation." Formulaic stereotyping is not only a characteristic of concepts but equally typical of "our gestures and sensual impressions, which after a couple of repetitions become just as habitual as imaginary processes tied to words."

The conceptual realism of the 1920s that we just observed in Brecht, and in Jünger and Schmitt as well, transfers the claim of perceptual acuity onto the alleged precision of the concept. Acuity works its effect in their thinking by way of a maneuver identical to that by which the bracketing of moral judgment aims to make human beings visible as physical objects. The position of the conceptual realists on perception—which we continue to find today in rationalistic theories of perception[126]—runs as follows: the eye, because of its biological structure, cannot be unbiased. "Pure" vision is a fiction. Every visual perception is a goal-oriented act, which involves scanning the environment for regularities; observation is a problem-solving activity, guided by a complex of expectations. Visual perception is like a spotlight trained on the organism.[127] It lights up phenomena within a certain compass, allowing a purposeful examination. If perception is to be sharp, criteria implicit in the goal of perception must determine its field.

The phenomenologist Alfred Schütz assumes that an "intentional ray of reflection" interrupts the stream of formulaic repetitions that suffuse daily life: a concentrated packet of light illuminates a circle in the environment, which is filled with the darkness of unconsciously experienced schemata. But for phenomenologists, the overall perceptual space outside what is intended remains filled by a fog of reflexes, anonymous noises, tactile impressions, and smells. The horizon surrounding the core area under visual inspection is permeable and "soft."[128]

The boundary line for conceptual realists, however, is "hard" and impermeable. The conceptual realists among the artists of the 1920s intervene into the perceptual space, in order to cut away the soft edges of phenomena, arrest fluid movement in freeze frames, and do away with ambivalences. They scan the visual field, concentrating on the isolated parcels in which their "specimen" is captured for examination.[129] Figures are separated out from one another until there finally appear "pure" phenomena. While it is indeed no longer possible to have any palpable experience of these phenomena, conceptual realism maintains the claim, as in Jünger's construction of the worker, that they are the result of perceptual acuity carried to an extreme.

The contemporary aesthetic appeal of the focus on sharp contours is not to be underestimated. In opposition to the impressionist blurring of boundaries and loosening up of subjective unity, the "calendrical objectivity" of conceptual silhouettes resulting from these surgical interventions into perception appeals to advocates of the cool gaze because it aims at the effect of the uncanny but uses a quasi-scientific manner: "So also in the bright transparency of loneliness does everything become clearer and larger, but above all it becomes more primal and demonic."[130]

Carl Schmitt's friend-enemy theory imposes a perceptual grid on the amorphous bodies of liberal society. It lights up areas of semi-darkness and assigns all vacillation and wavering to the category of betrayal. The métier of the cool persona is to isolate elements in the mix, *distinguo ergo sum* its slogan (see Figure 11).[131]

Since this attitude implies a claim to perceptual acuity, it is not surprising that conceptual realists go around with cameras around their

11. *Distinguo ergo sum*

(August Sander, *Künstlerehepaar* [Artistic couple], Cologne, 1925. With the permission of Photographische Sammlung/SK Stiftung Kultur, August Sander Archiv, Cologne; VG Bild-Kunst, Bonn.)

necks: ideograms, so it seemed, could simply be photographed. Critics suggest that Jünger's *Arbeiter* offered snapshots of the *universalia in re*. Jünger himself identifies the real opponent of his sharp-eyed gaze as an "impressionistic" vision, which he accords to the epoch of liberalism. Nineteenth-century art, he continues, reproduced and encouraged the decay of the social physiognomy mimetically in the dissolution of contours:

> We encounter here the individual, whether alone or in a group, in a strangely slack and nonreferential bearing, needing twilight all the more as a way to make excuses. Thus the love for such motifs as gardens in the glow of Chinese lanterns, boulevards in the artificial light of the first gas candelabra, landscapes in the fog at dusk or in the shimmer of sunlight. (122)

Impressionism had gone beyond the clear distinction of significant objects from the environment and atmosphere. Its observation put the "meaningless" on a par with the "meaningful"; dispersing attention over the surface, it no longer established the core area of meaning. Jünger takes this achievement of the impressionist school of vision to be a moment in "the process of decomposition," as a "clinical station" of decline that necessarily ends in nihilism. The spaces of twilight, of fog and shimmering sunlight he confronts with the "cool and dispassionate gaze of the artistic eye." The camera, according to Jünger, is capable of banishing the meaningless from the excerpts it produces, yielding an apprehension of pure types. Since the physiognomy of the type is not unique but endlessly reproducible, it can be captured in photographs and films.

Jünger's attitude toward photography draws on motifs that Vilém Flusser describes a half century later.[132] Jünger's use of hunting metaphors draws our attention to the importance he accords to the distinction between mere visual perception and "scouting." Arthur Schopenhauer referred to the difference between the two, explaining that scouting, as opposed to looking, is an act of seeing that is subordinated to the will.[133] Flusser associates photography with "being on the lookout":

> It is the prehistorical stalking pose of the Paleolithic hunter in the tundra. Only the photographer pursues his game not in the open grassland, but in the thicket of cultural objects, and his secret paths are determined by this artificial taiga.[134]

The photographer's thicket is made up of cultural objects, "which have been 'purposefully placed'":

> Each of these objects obstructs the photographer's view of his game. He sneaks through them in order to stymie the intention hidden within them. He strives to emancipate himself from his cultural condition, strives at all costs to capture his game.[135]

Since for Jünger the "purposefully placed" cultural objects that threaten to obstruct the photographic gaze consist primarily of the nebulous things of "modern humanity," the initial task, if the aim is to get a snapshot of reality, is to get them out of the way. Flusser, however, refers in this connection to the way the photographer by and large surrenders himself to the categories of the apparatus. He also comes to the conclusion that photography delivers "an image of what has been conceived," but the concepts in Flusser's case are those for which the photographer has been programmed by his apparatus. While Jünger ties the photographer's habitus to the bearing of the cool persona, which uses the camera to rip objects out of their cultural conditions "without pardon" in order to alter their symbolic meaning, he also handles the same apparatus like a "machine" that drags the photographer along like an appendage.[136]

In his reasoning about photography, Jünger races through several fields of thought, here pointing out the "predatory nature" of the apparatus,[137] there emphasizing the photographer's philosophical capacity to observe the world through a categorical apparatus, to demarcate visual fields, and record a series of distinct pictures;[138] then again he makes the photographer into a "functionary of the apparatus."[139] In any case, the technological instrument delivers pictures with sharply defined contours (122).With this conception Jünger puts himself provocatively at odds with Kracauer's theory of photography.

In 1927, Siegfried Kracauer complained that the story of an individual lies "buried under a photograph as if under a blanket of snow."[140] Now Jünger praises the capacity of the camera to freeze the visible in the unequivocality of the sign. Jünger seems to have read Kracauer's essay; it is not without a provocative gesture that he praises the aspects of a camera that Kracauer criticized, while devaluing the specific accomplishment of photography that Kracauer praised as characteristic of the nineteenth century. Thus Kracauer discovered the camera's ability to record meaningful debris—refuse material that no theory or pictorial tradition had yet captured. The new technological medium encompassed society's "previously unseen natural fundament" unregistered in existing sign systems, the detritus of visibility not yet permeated by concepts, the space of the visually unconscious, optical noise: "The photographic archive gathers together in illustrative form the last elements of nature estranged from meaning."[141] For Jünger, the conceptual realist for whom the notion of types has put its stamp on every item in his visual inventory, this salvage operation does not occur.

The 1920s offer a favorable climate for conceptual realism. Its practitioners offer countless theories as devices for "sharpening" perception: theories of physiognomy and mimicry; typographies of functionalist psychology distinguishing the "introvert" from the "extrovert"; sociological theories categorizing people according to social roles (secretary, tax accountant, pastry cook, and so on). Probably the most popular and the catchiest of them all is Ernst Kretschmer's constitutional psychology, which correlates character variations with measurable physical traits. Kretschmer makes it possible to see in a stocky passerby of medium height with small, deep-set eyes the "cyclothymic pyknic type," who, while harboring a certain good-heartedness, is decidedly ill-disposed toward theoretical systematicity; the slender sort with thinly muscled arms and bony hands, in contrast, presents the "lepto-schizothymic type," who is easily agitated and introspectively inclined.

Typologies turn the body into something that can be read. Their attractions are endless: typologies bypass the stress of *pre*predicative experience, stripping the other's orientation of ambivalence; they make judgments easier to form, clarify lines of opposition, and accelerate the decision-making process. Typologies thus provide the ideal framing conditions for decisionism. They take over the fatal tendency of the "physiognomic gaze," for which Ursula Geitner offers the formula: "Exclusive intimacy, with anxious pigeon-holing as the outward orientation."[142]

Typological thinking dominates the human sciences of this period, which would be little cause for concern if, as in Max Weber, types remained the products of a critical epistemology distinct from an unfathomable substratum of life. Martin Lindner draws attention to the way these years give rise to a "conversion of heuristic typology into ontology."[143] Now each individual type becomes a variation on the general structure of life. Only such an ontological perspective explains the "mythical" image of human being—such as Jünger's worker—that does away with individualistic psychological explanations of individual beings. Kretschmer's *Körperbau und Charakter* (1921) is an indicator of this ontological conversion of typological thinking. It becomes deadly when combined with a new historical metaphysic, which is what occurs at the beginning of the 1930s.

"Type," according to the *Philosophisches Wörterbuch* of 1934, also means "primal form."

> If the type itself represents an objective structure of life, it takes on a particular meaning in a historical situation in which one human type (in the descriptive sense) seems to be crystallizing and superseding another type. It is precisely this of which many observers in the 1920s felt themselves capable: The collective type was superseding the bourgeois type. This process alone was enough, according to the conception of history by vitalist ideology, to show that "life" was behind the new "type."[144]

Aside from Jünger's *Arbeiter,* one of the most extreme literary examples of this ontological conversion that blends typological thinking, historical metaphysics, and aesthetics is Gottfried Benn's essay "Dorische

Welt" of 1934. Benn claims here to be charting the contours of a new anthropology:

> The state, power, purifies the individual, filters out his irritability, makes him cubist, outfits him with surfaces, makes him capable of art. Yes, that is perhaps the way to put it: the state makes the individual capable of art.[145]

What the ontological typologies have in common is an emphasis on visible phenomena, on processes and behavioral patterns, and a resistance to introspective psychology. Jünger adopts Malinowski's ethnological slogan "Study ritual, not belief" when he remarks in *Der Arbeiter*:

> The gesture with which someone opens up a newspaper is more informative than all the lead articles in the world, and nothing is more instructional than standing for a quarter hour on a street corner. (132)

The automaticism of traffic, which he is observing here, is for him a sign that people are in motion about some secret center in accord with "silent and invisible commands." Jünger's ethnological gaze seems to bind signs to the body but counteracts the effect by a simultaneous dissolution of the physical; it stamps meaning so blankly on the brow that the body disappears behind the sign. Jünger, when he wants to, sees nothing all about him but allegories of his theory of mobilization.

It is the deadly tendency of typologies to have anchored the ordering model of the system of writing in the obscurity of the bodily world, and this in a historical situation in which the monopoly of writing is being called into question by the magic of technologically produced images. For a time, typologies can also seduce a writer like Robert Musil: "More is said to me today by the three words, 'asthenic, schizothymic type,' than by a long individual description."[146]

The omnipresence of typologies in the 1920s forms the background and medium for the elaboration of conceptual realism. Political camps tend to their respective typologies, giving form to frightening schools of perception in which people learn how to order racial and class physiognomies. The capacity for drawing distinctions takes on a dreadful "sharpness": people learn how to distinguish, on the basis of physiognomy and behavior, labor aristocrats from proletarians, lumpen proletarians from Social Democrats, Trotskyites from social fascists, white-collar employees from bourgeois, Jews from Aryans, friend from enemy.

A body's role is so distinct that a photographer like August Sander can snap its photograph. This "bourgeois" artisan, to be sure, does not come quite up to the standards of the conceptual realists; critics reprove him for leaving too much in the shadows, for keeping spheres not wholly penetrated by the concept, for not having stepped beyond the immaturities of impressionism. Thus the critique of Sander's *Antlitz der Zeit* by the Rhineland constructivist Franz W. Seifert:

> If our position on Sander's work in itself is thus completely positive, still we might wish for a sharper and clearer sociological formulation in regard to classification. Here the goal must be a herbarium, so to speak, of human existence: standpoint, year, activity, class affiliation, as we understand it in Marx's definition: "but we have here to do with persons only insofar as they are the personification of economic categories, the bearers of specific class relations and interests."[147]

What we see here is the reconnection of a new medium, which delivers "meaningless" visual impressions, to language, as described by Jünger in *Der Arbeiter,* in its ability to draw distinctions. Jünger later acknowledges that his tendency at the time was to use the "scissors of the concept," to cut life to a predetermined pattern.[148] The silhouettes offered by the type are practical: they unburden; they orient; they facilitate decisions. In the hand of the dandy-soldier, they are part of the "cult of evil."

In Jünger's essays toward the end of the republic, the striving for perceptual sharpness combines with conceptual realism in spectacular fashion. His writings also demonstrate, however, that his belief in the actual existence of concepts unwittingly conditions the fixed boundaries of things. Benjamin shows in reference to the French surrealists how easy it is to slip "from the logical realm of the concept into a magical realm of words."[149] He refers to the dadaists' "impassioned phonetic and graphic games of transformation." And in *Das abenteuerliche Herz,* Jünger steps into the magical. But is this kind of magic not simply the dark other side of his classification frenzy?

What we find in Jünger's magic is much more what Arnold Gehlen designates as a sign of magical thinking: the overestimation of order in nature, so that a secret center guides and interprets any nocturnal flapping of wings, flash of steel, dream, or gesture. This magical order also explains the formal intactness of Jünger's verbal construct. His work is not subject to the distorting aim of mediating the experience of complete alien determinacy with the assumption of the autonomous subject, which was responsible for the deterioration of the grammatical structures of other writers in Jünger's generation.[150]

The Cool Persona and the Sensation of Pain

Jünger's problem is the century's problem: Before
women could become an experience for him, there
came the experience of war.

Heiner Müller, *Krieg ohne Schlacht*

The juxtaposition of Jünger's essay "Über den Schmerz" with *Der Arbeiter* demonstrates the way that the call for perceptual sharpness, on
the one hand, and the construction of the object of observation from
within the cool persona's code of conduct, on the other, condition each
other reciprocally. In both texts we encounter the same parallel process:
the *de*moralization of perception goes hand in hand with the *de*psychol-
ogization of the observed object, which then behaves in the manner of
a physical body. The latter not only slips out of sight from an ethical perspective but in doing so loses its organic quality. All the while, thus dis-
embodied, the object under observation is supposed to gain in substance.

In "Über den Schmerz" the mutual conditioning of perception and
the construction of the object is especially palpable. "At all times,"
Jünger maintains here,

> the uniform encompasses an act of armoring, a claim to be protected in a par-
> ticular fashion from the onslaught of pain. This is already obvious in the way
> it is possible to observe a corpse in uniform with greater coolness than, for
> example, a civilian who has fallen in a street battle.[151]

The armoring of the gaze also allows the object of the gaze to claim the
uniform as a shield.

It is no surprise that Jünger's diagnosis of the era agrees with the cool
persona's code of conduct, which requires any person who would exercise power to transform his counterpart from an organic and moral en-
tity into a physical object. The cool persona must learn "to treat the
body as an object":

> This procedure admittedly presupposes an elevated site of command from the
> perspective of which the body is regarded as an advance outpost, which the
> individual, from a great distance, is capable of sending into battle and
> sacrificing.[152]

In contrast to Brecht and Serner, Jünger "covers the tracks" of the classic *Art of Worldly Wisdom*. Nevertheless, it is not difficult to distill from
his essay the following precepts:

Adopt an appropriately cool gaze, which can penetrate the fog banks of morality, gain distance from the hazy influence of compassion, so that things can once again be seen as horrific and demonic, and therefore made subject to command.

Prepare yourself for a life of pain, but don't let it come to expression.

Avoid resorting to the narcotic of humanism, which represses the knowledge of pain from your consciousness.

Learn to accept discipline as a form capable of eliminating the presence of pain from your consciousness. Then you will be able to develop the "cooler consciousness" that allows you to perceive yourself as an object.

The burden of the essay "Über den Schmerz" is not to set the conditions of perception. Jünger is primarily interested in articulating a typology of pain-resistant persons, as he observes them in the republic's civil wars: the lumpen proletarian, the partisan, and the worker-soldier. If these identifications are surprising, it is because Jünger overlooks the social space where more obviously cool candidates gather. Renaissance princes, field commanders or generals, martyrs or hermits lack the requisite ideal traits. Jünger is not searching for exceptions. For the phenotype of transgression in the bourgeois world, he looks in the sphere of labor. The criterion according to which Jünger measures the otherness of this type is its relation to pain.

The critique of the expressive cult of pain, which we already encountered in Plessner's early anthropological text, takes its most radical form in Jünger's essay. It not only confirms the prohibition to which Plessner's conduct code subjects "eruptive expression," as a relapse into the animal realm, but uses the prohibition to draw a sharp boundary separating the world of the worker from bourgeois society. The bourgeoisie's "world of sentimentality" takes the body as a value in itself and derives principles of "humane" treatment from the core idea of the inviolability of the body. But Jünger points out that the bourgeoisie has an ambivalent attitude toward pain.

The bourgeoisie's strategies for avoiding pain set up a disguised form of the division of labor. Confined on the margins of sentimental societies, in barracks, clinics, and cloisters, is a type that specializes in pain, that constantly awaits its application. In the nonviolent intermediate zones, the individual can repress the surrounding world of pain or—occasionally exposed to it—complain loudly and expressively. He devotes himself to the economy of pain avoidance, occasionally compensating the emptiness, which is filled only by the diffused light of the media, with a relapse into "psychological pain." Such an individual enjoys the artificial comfort of a life from which pain has been removed, even while being supplied by the media with images of pain that are part and parcel of the "dreamy, painless, and strangely unfocused contentment" and "fill the air like a narcotic." Jünger's sharp gaze exposes the dualistic structure of this condition: narcoticized islands of humanity with pain specialists permanently on call, surrounding, surveilling, or threatening them with destruction.

Jünger searches instead for a type that has set up a "life with pain" at the center of society, without allowing it the ritual vent of plaintive expression. In the civil war landscape, he finds two uncanny embodiments of the desired type—the lumpen proletarian and the partisan. Both violent types stand out against the diffuse, easily outraged masses, since they appear to be immune to pain; they remain uncanny, because their actual strength consists in their ability to disappear at critical moments back into the "amorphous body of the masses." They lack the clearly defined contours of the external enemy, in Schmitt's silhouettelike portrayal. They infiltrate the body of the state, make their armored appearances when their moment comes but then vanish from sight whenever they run the risk of being overpowered. Whereas an armored vehicle can easily disperse protest demonstrations, it must search out the rioting lumpen proletarians in their hideouts. In all cases of modernizing transformation, the lumpen proletariat takes an important role, forming, as Jünger observes, a "subterranean reserve" at the end of the Weimar Republic. With a side glance at the National Socialist movement, Jünger notes that the measure of a modern political movement's elemental force is the extent to which it includes such people as these, who are "familiar with the pleasures of torture."

The defining activity of the partisan as a type also takes place outside the ordered zone of legality. Nor does it adhere to the rules laid down by the friend-enemy definition, so that its contours are lost in the sea of the urban population. The figure of the Communist cadre operating illegally appears in Jünger's work in the mask of the partisan, displaying a bedeviling similarity to Brecht's character from the *Reader for Those Who Live in Cities*. "Cover your tracks!" is a slogan that can drive the distinction artist to distraction. In Jünger, the partisan must extinguish his bourgeois identity, simultaneously falling outside the honor code of the uniformed soldier:

The partisan has no cover; short shrift is made of him whenever he is caught. As he is deployed in war without a uniform, in civil war he turns in his party card before taking action. The affiliation of the partisan, accordingly, always remains uncertain. It can never be determined whether he is spy or counterspy, belongs to this party or the opposing one, to the police or the vigilantes, or to all at once—indeed, whether he acts on behalf of anyone at all or is simply engaged in his own personal criminal deeds. This twilight is part of the nature of his task.[153]

This blurring of contours strikes the cool persona as a provocation— and truly so when it turns up inside the state apparatus and in the "amorphous body of the masses," becoming conspicuous in the commotion of Sundays and holidays, in the tumult of the streets, or in the "gray hordes of demobilization" as the "ferment of decomposition" (110).

The outlines of the worker-soldier type, which Jünger juxtaposes to partisans and lumpen proletarians, never blur. They have been tempered in war's "death zone." Wherever this type appears, all the usual distinctions of race, class, estate disappear. A modern human being, the type realizes the dream of synchronization between organism and technical apparatus. Its being is integrated into technology. Enclosed within an "armored cell," it is the intelligence of a bullet; an electric machine replaces the functions of a central nervous system. Jünger presents the type in centaurlike images, in the concentric encasement of body and machine, as an "organic" construction. The images Jünger paints of this electric human crustacean correspond to his ideal of heroic realism: we encounter this figure in the troops encased in an armored police van on Alexanderplatz, cutting through the protesting crowds—like a "human sea"—we see how "inconspicuously" it operates the controls of its fighting machines or, "masked and enclosed in defensive shells, it marches through clouds of tear gas" (98); it pilots a Japanese torpedo;[154] or it crouches "in the fiery vortex of a falling fighter plane, in the air pocket of a sunken submarine on the bottom of the sea" (107). Radio signals inform us that a being yet lurks inside the metal shell. Or is it just the radio simulating its presence?

Perception has created the fitting object for the cool persona. It gazes indifferently back.

Armor from a Different Perspective   To replace this military vision of the persona trapped in the metal shell of organic construction for new objectivity images of civilian life offers a certain relief. But the habitus we

encounter here is not unrelated to war. "Not to be injured anymore"—
the soldier's trauma prompts civilians as well to don their armor:

> New objectivity painters prefer representing the individual fully clothed,
> packed in as many casings as possible. They paint people defended by suits,
> vests, ties, leather jackets, coats, by gloves, hats, and caps. Räderscheidt
> shows us a young man standing in a black suit, with yellow gloves and a
> bowler, alone on a vast square before a geometrically standardized architec-
> ture taken directly from the *pittura metafisica* of Giorgio de Chirico, appar-
> ently transposed into the modern world. He wears his closely fitting clothes
> like armor, protected from fear and cold, but for that the more isolated from
> his surroundings, and the lonelier.[155]

In Plessner, the social role forms a protective shield, maintaining distance, filtering expression, reducing friction. In Jünger, masks protect
people in daily life, evoking "for men, a metallic, and for women, a cos-
metic impression" (171). Everywhere we find the desire for an impenetrable shielding—against external danger or against internal decomposition and daily shaming.

Panzer, which in English means armor, shield, and tank, is one of the
magical words in the republic's masculinity cult. On the one hand, it recalls legends of the fallen warrior, overcome only by dint of material
superiority; on the other, it accepts the necessity of a form of resistance
that assimilates the tools of the aggressor. Mythologized in this way, armor also takes center stage for the enlightenment discourse of the republic, which sought to demystify it.

For psychoanalysts, the formation of a "cool armoring" begins early,
as a reaction to birth trauma (Otto Rank) or occurs as an element of
the "collective neurosis" of a society become fatherless following the
collapse of Wilhelmian authority.[156] Toward the end of the republic,
Wilhelm Reich, discussing his theory of character analysis, speaks of
"ego armoring" as a defensive apparatus intended to mount an offense
against the stimuli of the external world and intercept the libidinal
transgressions of the id.[157] He sees a neurotic element in the armor, because fear is continually involved in maintaining it. Its sole function of
averting "disgrace" draws ego armor into the "catastrophe of ridiculousness" that the cool persona tries at any cost to avoid and can lead to
severe neurotic idiosyncrasies.

More popular than Reich's explanations of neurosis, however, was
a finding of individual psychology according to which the superiority
habitus of the armored ego implies the compensation of an organic

inferiority. In Alfred Adler, the experience of inferiority becomes an elemental force in human evolution, which is responsible for cultural achievements. The individual, from the moment of birth, lacks what is responsible for making other sorts of creatures more powerful than he. "The influence of the climate forces him to protect himself from cold with materials taken from better protected animals. His organism requires an artificial encasement."[158] Sigmund Freud, in contrast, rejects the derivation of the inferiority complex from organic defects and refers (to put it in abbreviated form) this feeling's power to experiences of being deprived of love and fear of castration.

Others have put psychoanalytic insights to persuasive use, explaining certain of the types in our portrait gallery of the cool persona.[159] I summarize this approach here primarily to introduce a story that develops an explanation of the superiority complex into a satirical text about organic construction. Jünger, in "Über den Schmerz," remarks:

> Just the fact that the individual is closed up inside rolling vehicles lends him the appearance of greater inviolability and does not fail to work its effect on those being attacked.[160]

In his story of "Der Riese Agoag" (1936), Musil transfers Jünger's heroic notion of a "living torpedo" to the banal psychology of everyday life.[161] The hero of the story, attributing his scant attractiveness to women to his skinny body, compensates first by reading the boxing news and later by devoting himself from morning to night to body building. Always, after using his day to the fullest in just this way, he goes to sleep, first

> spreading out all the muscles he can muster all at the same time, then lying there in his own muscles like an alien piece of meat in the claws of an eagle, until, overcome by fatigue, the grip loosens and he falls straight down into sleep.

The image of Ganymede in the grip of the eagle (*Adler*) suggests that our hero leaves something to be desired on the aggression scale and that he might more securely fantasize being wrapped in the wings of homophilia than confronting the woman (if the mention of bird of prey does not refer only to Adler's compensation theory). In any case, it is no surprise that our bodybuilder gets beaten up shortly after by a "fat blob of a person," an incident which causes him to lose favor with the woman once again. Only now is he in a position to appreciate the advantages of an "organic construction." When he chances one day to witness an accident in which a city bus runs over an athlete, our hero seizes the opportunity and "climbs right up into the victor" (incidentally, the Berlin transit system used the acronym ABOAG). Now he is rendered "invincible by the apparatus of power." If other heroes put on their armor (*Panzer*), why should he not put on a bus? From a superior command position in the upper deck he feels himself able to scatter the masses on the street "like sparrows." Yet before he realizes his dream, which he optimizes by acquiring a bus pass, he cannot help seeing that he does not in fact gain the irresistible appeal he attributes to becoming an element of an organic construction. Out of his armor, he seems castrated. After he recognizes that woman, on account of "her lesser cognitive daring," is unable to make the conceptual leap from the armor to its inhabitant, he resigns himself to his lot—not, however, without adding a triumphant summary: "The strong are mightiest on their own."

Electric Fins for Leviathan   What separates Helmuth Plessner's construction of the duelist from Ernst Jünger's construction of the worker? And is the distance between the landscape of Jünger's "electromagnetic force fields" and Walter Benjamin's sketch "Zum Planetarium," the concluding piece of his 1928 book *Einbahnstraße,* one between disaster and welfare? [162]

In Jünger's book *Der Arbeiter: Herrschaft und Gestalt,* the icon of the warrior fascinates the gestalt of the cool persona. The warrior's physiognomy—beneath a steel helmet or a crash helmet—is metallic, "galvanized, as it were." "The gaze is steady and focused, schooled in the observation of things that can be captured in high velocity conditions" (107). This icon appealed to readers on the right, while the modernism of the diagnosis put them off. Readers on the left, who registered Jünger's sympathy for planning and his quasi-Marxist theory of simultaneity, did not know what to do with it. Theorists, finally, who admire the way Jünger's book reveals the relationship between war as an instrument of modernization and the domination of the technical media, tend to distance themselves from his horrific images of "heroic realism" by relegating them to the status of contemporary coloration. [163] Ideology critique, for which the book has become easy prey, deprives it of any diagnostic value, although its findings are as proximate to Günther Anders's *Antiquiertheit des Menschen* as to the chapter on the "culture industry" in Horkheimer and Adorno's *Dialectik der Aufklärung.*

The book's foreword of July 1932 names all the elements we have come to expect from a new objectivity code of conduct. Jünger connects the demand for perceptual sharpness, which is supposed to render vis-

ible the critical aspects of power ("Leviathan's fins" [7]), to the form of
the soldier's spiritual exercises, which seem designed to train him in an
instinctive security of action.

Jünger's book aims, like the other conduct codes, at a lifestyle. Once
again we encounter the fundamental motif of the codes, which is to
cultivate a distance from the body. Jünger's spiritual exercise aims at a
"metallic coolness" of consciousness that enables the individual, in the
extreme situations of the death zone, "to treat the body as a pure instrument, forcing from it a range of complicated accomplishments beyond the bounds of self-preservation" (107). The book offers instruction
in the habitus of the sharp gaze, counting "high treason against the
mind" as one of the "horrible pleasures of our time" (39). Like all codes
of conduct, Jünger's works with a theory of masks, so that a series of
precepts can be distilled from the book:

> The hardness of society can be mastered only by hardness, and not
> by any form of trickery (28).
>
> The more cynical or spartan, Prussian or Bolshevik . . . a life can be,
> the better it will be (201).
>
> Reality is determined, not by moral precepts, but by laws. There-
> fore the decisive question to be posed is this: is there a point from
> which it can be authoritatively decided whether a particular means
> should be employed or not? (191).
>
> There is no escape, no move sideways, no move backward; the point
> is much more to increase the fury and the speed of the processes in
> which we are caught (194).
>
> Nothing is as constant as change. . . . When unrest comes to a stop,
> every moment becomes a starting point of an Asiatic constancy
> (172 f.).

By listing *Der Arbeiter* among the conduct codes examined here, we
risk obscuring its novelty. Jünger's compendium, like the others, serves
the education of an "aristocracy" and an "order." But his nervous gaze
discovers it in incipient form in tank and submarine crews, in the ranks
of the security troops of a political movement or cadre—in a type that
can be reproduced in masses, not in the individually prominent dueling subject. The habitus of this type corresponds to its metaphysical
"stamp" (*Gestalt*). If the cool persona of the art scene comes into view,
Jünger delivers it up to the derision of his type, which finds amusement

in how clumsy the old sort of duelist looks in a landscape of the technical media:

> A special ceremony has been developed in which the modern individual, in the disguise of a quasi-aristocrat or quasi-abbé, to the sound of what has become very general applause, executes the practiced mortal thrust according to all the rules of the art. This is a game for which existential quantities have become two-edged concepts. More important for us is the hand movement with which the streetcar conductor rings his bell. (229)

In the world opened up by this book there are no reserves left over, no "last bits" of "something dangerous" preserved "as a curiosity" (52). The activities of the artist shift from the periphery of the romantic space into the sphere of power. Only here, according to Jünger, is it possible to experience the "elemental."

The individual as the "intersection" in a "network" of "cross-cutting currents"—this viewpoint is registered, without the reservation of cultural pessimism, for the first time by Jünger. The individual is hooked into the system by a cipher code:

> The power, traffic, and news services appear as a field in the coordinate system of which the individual is to be understood as a specific point. One "gets a bearing on him," for example, by turning the dial on an automatic telephone. The functional value of such a tool rises with the number of people connected—but this number never appears as a mass in the old sense but is always a quantity that can be expressed in precise numbers at any moment. (139)

A person in the modern media landscape who remains "immersed" in printed material, Jünger could only say ironically, will be made aware of the connections that nevertheless persist to general power circuits. The newspaper reader Jünger observes pursues a "different kind of reading," that is not to be understood in the sense of immersion:

> This becomes clear where one has the opportunity to observe the reader in situations, especially situations of public transit, in which merely making use of it already means going to work. An observer here will register a simultaneously alert and instinctive atmosphere, in which a news service of the greatest precision and speed is appropriate. One seeks the impression here that the world has changed during the reading, but this change is at once constant, in the sense of a monotonous change of colored signals flying by outside the windows. This is news inside a space where everything that happens involves the presence of atoms bombarded at the speed of an electric current. (264)

Jünger's praise of precision is for the technical medium. The news itself (for instance, a launching, a mining accident, or a motorcycle race) and the place to which the media turn their attention have no particular import. What suddenly occupies the center of attention is remote from the influence of the individual. Occasionally—having scarcely gotten used to the news service as a purely functional accompaniment to a habitual pattern of movement—the individual suffers a shock; without him, circulation would come to a standstill. Nothing the reading material contains can bring the reader to remove himself from the transport system in which he reads the paper. The all-encompassing dream created by the media has no fixed focal point. The attention of the newspaper reader, like that of the chess master playing simultaneous games, is always on call:

> There is something anxiety inducing, recalling the mute glow of a traffic signal, when suddenly one or another excerpt of this space—whether a threatened province, a big trial, a sporting event, a natural disaster, or the cabin of a transoceanic airplane, becomes the center of attention and thus the effective moment as well, and when a dense ring of artificial eyes and ears closes around it. (256)

If we look for the stylistic move that allows Jünger to produce the images of networking circuitry, we come on a maneuver that is as simple as it is astonishing: he changes the central technical metaphor. Jünger is one of the first writers to place the model of the electric circuit at the center of social analysis. Electricity, with its force field, network, connection, replaces the steam engine, the model of a psychologically oriented literature. Whenever he singles out a phenomenon's systematic quality, electricity is the dominant image; the combustion engine serves better to emphasize the dynamic quality. The electric topos recommends itself when one element in the total space requires an explanation: "The arrangement of atoms thus takes on the sort of nonambiguity that prevails in the electromagnetic force field" (266). Jünger attributes a special status to the electric media; they possess the quality of machines that replace, not only muscle power, as in the case of the older generation of technical apparatuses, but the functions of the central nervous system. Alongside these characteristics derived from electricity, Jünger finds an additional reason to elevate them to the central metaphor of his systematic thinking: the electric network comes under the administrative authority of the state, which controls all the connections and integrates every user of current into an "energy association" (215). The individual automatically has the status of an "organic construction" (275).

The metaphor of the electromagnetic force field, incidentally, enters the work of Walter Benjamin, Bertolt Brecht, and Joseph Roth. Research has made us aware of the great influence of the concept of the abstract, nonexperiential descriptive and explanatory model of the force field in physics on the epistemological discussion carried on in Vienna at the turn of the century:

> In terms of content, the invisible electromagnetic force field, which, for example, arranges a previously chaotic pile of iron filings all in the same direction, opened up the possibility of an analogous assumption of energies operating supraindividually, as in the formation of structured communities out of masses.[164]

The penetration of electric metaphors into philosophy and literature stems from the way in which they lend expression to the otherwise ineffable quality of the *élan vital*. At the core of the force field metaphor is an image:

> the existence of energetic tension between two opposed poles. This datum could be used to connect the polarized thought of classical Rome with the specifically vitalist idea that a life of intensity can only take place between two extremes.[165]

Jünger relocates this vitalist idea, using the electric metaphor only to characterize the monodimensional, systemic quality of the society of the worker.

Electricity, for Jünger, is an index of simultaneity: Those who sit under an electric light discussing the return to nature (223) or put the body of Christ next to a microphone or broadcast an encyclical over the radio (73) are hooked into the network of modernization. The synchronization of divergent mentalities with the highest technological level is already a fait accompli, even while it is still being vigorously called into question. Like his Marxist contemporaries, Jünger has in mind the lightbulb—hanging on a public utility wire—when he recalls a famous sentence from Marx's work *Zur Kritik der politischen Ökonomie* as he interprets society: "It is a general light into which all other colors are dipped, which alters them in their specificity" (98).

The new media are the leviathan state's electric fins. Even in extreme situations—in the air bubble of a submarine on the ocean floor, in the cockpit of a crashing fighter plane—the electric media remain connected to the all-encompassing network, with which the individual can break contact only at the threat of being extinguished.

What drives the cool persona in the "electromagnetic force field" of such a space? Networked and run through with circuits, it might well fizzle out to nothingness. But this is a wild guess. Nothing animates the cool persona like the images of nothingness it itself produces. And so the system's present moment also belongs to the cool persona.

In the landscape of the electric media, we see the cool persona in a man "bent over his cards to the hum of the telephone and the clatter of the news agency teletype."[166] He resists distractions but cultivates the awareness of the chess master; in fact, the cool persona ignores any sound that cannot be clearly deciphered, any amorphous acoustical signal. But the technical channels' white noise triggers a state of permanent unrest. On the battlefield, the persona is forced to probe even the most insignificant sounds for their meaning. There are reports from the First World War of the use of aural locator devices, equipped with giant reception horns and superhuman frequency ranges, which allowed soldiers to identify enemy artillery installations from twenty miles away.[167]

The new media open up new possibilities. They do not, as writing does, filter whatever the screen of the symbolic order allows to enter but are automatically part of "the roar of the real."[168] Their deployment in war only reinforces the ordering function of writing. No detritus of meaning remains, as meaningless undergrowth, optical garbage, or acoustical nonsense: the media register everything. A final corner of the perceptual field not yet occupied by meaning—a deserted bit of woods, the rustling of a newspaper page, an unknown tonal frequency, the irregularities of a crater landscape—comes clear. "Meaningless" disturbances of regularity are especially in need of decoding, because they might well be points of enemy incursion.

With the help of the electric media, the mesh of the symbolic becomes finer, the environment of understanding perception more hermetic. In Jünger's system, every sound is under the high voltage of meaning. An American study claims that Jünger's "fascist modernism" promised "to liberate the imagery from the Jacobin tyranny of the symbolic order";[169] nevertheless, in 1932 Jünger did more to reinforce the omnipresence of the symbolic order, by binding the electric media to writing.

When Jünger's cool persona steps into the field of reality where Schmitt's *distinguo ergo sum* resounds, fuzzy contours suddenly clear. Everything becomes a clue pointing to a secret center. The new media amplify the power of distinction. Probably a statement like Musil's at the end of a puzzling story—"But it is like whispering you've heard or merely a rustling, without being able to distinguish it"[170]—is irritating to the cool persona. The latter demands clear, if possible, sharp articulation. If sounds are to reveal enemy conditions, they must be audible and undisturbed by background noise or technical distortions, which could garble the message. "Electricity," Marshall McLuhan will remark three decades after *Der Arbeiter,* "points the way to an extension of the process of consciousness itself, on a world scale, and without any verbalization whatsoever."[171]

Jünger cannot do without verbalization in the imperium of the worker. Nevertheless, it is possible to identify in his work a double movement in regard to language: he ascribes to the new media all the restrictive characteristics that present-day media theory attributes to writing, in order, at the same time, to present as the music of the future a form of archaic communication in which the auditory is primary: the anxious attending to the voice coming from the secret center. Jünger's desire for a "competent reserve of illiterates" (203), necessary for the empire of the worker to function, is understandable. Only illiterates, he hopes, will submit absolutely to the commands of the literate stratum of rulers.

The language that Jünger admits into his system does away with the openness of verbal references, the instability of meaning and meanings, the ambivalences of expression, the labyrinth of correspondences, in short, the entire potential range of speech and thus all that is emblematic of linguistic life. Language keeps only its function to signal and warn, to instruct and command; it is always referential language, an element of a "secure and closed world of forms." Fearing "endless dialectical talk" (227), Jünger seeks to disempower speech. He mistrusts all texts that admit ambiguity: "There is absolutely no doubt that a textbook today has more meaning than the latest spinning out of unique experience by the bourgeois novel"(141), he comments.

Since Jünger regards books that make up an individual's memory system as so much ballast, he gives his own book an appropriate form. Although prompted by countless findings in books in libraries, he eschews references of any sort, names no names that might remind the reader of alien, strange, or canonical influences.[172] Thus the book suggests that it is itself "marked" as "metaphysics," which is also supposed to be registered in the form. That accounts for the book's curious individual qualities that amount to the author's handwriting.

We saw one theoretical component of Jünger's "total artwork" in the avant-garde movement. The world disintegrates into meaninglessly disparate component parts, glaring nonsimultaneities, dingy twilight spaces, craters, trash, and magic only—in an audacious move on the part of avant-garde thinkers, joining this perception to the circuit of modernization—to sparkle like a crystal in the "icy geometry of light"

(166). First all immanent meaning vanishes from the world and the characters populating it, then from a heavenly stage set modern gadgetry and the media crank down the center of meaning like an artificial sun.

Jünger's topos of modernity as an earthquake landscape—in which "ruins appear to be more significant than the fleeting quarters that get abandoned every morning" (83)[173]—displays certain similarities with the landscape of baroque tragedy, as conceived by another avant-garde thinker, Walter Benjamin, at the same time: decaying landscapes, squares both abandoned and overpopulated, the whole overcast by the cold heavens; rebellion offering no escape from this disconsolate earthly state. "The earth," as Jünger puts it, "is covered by the rubbish of crumbled images. We are taking part in a spectacle of decline comparable only to geological catastrophes" (74). A desolate space through which generations have passed, leaving behind "neither savings nor monuments, but solely a certain stage, the flood marks of mobilization" (165). As soon, however, as Jünger illuminates these images in his *laterna magica* from the "constant light source" (99) of a center, everything makes sense. Everything takes on the coloration of the "crystal," the total work space. Every bit of grenade shrapnel becomes an allegory of strategic meaning; every bodily movement occurs in the service of mobilization; to the keen observer, the broadcast signal, however distorted it may be, holds an encoded reference.

"There is nothing more regular than the axial orientation of the crystal" (220), we read in *Der Arbeiter*. Carl Schmitt terms the hermetic system constructed in his 1927 philosophy of the state a "Hobbes crystal." Jakob von Uexküll presupposes in 1930 that life develops like a "crystalline formation."[174] For Arnold Gehlen, a "crystalline structure" is the defining aspect of the standstill of history.[175] From modern biology we learn that total symmetry of this sort—however fascinating aesthetically—means death in the world of living organisms. Ernst Jünger was never one to promote the "myth of the avant-garde's innocence."[176]

COOL PERSONA—IN THE BELLY OF THE FISH

Nothing so threatens the cool persona's sense of Luciferian grandeur as the "banality of evil." How can its habitus survive dictatorship, holocaust, and war? Does a point come when attitude must be put at risk for the sake of experience, or does focus on such a point simply reflect a desire for expression? Further, does the cool persona's refusal to mourn after the Second World War compulsively repeat an attitude after the First

World War that found increasing resonance in the public sphere? In Carl Schmitt's *Glossarium,* amid the rubble, we see the cool persona's final stand.

No other intellectual of the 1920s acted out objectivity's trademark role—gambling with the devil—more consistently than Carl Schmitt. No one managed to contrive such an alliance with moral evil on the lofty plane of the state. Our question now concerns what remains of this Luciferian figure after the Second World War. Does it ask, like the exhausted Lindbergh after his transatlantic flight, to be carried off "to a dark hangar, so no one sees my weakness"?

The Diary   Schmitt's diary, published in 1991, begins after his release from an American internment camp. The entries run from late summer 1947 to August 1951. He writes as the Cold War was beginning to spread its atmosphere of bitter enmity over all debates, and it comes as no surprise that in his diary Schmitt refers sarcastically to the taboo against taking international animosity as the starting point of theoretical reflection. Schmitt draws a straight line from the taboo to artless talk of the "just war," in which, according to Schmitt, fundamentalism blends with unregulated killing. His thoughts return insistently to the question of whether putting an end to the political definition of enmity might not enhance the possibility of civil war and the ritual atrocities that accompany it. And he ponders, as could hardly be expected otherwise, the problem of depriving the vanquished of enemy status in order to subject them to hearings and judicial judgment as criminals.

The diary's appearance undermined the assumption humanistic Schmitt scholars had cultivated of a turn marked by the publication of *Der Leviathan in der Staatslehre von Thomas Hobbes* in 1938. With this book Schmitt supposedly broke off his dalliance with state fetishism, which dated from 1919, in order then, in the 1942 text *Land und Meer,* to carry out a kind of "mourning."[177] The diary disappointed expectations, maintaining with undiminished vigor all of Schmitt's theoretical motifs, from his 1916 hymn of praise to Theodor Däubler's *Nordlicht* to the enemy formula of the 1920s, from reflections on linguistic magic, taken over from his friend Hugo Ball, to the anti-Semitic outbursts of the 1930s. Any break in the continuity of his thought, writes Schmitt, indicates nothing more than a "mental disturbance" (105). A diary necessarily produces "photocopies of the palimpsest character" (130) of thinking, he maintains, offering a definition we could work with, were it not part of a defensive strategy that allows him to determine which of the successive layers of thought is the fundamental one.

The manifest outrage many reviewers expressed over the diary's publication reflects their disappointment. They expected a document of the guilt culture and got unrepentant effrontery. While the reviewers' moral indignation was no doubt justified, a thoughtful look at the ideas expressed in the diary would not have hurt them. These ideas revolve monomaniacally around the principle *nullum crimen, nulla poena, sine lege,* which is the title of a verdict that Schmitt had circulated in hectograph in 1945. The diary's contents include a collection of timely maxims. Infamous maxims, too, can instruct:

> A good conscience that is expedited by the judiciary is the worst. (90)
> Most people think taking off a fake beard is a metamorphosis. (107)
> Whoever is right a few years prematurely is wrong. (144)
> Scholastic asceticism is an ethical plus, but it falls short of theoretical accomplishment. (113)

Reading the book historically, we can ask what became of the cult of evil after the Second World War, which had held in its spell such disparate minds as Helmuth Plessner and Ernst Jünger, Gottfried Benn and Walter Benjamin, E. R. Curtius and Bertolt Brecht. Of greatest interest in this connection is the combination of self-enactment, compulsive brooding, and complaining that always turns the *Glossarium*'s lofty figure of the cool persona into a infantile ventriloquist. Schmitt's diary shows as well how the cool persona and the creature are uncanny doubles: "What is man! The circulation of blood, cast in the light of a poor will-o'-the-wisp" (314).

A few basic motifs of the old avant-garde made it through the dead of winter to sprout in the diary: the "joy in the acceleration" (31) of fatal processes, which Schmitt shared with the intellectuals of the left; the return to seventeenth-century anthropology, which welcomes in the state a great machine for keeping the "terror of drives" (207) in check; scorn for the faith in law as the "instinctlessness of a living being condemned to decline" (23, 50, 301), in which he marks his agreement with Brecht, Lukács, and Lenin;[178] and the pleasure involved in having a "satanic" (5) reputation. In these notes we find slogans (e.g., "The primitive thinks in substances, the civilized man in functions" [161]) in which the new objectivity jargon lives on. Also the pathos of invulnerability and mobility that surrounded the new objectivity's mechanical man comes back into force: "Best is when the enemy who shoots at me hits the spot where I stood a second before" (190).

The classic characteristics of the cool persona remain present in the years from 1947 to 1951; boastful and fascinating in public presentation, subdued in private notes. For the diary bears the remarkable characteristic of that "compulsive brooding" Benjamin saw in Jesuit spiritual exercises:

> This torment of intellectual consciousness is predestined for authoritarian rule through its complete lack of substance. It has lost all relation to the essence of individual being and it offers absolution, depending on how one wants to look at it, either mystically or mechanically, like a sacrament. The tension of penitent torment, displaced to that purely intentional zone, at the same time leaves moral life resting in a certain apathy, in which it now reacts not to its own impulses but rather to carefully weighed and considered stimuli of spiritual authority.[179]

The habitus that undertakes spiritual exercises with no grounding in morality coincides, predictably, with the attitude of the mendicant creature. Tossing aside Gracián's precept no. 129, "Never complain," the *Glossarium* engages in a plaintive discursive ritual: "Injustice is always ever again my lot" (252).

From the angle of Benjamin's book on German tragedy, Schmitt's self-portrait in the diary is that of an ousted intriguer who mopes, while refusing resolutely to adopt the role of the melancholic. Schmitt slips on all the masks of the poor supplicant creature he finds in his extensive reading, from Kaspar Hauser to Kafka's defendant in *Der Prozess*, from victims of ritual murder to the prophet Jonah inside the whale:

> Three times I was in the belly of the fish. I have tasted the defeat of the civil war, inflation and deflation, revolution and restoration, changes of regimes and burst pipes, currency reform, air bombardments, and interrogations; camps and barbed wire, hunger and cold, ragged clothes and hideous bunkers. (81)

Schmitt's Shame Culture   After 1945 Schmitt repeats an attitude that corresponds to the post–World War I zeitgeist: he does away with elements of the guilt culture—troubled conscience, remorse—and erects once again the artificial realm of a heroic shame culture. The difference that springs painfully to the eye, of course, is that the idea of a post–World War II shame culture is a phantasm, with no corresponding public discursive space in which to unfold. In the context of the Nuremberg trials, the statement of the Protestant church, and denazification, a guilt

culture is a matter of official prescription, so that Schmitt's shame culture has to articulate itself outside the public sphere.

The key concepts of the shame culture are honor and disgrace. After
World War I the issue was the "disgrace" of imperial collapse, which,
according to the rules of male association and bonding, had to be re-
versed. At issue now for Schmitt is the "honor" of which he was deprived as a vanquished foe. Everything that the Allies undertook with
Schmitt, during his incarceration and afterward, he experiences as a
shaming ritual, in which he, suddenly abandoned to the resentful gaze
of the enemy, isolated from his fellows and discriminated against, must
armor himself. He experiences his stay in the cell of an American camp
as exposure. "Man is most naked when he is stripped and made to stand
in front of another who is clothed," he writes in April 1947 in his "Weis-
heit der Zelle." "The clothes that were left to me," Schmitt continues,
"only confirmed my objective nakedness."[180] The effective factor in a
shame culture is not the admonition of the individual conscience but
the scorn of others, enacted in the form of public disgrace. Following his
release from the Nuremberg prison into the American zone, Schmitt,
rather than return to Berlin and the forum of a despising public, goes to
Plettenberg, where he believes that he is immune to disgrace. From here
he fires off condemnations of the Protestant guilt culture, striving to
keep his distance from its "spectacle of a brawl between preachers of
repentance" (30). He is "disgusted" by the pathos of moral indignation,
and he notes bouts of "depression," because people expect "from me
tips for memorial inscriptions in the confessional style." On "Der Fall
Jaspers" (the case of Jaspers), he later records the derisive verse:

> How his penitential speech offends me
> How disgusting are his rotten fish
> Now he's gotten where he ought to be:
> In the news and on the German telewish. (104)[181]

"A jurist," Schmitt reflects during the summer of 1946, still in the American internment camp, "steers clear of psychological self-depiction. The
impulse to offer a literary confession has been spoiled for me by such
ugly examples as Jean-Jacques Rousseau and poor August Strind-
berg."[182] Schmitt is not among the public "self-torturers." "If you want
to make a confession, go find a priest and do it there" (77).

He unrolls once again the old banner "Tout ce qui arrive est ado-
rable!" (8), carried by the avant-garde and the militant Catholic Léon
Bloy too; but the slogan he writes in his diary presumably has little to

do with the fate he himself experienced. For he had been "dishonored."
Carl Schmitt seeks comfort in the "all-surpassing objectivity" (119) of
Thomas Hobbes and finds himself vindicated: "Hobbes would say: as
long as one finds honor among men . . . , he will regard this life as splendid" (44).

But the treatment Schmitt experiences in no way accords to his status; what he has to say has been banished from that space of consensual
resonance, so that he screams "with no voice." Since he is not prepared
to repent, he receives no license for publications. His power of definition
lacks a place to be exercised in public; worse yet, he has lost that power
to the "enemy." And the latter, by virtue of its monopoly on making
distinctions, incriminated his practice since 1933 —which is for Schmitt
a serious logical error.

The power of definition had been Schmitt's elixir, the axis of his sovereign consciousness. At the center of his *Glossarium* we find the motto
that also belonged to the creed of Weimar's leftist intellectuals:

> Understand the power that is trying to get you in its grasp; do not confront
> it with countermeasures on the same level; rather, test your power to under-
> stand against that power. It will also try to grasp your understanding. But let
> it. It will cut its paws. (145)

Nor can he, in the seclusion of his refuge in Plettenberg, resist circulat-
ing "dangerous definitions" in letters. Still in the role of "hunted game"
(174), he wants to classify his hunters. Sometimes he manages to get his
views—as a kind of smuggled contraband—published in an organ ap-
proved by the occupation powers. Then he rejoices that his contraband,
in good new objectivity manner, is allowed to ride on a commodity:

> In the weekly journal *Christ und Welt,* a nice little gloss of mine has been
> printed, via an advertisement for Nivea cream. It is good so. In czarist times
> the Russian nihilists hid their bombs in flower pots. Why should I not frame
> my analogous concerns with Nivea cream. Or, conversely, make my own ap-
> pearance as the frame for Nivea cream, so as not to agitate the persecutors.
> (111)

Schmitt directs his attention to the unsecured terrain of postwar society
and, as in the 1920s, it remains now: when orienting parameters collapse, it's time for codes of conduct.

On 1 May 1948 Carl Schmitt, following the familiar model of
Gracián's *Art of Worldly Wisdom,* notes seven maxims, to which he
will later add a few others. The Spanish Jesuit, we recall, replaced the
internal regulator, the conscience, with an external voice—a code of

conduct. Three of these tactical rules, in Schmitt's version, are as follows:

> If you end up in a loudly screaming chorus, you must scream the text yourself as loudly as you can. Anything else would mean your certain ugly death. Your hearing and brain would be shattered from without if you didn't defend yourself from within by screaming along; I can only recommend to you then a purely physical means of defense against annihilation by sound waves. (144)
>
> Go into the shelter when the signal calls for it; raise your hands when you are ordered to; don't forget that the relation between protection and obedience is no longer certain and self-evident; the shelter can be the gas chamber. (144)
>
> Beware of every loudspeaker; beware of every microphone that conducts your voice into the false public sphere [see Figure 12]. Every amplifier is a meaning counterfeiter. . . . But beware of the false echo that arises in the byways of the catacombs. (172)

Borrowing from Thomas Hobbes's theory of the state, Schmitt assumes from the outset a reciprocal relation between protection and obedience. Just as the protector can demand obedience, those who obey have a right to protection. Where this arrangement is violated, behavior can no longer be steered in a way that ensures protection. The result is that everyone is delivered up defenseless to circumstance. Schmitt thus formulates rules for situations that, from his perspective, are no longer subject to regulation. Bitterly, he elaborates his precepts ad absurdum; for their validity is restricted to honor-based social groups. He lays responsibility for his rules' absurdity at the feet of the dishonorable victorious powers.

Phonomania and Creature   Schmitt's behavioral rules recreate the world of mobilization as an acoustic space. He advises in favor of purely physical defensive mechanisms, which are supposed to guarantee survival, while the command's substance or the song's text is of no matter. Schmitt's diary thus documents a remarkable form of phonocentrism. It reflects his resistance to the concept of law and clarifies his childish fixation on the "voice of the father."

Through three hundred and twenty pages of diary entries, there is scarcely a reproduction of a visual impression to be found. The diary leads us into a world of acoustic phenomena, into a laboratory of echoing voices. Ultimately, the friend-enemy theory receives a phonetic basis. Even close friends appear without facial features; in the case of Jünger, Schmitt registers the "pathetic larynx" (104); for historically more dis-

12. Beware of every microphone!

(Carl Schmitt. With the permission of Ullstein Bilder-
dienst, Berlin.)

tant associates such as Max Stirner, he occasionally remarks on a "pu-
erile crowing" (36). In the auditory space of the Schmittian world, Hitler
is an "empty amplifier" (111); the ego, a figure (*Gestalt*) of the "echo"
(17); the worst characteristic of the contemporary world, its "deafness."
Schmitt feels himself beset by "eavesdropping nonjurists" and jurists
who do not listen (85); his strongest affect consists in the "shudder and
outrage" that overtake him when he hears the word "law" (23). "Timely
silence" counts for him as a classical virtue. His favorite role to play in
the vicissitudes of life is that of the "blind harbinger" (152; cf. 16). The
figure of the "noble blind man" (Jürgen Manthey), who succumbs to neither the seductions of narcissism nor the illusions of visual appearances
but "listens," suffers, and speaks, hoping to get a hearing, is his idol.

Schmitt reacts idiosyncratically, as if irritated and impatient, to any
argument based in any way on appearance. It pains him, leaves him

dumbfounded to register that the persuasiveness of his voice could be undermined after the war by the horrifying evidence of film (204). When he reads that the new Bavarian constitution begins with the words "In view of the rubble around us," his condemnation is complete (235). Those who would accept visual appearances as evidence make optical illusion the basis of constitutional principles.

If the goal is to arrive at principles of law, the eye must be eliminated as an organ of moral judgment. While visible facts have no argumentative status (with the exception, incidentally, of the "visibility" of the judiciary itself, which he sees as establishing its "substance" [235]), every conceivable acoustic signal prompts thought. No excuse is too paltry. On 19 February 1948 he writes:

> I hear (mornings at 6:00, in the dark, still half asleep) a factory siren, accompanied by a vision of the wide-open jaws of a huge fish. I would like to pursue the immediate simultaneity of an acoustic impression with a visual image. That would likely be more productive than researching the problem of radar. It would offer a glimpse of our inner sensorium. People who hear, instead of church bells, only factory sirens are supposed to believe in the God who is worshiped in church. They are more likely to believe in an iron-hard Moloch. (110)[183]

The foreground point raised in Schmitt's depiction of his acoustic space is the sovereign's voice, which is supposed to reach the ears of the subjects undistorted by the medium. At issue is the problematic written medium of the laws, which distort, absorb, or extinguish the voice, allowing it to reach the ears it is intended for only in diffuse, ambiguous form—the ears of "nonlistening jurists," who occupy themselves producing technically neutral analyses of reigning opinion. In his construction of the state's acoustic space, his thoughts return to ways of regaining the sovereign voice and eliminating legal positivism. Actually, however, as Sombart suspects, the real point is for the voice of the tone-setting constitutional law expert to reach without impediment the ear of the ruler.[184]

Setting down his thoughts on the omnipotence and wretched impotence of the sovereign, on 23 May 1948 Schmitt paints the melancholy picture of a ruler who seems to have migrated directly from baroque tragedy into the Cold War: "Ultimately, the sovereign, blocked off by the anteroom and his chief of staff, sits in the icy solitude of his omnipotence" (152). What Schmitt is tracing here is the mirror image of the lonely prompter, who has been unjustly dismissed from service. For the sovereign's loneliness derives from the way the incompetents who populate the anterooms distance him from his best advisors.

Schmitt's image of the sovereign recalls an anecdote from Pushkin, told by both Ernst Bloch (in *Spuren*) and Walter Benjamin (in his Kafka commentary), which explains the conditions of sovereign rule. In Benjamin's version, Potemkin (according to *Meyers Enzyklopädie* of 1906, a skillful courtier who "combined deceitfulness with old-fashioned Russian brutality but was altogether unfamiliar with noble moral ideas"), governor-general and ranking military officer for Her Grace, Catherine II, suffered from severe depressions, during which access to his chamber was strictly forbidden. One day, with stacks of unprocessed files reaching alarming heights outside, an insignificant chancellery bureaucrat chanced into the palace anteroom, where the councilors of state stood wringing their hands. Scarcely waiting for an answer to his question, "What's up, Excellencies?" he took the files in hand, heading off with the bundle under his arm through galleries and corridors to Potemkin's bedroom, where he turned the doorknob.

Having found Potemkin, dressed in a tattered nightgown, chewing his nails, hunched over in bed, he—"wasting not a word"—dipped Potemkin's quill in ink and slipped the files one after the other onto his knee, whereupon, as if still in sleep, the latter applied the required signatures. Triumphantly, swinging the files in his hand, the bureaucrat made his way back to the councilors, who, having ripped the eagerly awaited papers from his hand, stared back in horror. Only now did the little man have a look at the signatures, discovering there that, instead of Potemkin's, his own name had been written.[185]

That could not have happened to Schmitt, because he knew that it was necessary to gain the ruler's ear. The bureaucrat would have been for him a typical example of the "nonlistening jurist," who is fixated on handwriting. And with this, we come to the central motif in Schmitt's assessment of the ear and the voice: his visceral reaction to "the law."

In the draft for a letter on 19 January 1948, Schmitt writes as follows:

> I would like to say, right away, in surrealistic openness, that the word, and now for the first time properly, the concept of the "law," unleashes in me all manner—conceptual, theoretical, associative-psychological, and, *last not least,** phonetic—of shudder and outrage. Outrage namely at the orgies of the typesetter and the terror of the "settings of the settings." (185)

---

* The italicized words are in English in the original.

As Raphael Gross has demonstrated, a "hatred of the concept of law" runs from the earliest writings all the way through Schmitt's works.[186] Already in his second legal publication, in 1912, we find, "The law is always full of holes. That opens the opportunity for the judiciary and the levying of judgment."[187] Our misfortune, according to Schmitt, lies in our being ruled, as the legal positivists would have it, by the "sovereignty of the law," which could never be anything more than an "overcompensation for the absence" of the actual sovereign.

The question of who is responsible for this cursed confinement of the judicial function to the letter of the law leads directly to the problem of Schmitt's anti-Semitism, for this concept of the law, according to Schmitt, is a product of the mental type of the Jewish people.[188] Law in this conception, as Schmitt would have it, becomes a technical means to restrain the all-powerful leviathan, cut it into pieces, and consume it. The fact that Schmitt, both in the Weimar period and in occupied Germany after the Second World War, feels besieged by positivist legal technicians appears to him proof that the Jews' assimilation was successful; for when one Jew was assimilated in one village, then the village had become Jewish. Yet the Jewish victory instanced in legal positivism could, as Schmitt continues, be no more than provisional, for faith in law is part of the "instinctlessness of a life-form condemned to decline" (23).

The ear of the ruler and the role of law—here are surely two important aspects of Schmitt's phonocentrism that, remarkably enough, evade his own reflections on his phonetic obsessions. The latter revolve instead around three other critical elements in Schmitt's construction of his acoustic space, namely, the command, conceptual realism, and speech magic.

Potemkin, in the grip of his melancholy, was in no condition to issue commands; the handwriting that the petty bureaucrat managed to get from him strikes back at those who, by virtue of the office they held, were fixated on writing. At the center of Schmitt's acoustical space, we find the command. An oral command is a form of language, establishing a direct connection between sender and receiver. The possibility of splitting speech between the speaking subject and the subject of speech, which characterizes written forms of language, is excluded by the command. With a command, the translation of the verbal appeal into action is regarded as unproblematic, or at least potentially possible. Schmitt's appreciation of the command relies on the state theory of Thomas Hobbes, who had held it to be "the greatest charity of language, for without it there would be no community among people, no peace, and as a result no discipline, but, first, wildness, second, loneliness, and, instead of places to live in, hiding places."[189] Schmitt can only agree: "The best thing in the world is a command, rather than a law; a command is direct speech" (274). He criticizes Hegel's master-knave dialectic for its crudeness, calling the dialectic of commanding and obeying, which is geared to speaking and hearing, endlessly more subtle (159). In *Der Arbeiter,* Schmitt's friend Jünger had already offered a definitive analysis of the subtlety of obeying: "Obedience, that is the art of hearing, and order is readiness for the word, readiness for the command, which, like a streak of lightning, runs from treetop to roots" (13).

Schmitt's conceptual realism is another of the constituent elements of his acoustic space. In retrieving the term realism in its medieval sense, Schmitt assumes that the truth contained in the spoken word does not reside in the thing it refers to (116). Unlike writing, which is characterized by the capacity merely to produce the illusion of the presence of the absent subject of speech, the spoken word is inseparable from the instance of speaking. Only in sound does the word take on its corporeal reality; only in sound does it create space. When Schmitt then terms himself a "concept-ballistics man" (*Begriffs-Ballistiker*) he is attributing to his definition the material quality of a projectile.

Schmitt's view of conceptual realism acquires its uncanny dimension in combination with his reflections on speech magic. Every word, as he puts it in the diary, is a "phonetic hieroglyph," an "echo of primal worlds" (159), which "impresses itself on memory with hypnotic power." The point, therefore, is to find key words that articulate a fundamental experience—like *Dezision* (decision), *Raum* (space), or *Feind* (enemy)—and have phonetic qualities that stamp them on the memory. The purely phonetic qualities are ineffaceable. Schmitt believes that his key concepts achieve such a result, so that the cut of the umbilical cord is present in *Dezision;* that the primeval land is available for perception in *Raum,* bounded by the sea, defended by the father, and cared for by the mother; and in *Feind,* on the purely phonetic level, he hears the full intensity of one's separation from the other (16).[190]

His enhanced sensitivity for the tonal aspect of words (76), his attentiveness to the phonetic qualities of speech, stem from a time in which he was on friendly terms with Theodor Däubler and the dadaist Hugo Ball. Ball also remarked, referring to his famous performance of sound poems in the Cabaret Voltaire in Zurich during the First World War, that his voice, as soon as he surrendered to the mere sound of the words,

took on the "ancient cadence of the priestly lamentation . . . the style of
a song sung at mass, as it rings plaintively through the Catholic churches
of occident and orient."[191] The origin of Schmitt's remarkable sensitivity to the aural qualities of language no doubt predates dadaism and
could well be rooted in his childhood experience of Catholicism.

The provisional results of our reconstruction of Schmitt's acoustic space
suggest that the structure of command stills the furor of his logocen-
trism, that rites take up (when possible) the magic of the word. The
acoustic space seems to be a very stable construction—which it is *not*.
Schmitt sees threats stemming from two sides: from technology and
from the body.

In the diary Schmitt repeatedly proclaims his favorite motto—*distinguo ergo sum* (69)—but also knows that the certainty it suggests is il-
lusive. Space—even in the mouth, at the threshold of expression—is
always crisscrossed with other sound waves (60, 63). Permanently at
play in acoustic performance is "something wildly alien," a "mass" that
bends the word and distorts meaning (52). Between "microphysical
sound stimuli" and "macrophysical sound amplification" lies the disaster of the technological world. Thus the advice, in one of his behavior
precepts, is to "avoid the microphone."

A suspicion naturally dawns that this point of cultural criticism serves
in the first instance to relieve Schmitt of a certain responsibility. He
counts Hitler a "sound amplifier," the National Socialist dictatorship a
technocracy that necessarily distorts every word. And since Schmitt per-
force used a microphone to deliver his commencement speech to a group
of teachers in the national legal association, the speech necessarily took
on the quality of a call for a purge of Jewish lawyers from the association. To this extent, his dialogue with the diary (the problematic of writing as a technical medium occurs to him only in reference to law) provides an ideal terrain for the word.

Nevertheless, it becomes apparent that Schmitt, precisely in this refuge, feels the interference of a force that undermines his notion of autonomy; he recognizes somatic influences on the articulation of language,
even on his own power of definition (16 ff.).

In Helmuth Plessner's anthropology, we encountered the cool persona
as that highly reflexive dueling subject, its ego sharply distinguished
from the unconsciousness of bodily being. It needs, as we noted, to forget its body in order to present itself properly as a physical form. The
task of overseeing the boundary to the unconscious, with which the ego

assures itself of its identity, puts the subject in a state of chronic alarm. And if we transfer the image of Plessner's brightly lit fencing hall to Schmitt's *Glossarium,* the fundamental *distinguo ergo sum* equals the duelist's gesture with the foil. Using the principle of *distinguo,* the decisionist draws a line to mark off the spheres of what he can, and cannot, master.

Our experience with the decisionist as a conceptual type during this century suggests that the more precisely it circumscribes the space, the greater is its longing for the amorphous condition of the bodily. Schmitt notes on 22 June 1948:

> The fundamental precondition of the ability to make good definitions is a rare ability: to bound and exclude what cannot be circumscribed. . . . That is the first of all distinctions, just as all virtue for the stoic begins by marking off the sphere of our own power from the sphere in which we are powerless. (169)

As if echoing previous certainty, the inevitable comment comes a month later:

> I am not in control of what penetrates into my consciousness, and not of that which remains unconscious to me. . . . Nor, therefore, am I able, as the stoic would have it, to distinguish what is in my power and what is not, and, on the basis of this distinction, master the one and accept the other. (180)

Somatic currents, bodily impulses, and physiological conditions of articulation determine what penetrates into consciousness, and they come into force with the articulation of a word—for example, *Dezision* or *Feind.* The secure ego, from this viewpoint, is only a "swamp light," and when Schmitt repeatedly indulges the satirical verse *Cogito ergo sum, summ, summ, summ, Bienchen summ herum,** he also betrays his suspicion of the emancipated signifier, as could only please a deconstructionist: we seem to have found the vulnerable point in the steely structure of the command as well as the ritual structure of his acoustic space, in which language turns into indecipherable sound and command collapses. Here, we could maintain, Schmitt succeeds in punching holes in his definition discourse by way of Nietzsche's "guiding thread of the body"; here we have a lapse back to the literary avant-garde, or at least a case of geriatric anarchism.

And yet the evidence of the tie back to Hugo Ball's word experiments

---

* *Summen* = buzz; thus, "little bee buzzing all around." The rhyme occurs in German nursery rhymes.

cuts both ways. With Ball, the mythic-bodily function of sound remains embedded in a liturgical celebration that offers the babbling creature its great echoing architectonic space of the church. Exchanging the social contract bound to words for the comfort of an encompassing organism—the clan, the family, or the church (which needs no contract because of its apparent status as a superior ordering power)—the voice settles into the primacy of the auditory network, into McLuhan's "magically resonating world of simultaneous connections between acoustic and oral space."[192]

Vilém Flusser has coined the term "pyramidal discourse" for the kind of auditory communication Schmitt has in mind. It functions in societies that, while hearing, are not supposed to answer:

> That is the reason for having relays between sender and receiver. The sender becomes inaccessible to the receiver. This model presupposes pyramidal hierarchies such as the priesthood, within which the messages of a distant God are transmitted through authorities toward receivers. The mediator has a twofold function: to keep the messages free of noise and to block the receiver's access to the author.[193]

The point may be a surprising one: insofar as Schmitt's phonomania plays itself out in the context of a pyramidal discourse, it remains a creature of the technological communications paradigm of the interbellum, the radio. Confirmation for this point comes from another direction: making the human word absolute, we read in Horkheimer and Adorno's *Dialectik der Aufklärung,* is a "false commandment," which is part of the "immanent tendency of the radio."[194]

Schmitt's Kafka   If people face the decision of becoming kings or couriers, "in the way of children," according to Kafka, "they all [want] to be couriers." So the world is full of couriers running around, shouting out their reports to one another. But in the resounding absence of a king, their reports have no meaning. This is Kafka's space, founded on the murmur of couriers' voices.[195]

What could be more distant from Schmitt's acoustic space revolving around the command axis than this world of Kafka's? And yet Schmitt feels the magnetic attraction of a world in which the messengers can only get started with their task once the commanders—should they appear at all—have died, in which the couriers get lost in the labyrinths of palace hallways or dimly lit lofts, where those for whom the messages are meant are forever deprived of the true word or have to dream up the messages themselves. What is Schmitt to do with the telecommunications of a system of domination such as Kafka describes in *Das Schloß*?

> In the Castle the telephone works beautifully of course; I've been told it's being used there all the time; that naturally speeds up the work a great deal. We can hear this continual telephoning in our telephones down here as a humming and singing, you must have heard it too. Now, this humming and singing transmitted by our telephones is the only real and reliable thing you'll hear, everything else is deceptive. There's no fixed connection with the Castle, no central exchange that transmits our calls farther. When anybody calls up the Castle from here, the instruments in all subordinate departments ring, or rather they would all ring if practically all the departments—I know it for a certainty—didn't leave their receivers off. Now and then, however, a fatigued official may feel the need of a distraction, especially in the evenings and at night, and may hang the receiver up. Then we get an answer, but an answer of course that's merely a practical joke.[196]

Schmitt is fascinated by novels that measure the constitutional nation's lack of foundation, that create the sense of a permanent "state of waiting," which for him signifies the epitome of Judaization (37). The representation of decisions being made out of nothing unsettles him—while in Kafka the much ballyhooed "decision" amounts to a gesture, to a little finger smoothing an eyebrow.

The contrast between these two anti-worlds might explain Schmitt's fascination. Its basis, however, is more ominous than the model of the attraction of opposites can suggest. On 29 August 1950 Schmitt notes in his diary:

> But I (in contrast to Heidegger) name names out loud, like a child, and am for that reason predestined to be the sacrificial victim of ritual murder, like Kafka's defendant in *Der Prozess*. (309)

Schmitt believes he has fallen into the cogs of the legal machine, which lets him go on vegetating there, as he goes on to say, only because it is too worn out to carry out the traditional ritual murder.

Seven entries on Kafka document the way Schmitt follows the mores and customs of the constitutional nation in Kafka's novels. Kafka's writings illustrate for him the condition of a world in which the final judgment of the father is willfully nullified, so that people are left with no alternative but to feign his presence. It is a world in which faith in the law prevents the individual from perceiving the holes in the law, from which—in the father's voice—all that is good could be expected and in which —were the father's voice to be heard—it would demand nothing of the son but self-liquidation. In *Das Schloß*, Schmitt discovers the drama of assimilation, leading ultimately to the result that "the whole village mumbles." Schmitt justifies his fascination in rationalistic terms, with the judgment that Kafka wrote himself free of this world "satirically." He plays with the—for him—horrific notion that Benito Cereno, his beloved hero from the Herman Melville story, would be delivered up to a Kafkaesque trial, posing in this way a revealing thought experiment, with which he hopes to rescue his existentialism from its dilemma in a single shot:

> Franz Kafka could write a novel: THE ENEMY. Then it would become evident that the indeterminacy of the enemy evokes the fear (there is no fear but this, and it is the essence of this fear to sense an indeterminate enemy); in contrast, it is a matter of reason (and in this sense of high politics), to define the enemy (which always implies simultaneous self-definition), and with this definition the fear ceases, with only dread, at most, remaining.

But how—sighs Schmitt in this connection—how are we to snatch something from indeterminacy, "if we have no concepts in common?" (148). Shared concepts are lacking, no doubt, because no one else makes use of Schmitt's definition of the enemy, which demarcates the existential other.

For Schmitt, it is the font of all evil that humanity will no longer accept a paternal authority, and that instead in the father's place is the "objectivity" of law. There for him lies the disgrace of the November revolution and the failure of the majority of the Weimar Republic's legal scholars: "legal positivism," so he declares in the diary, "kills its father and devours its children." The worst form of "father devouring," however, he finds in "Americanism" (148), first in the new objectivity decade of the Weimar Republic and later in the postwar Federal Republic.

As children of this Americanism we have been trying for thirty years to stand up to a form of political romanticism that, as Paul Tillich formulated it, appeared "to create the mother from the son and call the father out of nothing." That is why it is no cause for sadness if acoustic conditions for the call for the father remain pretty bad during our lifetime.

Incidentally, Kafka did write a little piece about the enemy; it is called "Der Bau" (The burrow) and shows us an animal that lives underground and loves silence. The silence, in Siegfried Kracauer's commentary, "that prevails, or ought to prevail, in his lightless structure is also truly the only radical antidote to the true word."[197]

CHAPTER FIVE

The Radar Type

In the middle of the twentieth century the sociologist David Riesman observed a new character type in American cities. Speaking of the "other-directed character" in 1950, he noted how difficult it was to define.[1] And within the German tradition, familiar historical assumptions and cultural antipathy made the figure even more difficult to perceive: witness research into the gray hordes of white-collar employees in the 1920s, studies of the "authoritarian character" during the 1930s, institution theory in the 1940s and 1950s, and construction of "one-dimensional man" in the 1960s. The new objectivity generation identified an "other-directed" figure and accorded it the potential for autonomy. We recognize it today in the postmodern type.

We organize the discussion in terms of Riesman's model as a way of withdrawing the figure from a teleological perspective. In the latter view, mass society with its new characters—including the "market character"—is a preliminary to fascism and leads necessarily to dictatorship. As if democracy represented no possible future for such life forms. Riesman glimpses the rise of the new type in a struggle against an older figure, which is "inner-directed." If Max Weber saw in the older type an embodiment of the Protestant ethic, Freud the normal case of an individual under the sway of his superego, then Riesman sees in it a dying type. To distinguish the two, Riesman picks technical metaphors: the inner-directed individual behaves as if he has a built-in gyroscope; the other-directed type guides his behavior as if with a radar device. The guidance system of the inner-directed person allows for only limited maneuverability, but a psychological radar device need not point in a single specific direction to register the other's behavior, and in particular its signaling behavior.[2] An other-directed apparatus receives signals from near and far, in a situation of many broadcasters and frequent program changes. The interior compass is not quick enough to give guidance. The new means of mass communication surround both figures; the inner-directed type attempts to unify the welter of news through a single lens, in order to judge it in moral terms, while the outer-directed type uses information to orient behavioral patterns, in order to determine the appropriate habitus, learn, and consume—and, when it is functional, to maintain an attitude of indifference.

The new type is indeed in a "chronic state of alarm," but not in the sense of a mobilization against a hostile power or integration into a collective; alertness has much more to do with securing interrelational mobility, observing rivals in a "fair competition," registering the winds of fashion and others' consumption behavior. For its actual stage is not the sphere of production or the frontline of a collective, but the tertiary sector of consumption and strategies for regenerating labor power. To the educated bourgeois this is the domain of inauthenticity, beyond absorption in work that orients the inner-directed type's search for self-realization. Lacking inner direction, the radar type perhaps "lacks a conscience" too; still it does not indulge in the spectacle of amorality we know from the cool persona. It engages in tireless information-gathering, in a cult of nonchalance and "fun morality." The radar type relates cynically to institutions but sentimentally to fellow beings.

Of course Riesman recognizes the weakness of the radar type for dangerous collective enthusiasms. But in his construction the possibilities for autonomous movement do not rely on the model of inner-direction; rather Riesman dares to consider other-direction and personal autonomy as of a piece, without resorting to the figure of the armored subject. The autonomy of the radar type is never an all-or-nothing affair, but the result of a largely imperceptible struggle with varieties of conformity. Autonomy of this sort never produces heroes.[3]

The new type practically never speaks for itself (Irmgard Keun's novels appear to be a special case). Within dramatic tales of degradation dedicated to the inner-directed moralist—who, equipped with a compass still loses the way—the new type appears in supporting roles as the passerby. If the new character falls under the gaze of cultural criticism, it appears in the central tenets of a politicized—a black—anthropology as nothing but plastic in the hands of manipulators. And city planners have the figure in mind, in the surroundings of the new mass media, in the scattered urban public, or in the unfavorable light of a process of corruption:

> In addition to his talents, applied with far greater direct benefit, of course, than merely at the podium, there is also his evident expertise in society, and that he lives less in reference to the concrete matters at issue and more in his relations is unfortunately not to be doubted. A man among many to be seen walking about these days. They prosper in the big cities, where the most opportunities are to be had, searching out the points of least resistance.[4]

As we begin to sort out reactions to the radar type's appearance—a target for polemics or a welcome new phenomenon for which dwellings were designed, cities planned, theater created—one obvious question is how to account for its existence against the backdrop of the extremely unstable tertiary sector, from the inflation in 1923 to the economic crisis of 1929.

There are a number of reasons why, in the 1920s, the radar type takes on pleasing contours: the war had demonstrated that inner-direction could be done away with by fiat. Or, to put it another way, during the war the compasses of the majority of inner-directed sorts turned out to point in the same direction. Most of the postwar judgments pronounced against the "soul" and the "bourgeois psyche" appear to be reactions to the "failure" of inner-direction—well prepared by the intellectuals' reading of Nietzsche. Attention turns from discredited internal regulators to public rules of behavior. When talk turns to "de-coring" the individual and praising behaviorism;[5] when the word is that "man lives, not in substances, but in relations"; when it is attitude that sets the tone, character can be inferred from body type, and the "culture of the body" rises to a new prominence—these indicators reflect the assessment of inner-direction as more a pretty fiction of the nineteenth-century German bildungsroman than an intact means of orientation. Interrelational attentiveness becomes a new virtue.

Enjoyment and consumption, the sideshows of the passing epoch, take over center stage. A consumerist attitude becomes the dominant reaction form; the new type develops it also in opposition to politics. This approach, while perhaps depriving its adepts of the enthusiasm of "genuine" political engagement, has the virtue of making them relatively skeptical of political illusions. Since the new objectivity radar type inclines to a certain hedonism, it can count on being roundly criticized by all the expert preservationists of culture. The sense of shortage remains alien to this new type, even when it hasn't much in the way of material resources. People do not save money or accumulate things; they spend it to consume, to take part in the fashion competition, to cultivate lifestyle (the jargon of the new objectivity shows awareness of this new consumer type and even comes up with a few pert slogans). The older culture type registers with a certain shock the existence of characters who are able to welcome the new media without concern; they are at home with the phonograph, radio, and film. To designate this relaxed way of being in the mid-1920s, Kracauer rehabilitates the previously negative concept of distraction.[6] Brecht and Benjamin agree:

> In the decline of middle-class society, contemplation became a school for aso-
> cial behavior; it was countered by distraction as a variant of social conduct.[7]

"Tactile reception" acquires positive value, as the "distracted masses" begin making use even of avant-garde architecture, viewing it as a form in which attentiveness and habit are not mutually exclusive:

> The distracted person, too, can form habits. More, the ability to master cer-
> tain tasks in a state of distraction proves that their solution has become a
> matter of habit.[8]

As a negative image the radar type has sharply defined contours. From the description in the second volume of Spengler's *Decline of the West* to the chapter on the "culture industry" in Horkheimer and Adorno's *Dialectik der Aufklärung,* this "nomadic" type is deplorably visible, wandering in the signal world of the mass media and fashion. The critics fix on the circumstance of radar guidance in order to deny the type any possibility of carving out a space for itself between the pressure to conform and nonconformity. Horkheimer and Adorno's examination of American cities projects the old bogeyman of one-dimensionality, borrowed from anti-modernization texts of the nineteenth century, onto their inhabitants:

> Here there is no distinction made between the economic fate of a person and
> the person himself. No one is anything except his fortune, his income, his po-
> sition, his chances. The economic character masks and that which lies be-
> neath them correspond, for the persons in question as well, down to the
> smallest wrinkle.[9]

In contrast, we have many documents from architects and writers, portraying the radar type as the ideal inhabitant of their buildings or as a public tailor-made for their revues, films, and operas. They see in this "irresolute mass" a "cosmopolitan audience" that should get its money's worth; they see passersby who are fully capable of absorbing into their movement the signal system of a big city square; they discover that the radar type, dealing with the rotary press, telegram, telephone, radio, and weekly newsreels, has developed the consciousness of a chess master.[10] It seems that the camera will increase people's capacity for more rational perception. Moholy-Nagy sees it developing a "consciousness of simultaneity":

> The new rapid and real reflector of the world, photography, should operate to illustrate the world from all points of view, should develop the capacity of seeing from all angles. . . . The modern city, with its multistoried buildings, workshops, factories, and so forth, the two- or three-story display windows in shopping zones, streetcars, automobiles, three-dimensional electric billboards, ocean liners, airplanes—all of this . . . has necessarily altered to some extent the traditional psychology of perception.[11]

Architects design nomadic furniture:

> This corresponds to the mobility of today's individual, who regularly spends many hours of his life on the train, in the streetcar, automobile, or on a bicycle, who has moved a great distance from the sedentary life (in both the narrow and the broadest sense) of a rural farming people.[12]

The epitome of new objectivity furniture is the tubular steel chair designed by Marcel Breuer and then further developed by Mies van der Rohe. In line with behaviorist doctrine, the chair has the capacity to be both reflection of and stimulus for the distracted urbanite:

> It could perhaps be said that the only sort of person who would feel comfortable in this chair is one for whom the constant tension of modern life and the taut sense of high-speed energy have become necessities even in relaxation, have become indispensable parts of his feeling for life.[13]

New-style architects resort to weighty verse to document the range of action, the rhythm and rationality of existence at a distance:

> . . . research, define, and order the force fields
> of individuals, family, and society.
> its basis is an understanding of living space
> and knowledge of the periodicity of living space
> psychological distance is as important to it
> as the sort of span that's measured in meters.
> its formative tools—consciously applied—
> are the findings of biological research.
> because this doctrine is true to life
> its theses are constantly changing;

because its realization lies in life,
like life itself.
"being rich is everything."[14]

In view of the many novel projects, plans, and gadgets, we cannot easily dismiss the suspicion that the architects of the 1920s are still waiting
for the appropriate type of city dweller to come into existence en masse.
In new objectivity manifestos the radar type appears. We get a good
look at its lifestyle; we see its tools. But the type itself seems to escape
literature's grasp: it is a character still in search of a genre and an appropriate technical medium. Its discourse gets established behind the backs
of those who seek their identity in the printed word. And instead of
textual traces, the radar type leaves behind only views of itself as type,
which, should we wish to, we can photograph. Thus does it form that
negative image of the erosion of the subject passed on by the bildungsroman. Its profile vanishes in the craters of the electric media. Since the
literature of the educated classes stays firmly in the hands of the inner-
directed type, the new, Anglo-Saxon type remains a marginal phenomenon. It forges its way through more trivial genres, which are open to the
market: cabarets, crime novels, magazine stories, and revues. Its senti-
ment dominates Kurt Tucholsky's romantic novel *Schloß Gripsholm,* in
which distance and passion are cast in a comic light, which will also illuminate the radar type in Hollywood films of the 1930s.[15] Walter Mehring registers the capacity for simultaneous perception, cynicism toward
institutions, and a species of urbane hedonism.

Most conspicuous are the novels in which the life of the radar type is
described from the viewpoint of the moralist. Their hero—whose compass no longer provides orientation and who considers it disgraceful to
have to adapt his navigational skills to the new behavioral type's skills—
goes on trying to hold the lost fort of inner-direction. The hero may
experiment with a few attitudes of the radar type, but since he has no
handbook to guide his actions, since anxious alertness is not his talent
and he has no money with which he might otherwise take part in commodity circulation, he listens to the inner voice, checks out the traditions
of the enlightened bourgeoisie for guidance, goes back to his mother,
and drowns.

Erich Kästner's *Fabian* and Martin Kessel's *Herrn Brechers Fiasko*
formulate the confusions caused by the new consumerist attitude. Kästner had introduced the radar type's cult of nonchalance into poetry in
his early collections *Herz auf Taille* (1928) and *Lärm im Spiegel* (1929).

In his novel he signals the dark side of nonchalance: indifference in relation to the mass media, surrender to the circulation of news, commodities, bodies, a sense of sexuality as a consumer good that is supposed to save everyone from general disinterest. "Sex," Riesman will later state in reference to the market character, "provides a kind of defense against the threat of total apathy."[16]

The first appearance of the radar type, from Kästner's perspective, is necessarily amoral. The provocation is all the greater since women are the ones who show what it means to navigate the tertiary sector without a compass ("navigate" in this sense makes us aware of what the male "compass" means). The heroines of Irmgard Keun's novels *Gilgi: Eine von uns* (1930) and *Das kunstseidene Mädchen* (1932) use other-direction's mimicry as a weapon. These are people who constantly define themselves in the mirror of others' perception, who assess closeness and distance in terms of their own latitude for movement and use fashions as signposts and markers—chess players without fortune. The jargon these heroines speak shows how language must be forced in order not to decay into sentimentality. But they do not succumb to the existence of the creature or the proletariat; they know, when they wind up in cold train station waiting rooms or other stopgap destinations, that they cannot forsake their formation—though it offers them no security—if they want to remain mobile.[17] Nor is Riesman's diagnosis rosy. The psychology of the new type is based in a diffuse anxiety; it feeds the sense of chronic alarm and keeps the restless object of our gaze in motion. Demagoguery can turn it into panic.

As writers, sociologists, politicians, and cultural theorists observed the phenomenon of the radar type, they reacted. And they reacted like individuals who feel—as events take a sudden leap forward—that they are being run over.[18] The substance of their dilemma was that none of them understood the new phenomenon as something possessed of its own right and worthiness. All of them thought of it as transitional. It was a loose-knit formation and therefore destined to collapse. Some foresaw the formation finding its way home, after the collapse, to the proletariat; others fixed their hopes on the promise of an improved form of inner-direction (assuming, of course, a measure of self-discipline). Never were these new sorts simply to be themselves; "substance" was always stored elsewhere.

The Nazi regime did not threaten the radar type with collapse, did not demand of its exemplars that they rise to some other occasion. In

Benjamin's words, it helped them achieve "their expression." It organized them as mass ornaments, allowed them to take pleasure in themselves as a formation, having gradually squeezed off the republican latitude for distracted reception and thus removed the conditions in which
the radar type might develop autonomy. The critical sociologists of the
1930s made haste to outfit the new type with an "authoritarian character," hurtling toward the fate it deserved, thus closing off the potential
ascribed to the type by the new objectivity.

Riesman's concept picked up on the work of two exiled German
scholars. From Erich Fromm's *Man for Himself* he took over the idea of
the "market character"; and from Karl Wittfogel he adapted the metaphor of the radar set. Also present as an impulse in his work, as it had
been in that of many Weimar intellectuals, were Georg Simmel's observations on the sociology of conviviality.

The Creature

The creature illuminates the other side of modern consciousness. The opposition to the radar type, as manifest in their respective orientations toward the mass media, could not be greater. While the radar type moves among the mass communication media like a fish in water, the creature feels put upon. Unable to decipher the signals to its own advantage, the creature faces an impenetrable destiny.

The logic of a book that begins with conduct codes for the cool persona and ends with the creature nourishes an expectation that this final figure will emerge as the epitome of unmasked essence. It suggests that the path from the armored ego, from the diplomat's costume games and distorted voices, leads to a point where finally a subject will act without masks and speak in authentic tones.

Rather than throw out all notions of the authentic creature, we need to interpose the concept of the discursive mask. As in the case of the cool persona, the mask holds a spectrum of possibilities: the creature's mask, as an artificial device, also regulates closeness and distance; its physiognomy reflects a social situation, shields nakedness, overcomes shame, evidences a defensive reaction to mortal fear or an ambition to be demonic, striking a ferocious pose among the besiegers.

The creature, part of a powerful iconographic tradition in the modern era, gets embedded in the 1920s in the discourses of theology, psychoanalysis, and animal behavior research. In a current Catholic lexicon we find the following definition:

Creature designates that which exists through creation, therefore everything the meaning of which is superior to itself, which is mortal, threatened, open to God and at His disposal (see *Potentia oboedientialis*), which in turn allows the creatural to exceed itself through grace in the acceptance of divine self-revelation (see *nature* and *mercy*).[1]

WAR CRIPPLE

Before getting caught in the cool gaze of the 1920s and turned into an object of behaviorist observation, the creature was allowed for a while to be the medium of pure expression, the vessel of life. As we saw in our discussion of the loss of expressive functionality, the "scream of the creature" provoked vigorous polemic at the start of the 1920s. The critics' objections vary. Plessner excludes the scream from the register of civil and diplomatic behavioral modes because he fears overstepping the boundary into the animal world, while Brecht disdains it because he senses in this form of spontaneity the conventions of bourgeois law and theology.

The new objectivity assaults on the creature in expressionism may not do justice to it, but they correctly indicate the prominent position this figure occupies in the literature from 1910 to 1920. It apparently realizes the expressionist notion of the existence of the "essential ego," without "the incidental adulterants" of the qualities of the persona.[2] But what the new objectivity critics make their target is not expressionist writing's focus on marginal types such as beggars, prostitutes, and orphans, who as outsiders are immune to society's negative traces and pursue an entirely different existence outside it. Their target is the image that a few expressionist authors have of themselves as *poeta dolorosus,* as creature. Neither literary conventions nor social conditions inform its cries.

Since, as the crudeness of this sketch itself demonstrates, new objectivity's negative image cannot adequately represent expressionism—"And the father is ashamed of the son, whom all disdain"[3]—we turn our attention to a specific variant of the expressionist creature, the war cripple. His is a particularly precarious case: he has what remains of the cool armoring of the soldierly persona and embodies the creature's injured organic substance, which the armor was supposed to protect. His appearance necessarily recalls a situation that overwhelms the survivors with shame and disgrace. And thus society tries to conceal him, a strategy strained by the presence of 2.7 million invalids at the end of World War I and enforcing "restraint" (*Verhaltenheit*) on the cripples themselves to make their presence tolerable.[4] Embarrassments, whenever at all possible, are to be avoided: "There are no waiters with artificial hands employed in any Berlin hotel. The cultivated guests, who pay fifteen marks for a dinner, find that the sight of a prosthetic hand spoils their appetite." Nor is a person with a stump for an arm or leg, wheeled around "like an infant in a wagon," assumed to be a tolerable sight.[5]

Both images come from Leonhard Frank's story collection *Der Mensch ist gut*, published in Zurich in 1918, to which nearly all the polemics by new objectivity writers refer. What prompts their critique is the collection's underlying mixture of naive anthropology and theory of history with a Christian spirit: a waiter says to the author, "The good in man plus boundless horrific suffering will be what causes the [revolution]." Just as hard to endure for the new objectivity writers is the expressionist sons' willingness to generate energy from disgrace.

Frank uncovers and probes two aspects of the creature that are painful from the angle of the armored ego: its scream and its unmasked countenance. Frank's intense formulation of the victim's cry in the amputation hall rummages through the conventions of writing in a desperate appeal for relief:

> He went through the alphabet.   *E* didn't help him.   *I* didn't help him.   Only *U*. He roared with all the force he had in his lungs, "Uu!"[6]

Pain forms a semantic field in which words' only value relates to the physiological effort they involve. Frank describes another war cripple's face, the accustomed site of expression: "Everything is gone. Two holes where the nose was. A small, lipless, formless, scarred, crooked hole where the mouth was."[7] From a man robbed of traditional means of expression Frank fashions the container for a revolutionary "storm of emotion" that—under the staff doctor's direction—raises a rebellion against the war. Emblematically, the creature links the de-naturing of man to his redemption. Images of the creature, as they arose in the decade of the new objectivity, undermined this illusion.

DISCOURSE OF THE CREATURE: FROM THEOLOGY TO ANIMAL BEHAVIOR RESEARCH

In nineteenth-century literature the creature had a prebourgeois constitution, which was supposed to lend it a depth missing from the rational type. It stood apart from social models or categories: alternatively "noble savage" or lumpen proletarian, agricultural laborer or transport worker, maid or prostitute. If it tended toward asociality, it also had an anarchistic streak.[8]

Twentieth-century social schemata barely define the creature. But now it appears as a figure under extremely remote control, unlike the vagabond, who is untethered, or the anarchist, the last refuge of the individual conscience. No inner regulator is in place. As a rule, the twentieth-century creature is forced to sublimate drives through brute force or in some kind of asylum. It achieves discipline only in stable environments like the military. Its capacity for rationality is strongly qualified by a tendency to think magically, in images.

The fascination exercised by this "outward-turning" figure on a public undergoing disenchantment is easy to understand. As a being subject to external controls and impositions, the creature exposes the autonomous ego's reverse image in the discourses of self-determination. A sense of inescapable destiny answers the ambition to be history's agent. Prominent creatures of the new objectivity decade are Brecht's infanticide Marie Farrar and the parricide Jakob Apfelböck; Döblin's Franz Biberkopf; Arnold Zweig's Sergeant Grischa; Joseph Roth's Hiob; Robert Musil's Moosbrugger; and Ludwig Turek's Brother Rudolf, already dying in his crib, failing even to achieve the status of creature.[9] The great achievement of proletarian literature of these years was to sever the worker's image from the creature's, at the price of moving the worker closer to the cool persona.

Marie Farrar, in the *Devotions,* exemplifies the stimulus-response schema of a behaviorist animal researcher. Brecht shows that this bundle of reflexes is the object of legal and theological discourses.[10]

ON THE INFANTICIDE MARIE FARRAR

1
Marie Farrar: month of birth, April
An orphaned minor; rickets; birthmarks, none; previously
Of good character, admits that she did kill
Her child as follows here in summary.
She visited a woman in a basement
During her second month, so she reported
And there was given two injections
Which, though they hurt, did not abort it.
     But you I beg, make not your anger manifest
     For all that lives needs help from all the rest.

2
But nonetheless, she says, she paid the bill
As was arranged, then bought herself a corset

And drank neat spirit, peppered it as well
But that just made her vomit and disgorge it.
Her belly now was noticeably swollen
And ached when she washed up the plates.
She says that she had not finished growing.
She prayed to Mary, and her hopes were great.
    You too I beg, make not your anger manifest
    For all that lives needs help from all the rest.

3
Her prayers, however, seemed to be no good.
She'd asked too much. Her belly swelled. At Mass
She started to feel dizzy and she would
Kneel in a cold sweat before the Cross.
Still she contrived to keep her true state hidden
Until the hour of birth itself was on her
Being so plain that no one could imagine
That any man would ever want to tempt her.
    But you I beg, make not your anger manifest
    For all that lives needs help from all the rest.

4
She says that on the morning of that day
While she was scrubbing stairs, something came clawing
Into her guts. It shook her once and went away.
She managed to conceal her pain and keep from crying.
As she, throughout the day, hung up the washing
She racked her brain, then realized in fright
She was going to give birth. At once a crushing
Weight grabbed at her heart. She didn't go upstairs till night.
    And yet I beg, make not your anger manifest
    For all that lives needs help from all the rest.

5
But just as she lay down they fetched her back again:
Fresh snow had fallen, and it must be swept.
That was a long day. She worked till after ten.
She could not give birth in peace till the household slept.
And then she bore, so she reports, a son.
The son was like the son of any mother.
But she was not like other mothers are—but then
There are no valid grounds why I should mock her.
    You too I beg, make not your anger manifest
    For all that lives needs help from all the rest.

6
So let her finish now and end her tale
About what happened to the son she bore
(She says there's nothing she will not reveal)
So men may see what I am and you are.
She'd just climbed into bed, she says, when nausea

Seized her. Never knowing what should happen till
It did, she struggled with herself to hush her
Cries, and forced them down. The room was still.
     And you I beg, make not your anger manifest
     For all that lives needs help from all the rest.

7
The bedroom was ice cold, so she called on
Her last remaining strength and dragged her-
Self out to the privy and there, near dawn
Unceremoniously, she was delivered
(Exactly when, she doesn't know). Then she
Now totally confused, she says, half froze
And found that she could scarcely hold the child
For the servants' privy lets in the heavy snows.
     And you I beg, make not your anger manifest
     For all that lives needs help from all the rest.

8
Between the servants' privy and her bed (she says
That nothing happened until then), the child
Began to cry, which vexed her so, she says
She beat it with her fists, hammering blind and wild
Without a pause until the child was quiet, she says.
She took the baby's body into bed
And held it for the rest of the night, she says
Then in the morning hid it in the laundry shed.
     But you I beg, make not your anger manifest
     For all that lives needs help from all the rest.

9
Marie Farrar: month of birth, April
Died in the Meissen penitentiary
An unwed mother, judged by the law, she will
Show you how all that lives, lives frailly.
You who bear your sons in laundered linen sheets
And call your pregnancies a "blessed" state
Should never damn the outcast and the weak:
Her sin was heavy, but her suffering great.
     Therefore, I beg, make not your anger manifest
     For all that lives needs help from all the rest.

Bourgeois law fits out the creature with the mask of the responsible sub-ject; theology makes it the mirror of some distant seat of grace. The bourgeois criminal procedure respects the separation of powers. The ex-ecutioner, who has the task of liquidating the responsible legal subject, is accompanied by a member of the clergy, who entrusts the depraved creature to grace. Brecht attempts with his language both to portray and dispel the nimbus both discourses throw around the creature.

Brecht shows up the fiction of the responsible subject. Bourgeois society rips away a creature's chance to develop qualities of self-determination, subjecting it to physical torments, in order then to honor it with full responsibility at the precise moment that proper procedure calls for killing it. And Brecht displays what is left once the ideological implications of bourgeois law and theological language are gone. The tormented being must be removed from the web of worldviews that style it the creature before it can be outfitted with other sorts of potential—rebellion, for example.

When Arnold Zweig presents the creatural type as the hero of his Grischa novel, the prospect irritates Brecht.[11] In this hero Brecht sees a touchstone of compassion, which only prolongs the misery. He stresses in contrast—in Nietzschean fashion—how senseless it is to put oneself into the psyche of a man who is condemned to death.[12] Zweig's novel has for him the logic of an appeal for mercy to authorities who—unless they are of a theological sort—are nothing but legal illusion. Brecht is at one in this judgment with Walter Benjamin, who remarks that in dramatic tragedy the "trial of the creature" as a protest against death is in the end "only halfway processed and shelved."[13] Hopes for reopening the trial in the twentieth century are gone entirely.

GRISCHA IN THE ARMY

Zweig's Grischa character presents the greatest discrepancy imaginable to Brecht's creations. His development proceeds in a direction diametrically opposite to that of the packer Galy Gay in Brecht's *Mann ist Mann*. Grischa transforms himself from a soldier eager for battle into the very emblem of meekness, from a cog in the army machine into a paltry organic bundle in the death cell. And for good measure, hoping to recapture his human dignity by voluntarily dispensing with resistance, Zweig's hero turns down an opportunity to flee. No longer a prisoner with flight instinct intact, he becomes an adherent of *amor fati*. Yet the more the character disarms, in his striving after individuation, the more he falls into the control of others. Zweig explains this fatal circumstance in a Hassidic equation, as related by the carpenter Täwje:

> Two people cast lots. Then the outcome is important for the one or the other, but not for the lots.

The Grischa creature, as others have observed, is a reflexive form of the cult of the eastern Jew, which fascinated many intellectuals in the 1920s.

The legend of the good Grischa belongs to "philosophical physiognomies" generated by this kind of populism.[14]

At the same time Zweig's novel offers images of a shocking modernity, in which a mixture of institution theory and research into animal behavior explains the creature's functioning in the "artificial group" (Freud) of the army. The execution squad moves, Grischa in the middle, toward the gravel pit. In macabre fashion the writing evokes the rhythmic motions of an organism:

> The clattering of bridles, chains striking against leather; laced boots, sixteen pairs, crunching evenly in the colder snow. Sidearms strike in a steady beat against thighs, and rifles, sometimes butting off helmets, rise with a rustle and crack to the shoulders.[15]

Describing these "marching bodies," Zweig stresses the physiological elements. The signs of the group psyche's martial temperament emerge— behavioristically—in the way the soldiers' chin straps cut into their flesh. He includes the advance cohort of two sergeants on horseback. The one at the lead, on an elegant dark brown gelding, represents a cynical consciousness; the other, atop a fat, easy-going mare, is more troubled in his thoughts. Both characters on horseback belong to the working organism of the death squad, raising itself "in tender gold and white" against the indifference of the snowy field. The victim, too, is integrated into the "striding body," in which touch is the commanding sense. Grischa maintains his bearing in this formation because of the tight belt he wears.

Here, where Zweig illustrates the reasons for the smooth functioning of an organization in rhythms and physiology, lie the novel's extraordinary innovations, which he creates by going back to the genre of physiology. Shortly before writing it, Zweig studied Georg Büchner's drama *Woyzeck*.

Arnold Gehlen's theory of institutions forms an interesting contrast to Zweig's representation of the execution squad with its rituals. Zweig explains the frictionless operation of an apparatus requiring no legitimation by referring to meanings external to its own functioning. Gehlen, in his essay "Über die Geburt der Freiheit aus dem Geist der Entfremdung," later writes in praise of human institutions:

> People are able to maintain a lasting relation to themselves and their fellows only indirectly; expressing themselves, they must come to themselves by way of detours, and there lie institutions. As Marx saw correctly, it is these manmade forms in which the material of the psyche, also an undulatory material in its supreme richness and pathos, is objectified, woven into the course of

things, and in that way, and only in that way, made to endure. Thus are people at least burned and devoured by their own creations, rather than by raw nature, like animals. Institutions are the great preserving and devouring orders and destinies, which long outlast us as individuals, and of which people, with open eyes, make themselves part. Those who dare to enter into institutions achieve perhaps a higher freedom than obtains in the enclosure of Fichte's self-determining ego or that of his modern stepbrother, Erich Fromm's "man for himself."[16]

Sascha, the teacher from Merwinsk in Zweig's novel, takes issue with this theory on the level of its argument. As the businessman Weressejew waits downstairs for the priests and the execution train draws near the pit, Sascha formulates his view of the natural history of institutions as arrangements that people "themselves have not made but have carelessly allowed to grow from generation to generation."[17] The teacher from Merwinsk accords to nature what Gehlen celebrates as emancipation from brute natural forces. Sascha is to a certain extent correct. But in fixing on "carelessness," his argument is weak. It could not be termed Marxist.

Of greater analytical precision is Zweig's image. It reveals the way the marching body functions, because an institution like the army suppresses the individual's inner regulative devices sufficiently to allow physiological rhythms to absorb consciousness. At the same time, of course, the institution takes on the character of a "second nature," of something that has grown. With a triumphal note Gehlen lifts human destiny out of the animal realm. "Thus are people at least burned and devoured by their own creations," he declares, "rather than by raw nature, like animals." Zweig undermines pathos of that sort by delivering an adequate explanation of the course of things and the psyche in institutions like the army through an animal behaviorist's eyes, registering the motions of the creature. The logic of Zweig's images teaches that, in the army and other such institutions, critical differences between human and animal fall away. To emphasize the point, he builds one more aspect into the image of the execution squad's marching body. Within the group psyche bound together by chin straps, uniforms, and rhythms, one being loses its composure: the lazy mare, who bears troubled consciousness on its back. It loses control, and this collapse of self-discipline in the poorly trained horse—the only living thing that breaks ranks—is also the incident that so obviously "outrages" the squad that it moves the creature into the rearguard.

13. An ex-porter in the Grand Hotel, who ends
up in charge of the toilets
(Publicity still for *The Last Man*.)

> But you I beg, make not your anger manifest
> For all that lives needs help from all the rest.

In the first republican decade an assortment of creatures is on parade.
The repressed returns as photographic sensation. From war cripples to
asylum seekers, they appear in public as objects in need of social solici-
tude. Their voices matter less than their somewhat exotic, somewhat
compassion-inspiring surface appearance, and their mechanical motion.
Their appearance forbids overly optimistic replies to the anthropological question, What kind of thing is man?

   In art, literature, and film, the creature shows up as the final station
in a life story: as the soldier who has lost his armoring; as a defenseless
worker put up against the wall by Freikorps rabble; as a pitiful soul at
the mercy of the bureaucracy; as an ex-porter in the Grand Hotel who
ends up in charge of the toilets (see Figure 13); and "naturally"—barred,

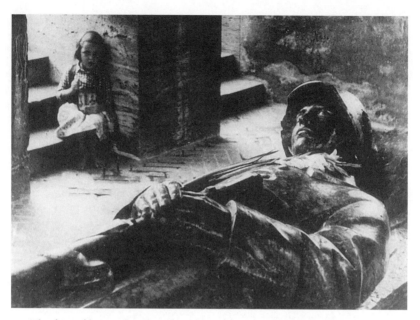

14. The fear of being abandoned is always present in a shame culture
(Bernhard Bleeker's memorial to the unknown soldier, 1925. With the permission of Stadtarchiv München.)

as we saw in Plessner's anthropology, from the sphere of artificiality—as the woman who turns on the gas, who endures life as a prostitute, who murders her child. The creature always figures as a being in need of mercy in a time that knows no source for it, since the creator has retreated to an impossible distance and bourgeois institutions cannot make up the loss. In the images of total mobilization, this being does not appear. Mobilization calls for metallic characters;[18] creatures cannot surpass their organic substance.

From the viewpoint of our typology new objectivity literature alternates between extremes, between the self-confident subject in armor, as soldier or dandy, and the living being, as organic bundle of reflexes, in mortal need (see Figure 14). Songs of the armored subject and legends of creatures in need of mercy fill the space of modernity. The narrative often records the change of armored subject to pitiable creature—and what a "disgrace" it is. A cosmopolitan public indulges its fascination for creatural legends and songs. It finds in these stories a ratification of its state of chronic alarm, of the constant threat of falling victim to social degradation. Its diffuse anxiety seems objectified in the fate of oth-

ers. And if, in the role of public in the 1920s, it is no ready source of
mercy, how much less so, in the 1930s, as *Volk?*

THE CASE OF ANGERSTEIN

The sense of security contained in the concept of the persona disintegrates in the image of the creature. In the persona there remains an ego
made autonomous by consciousness of what (through the mask) appears from the outside, while the creature makes its appearance only
once the artificial devices of the persona crumble into pieces. The judicial trial seems to be the preferred setting for this spectacle of destruction, because the contest pits the individual's moral responsibility, which
in bourgeois society enjoys such a secure status, against the creature's juridical incompetence. In the 1920s such cases capture the attention of
psychoanalysis, which attempts to rescue the accused from the grip of
the guilt culture, as institutionalized in the form of the tribunal. The effort is successful in that it undoes the fiction of the competent subject.
But, by simultaneously consigning the subject to the figuration of childhood, it occasions the return of the core family that the new objectivity
generation had so vehemently rejected.

Under the title "Tat ohne Täter," in July 1925 Siegfried Kracauer reported on the trial of the multiple murderer Fritz Angerstein. The case
became for him the symbol of the risk entailed in a world of "objectivity," in which relationships among people are guided by the functional
play of social roles.

> For the more relationships among people become objectified, with emanci-
> pated things gaining power over people rather than people seizing hold of the
> things and humanizing them, the more easily it can and will happen that the
> disfigured humanity that has been repressed into the deepest recesses of un-
> consciousness will reappear in hideous form in the world of things.[19]

What psychoanalysis represents as the id finds its mask in the creature.
The persona, in the form of the "authorized agent," conjures up one last
time the bourgeois illusion of the accountable subject; it remains the pur-
view of such social categories as petit bourgeois or manager. The Angerstein trial exposes the irreparable discrepancy between the person and
the treatment of the person:

> A deed without a doer—that is the provocative, the incomprehensible aspect
> of the Angerstein case. The deed is inconceivable: an orgy of ax blows and ar-
> son. Intimidating in its mere magnitude, the crime bursts the bounds of cus-
> tomary statutes as only an elemental event can. It is impossible to do more

than stare at it; it is not to be subsumed within existing categories. Nevertheless, there it is, an undeniable fact that, for well or ill, must be registered.

But where is the doer that belongs to the deed? Angerstein? The little, subordinate fellow with modest manners, a feeble voice, and a stunted imagination? In [Arthur] Schnitzler's play *Der grüne Kakadu,* a real murderer seeks to hire himself out as a criminal impersonator to a bar for the Parisian demimonde. But he is dismissed by the proprietor with the remark that the impression he makes is not bloodthirsty enough. The pseudo-perpetrator from Haiger resembles that man. At bottom a mere petit bourgeois, Angerstein can be outfitted with a vicious appearance only in retrospect by overheated journalists. Had one encountered him prior to the crime on the street, one would have asked him for a light and quickly forgotten his features.

Even today, or today once again, he remains stubbornly at home in the narrow confines of inborn mediocrity. His behavior during the trial has been minimal in every respect. There have been no sudden eruptions to help us chart a connection between the man and what he did, no outbursts to suggest a subterranean fiendishness, nor the kind of silence that would correspond to what happened. Instead, he has withdrawn into trivialities, into a dull state of shock wholly incommensurate with its cause, a confused acceptance of what he himself does not understand.

Angerstein, in Professor Herbertz's depiction of the events, did not commit the deed; the deed happened to him. Having transpired, it detached itself from him and now exists as a purely isolated fact for which there is no proper cause. It rose up out of nothing for the while of the murders, a dreadful "it" out there in space, unconnected with him. If the soup had not been burned— a triviality become a link in a chain of external causation—Angerstein's victims would have gone on living and no one but his fellow citizens of Haiger would ever have heard his name. The crime looms gigantically over him; he disappears in its shadow.

Interrogations and depositions have produced what information there was to produce. Unknown details have become superfluous; a crude whole has been constructed of a thousand statements. The picture is not false, but it is not right. It recalls to the light of day what has descended irrevocably into the darkness, offering it, in a form as inadequate as it is liberating, to judicial measurement.

A petit bourgeois like a thousand others plunged clumsily into atrocity. He married young, worked his way up, even became a manager. Trivial and respectable, not worth wasting a word. The signs of distress are serious, if not extraordinary: leftover adolescent anxieties, localized tuberculosis, a family in financial need, life with an ailing wife. He loved the frail, easily agitated woman—neighbors and visitors praise the marriage. She suffered one miscarriage after the other; she subordinated their erotic life together to the principles of Methodist piety. A life of churchly devotion, which was not easy for him. But, aside from a single sexual dalliance, he was faithful, on the whole anticipating the oversensitive creature's needs. She complained and suffered, her pietistic spirit tormented by morbid premonitions.

And now, in the winter of 1924, the event comes out of nowhere. Minor illegalities preceded it, a confusing swindle, no one knows how or why. Running amok, it seems that a physician's attentions merely added to the burdens. His previously neatly bounded world was slipping through his fingers. The woman of his obsession draws him with her toward a longing for death, for an end to it all. He may have been thinking of suicide as he stabbed her— but why the frenzy with the hunting knife and the ax, why the senseless bashing of the skulls of uninvolved others? What sucked him, the minor administrator, for a night and a day into the cyclone of devastating violence?

The psychiatric reports have neither sought nor found connections between the doer and the otherwise alien deed. They follow the clinical findings; it is not their job to do more. Only Professor Herbertz, the depth psychologist and a judicial outsider, identifies the paths leading upward and outward from the deeper layers of the unconscious.

What happened according to him? Well, petit-bourgeois Angerstein with the apparently easy-going nature must have had to repress mountains of dissatisfactions and worries. It is easy to imagine: the hysterical wife, who wants to be protected and cared for, with her dark biblical fantasies and complexes of her own; the need to keep them secret. Psychic dynamite piles up, while the container holding it looks fine. One day the story explodes—with a bang, impulses break through inhibitions. The bestial instincts, dark desires that have been nourished since childhood, unconscious hatred: all the explosive material in the nether reaches of the soul hurtles toward the surface to discharge like a volcano. It must be right, what Professor Herbertz argues: that during the catastrophe Angerstein was completely out of his mind. Certainly, he wanted to hide the outrage from the eyes of other people; but can it be called normal and customary when he undertakes the most intricate means to that end? Does it testify to sanity that he smashed five human skulls solely so that they would not register incriminating information? This logic is illogical; nor does it have anything to do with Angerstein the sober businessman.

Many details confirm the assumption that the quiet manager was caught unawares by some unknown something inside him. He admits that he himself cannot understand, cannot conceive, that the gigantic fact came out of him. His early attempts to deny it are ridiculously petit bourgeois. Now that he has acknowledged being the perpetrator, he gazes fixedly at what others designate his crime. His evasions from now on have to do with incidentals, his excuses with mere details. The actual misdeeds weigh on him like a block of lead he cannot cast off.

If he is conscious he flees into sleep, sleeping double the usual amount, because his memory wants to disappear. The fact outside there, which is undeniably related to him, is completely overwhelming; he does not like to taste or feel it. Suicide is also beyond the bounds of his horizon, now narrowed to a point. His reading is the Bible, which perhaps brings him by way of detours into contact with his wife.

A deed without a doer that has nothing, but nothing, in common with those great crimes committed by people whose names live on in popular memory. Those crimes were manifestations of a will, however misguided;

they were eruptions of unbridled natures, twisted minds, the expression of outsized drives and passions. They stemmed from a place in the guilty person, were not just there alongside him, existing inadequately in space.

The deeds that now go by the name of Angerstein lack a personal point of reference, without, however, that meaning that they were born of mental illness. That there is no sufficient reason for them in the consciousness of the doer is what turns them into a tormenting puzzle, what lends them the uncanny remove of mere facts. It may be that depth psychology is correct in claiming that they emerge to the light of day out of the craters of unconscious psychic life; it has not, however, solved the puzzle of how such a thing is possible.

Suddenness and isolation, the characteristics of disgrace, direct the court proceedings from Kracauer's perspective. The "perpetrator," overwhelmed in the public gaze, represents himself as creature. In doing so, he opens himself to all manner of dishonor, but that approach is also the only one with any prospect of protecting his life. Creature is the mask that must be relied upon to avert the threat of death. At the same time, Kracauer is required, in order to credibly convey the creatural image, to strip Angerstein of any talent for strategic self-enactment; for the accused must not possess the ability to reflect upon his role if there is to be any chance of avoiding execution. To accomplish this effect, Kracauer's report continuously rehearses the fall of Angerstein's persona into a realm so elemental that a masked performance is no longer a possibility. The defendant's psychological topography, as Kracauer sketches it, takes over elements of Freud's early description of the apparatus of the psyche but is in no way committed to the overall analysis. On the one hand, Kracauer's metaphors demand a thoroughgoing separation between the two spheres of the civilized and the elemental: "psychic dynamite" has piled up in the soul's "nether reaches"; the seeming composure of civilization itself becomes explosive, "volcanic," its outer shell burst asunder by "elemental events." On the other hand, Kracauer acknowledges that the natural force that turns Angerstein into a perpetrator is not so elemental but instead falls hostage to the unconscious, which, in turn, struggles in the inauthenticity of the social context— whereby the "hysteria" of the murdered spouse is taken as a given.

In the final passage of the report, Kracauer withdraws from the "demonic" aspect of the case, in which the contents of the "craters of unconscious psychic life" reach the light of day. With no transition, he reaches back to a motif from vitalist philosophy, which blames the deformations of the creature on the reification of the world of civilization. The claim with which he closes his article on the Angerstein case is just as enigmatically unmediated: "Only in a humane world does the deed have its doer."

BRONNEN'S *O. S.*

In his essay on Angerstein, Kracauer mentions in passing similarly elemental transgressions of the law, with the difference that popular imagination celebrates the doers in these cases as great criminals. Such malefactors earn admiration, as Walter Benjamin points out in *Kritik der Gewalt*, because their unlawful acts remind us that the rule of law is rooted in violence and that no new legal orders can be created in the absence of violence.[20]

Arnold Bronnen's novel *O. S.* attempts to create that kind of admiration for the postwar desperadoes of the Freikorps. But the heroes he depicts occupy an intermediate position between those great authors of misdeeds who want to destroy the system and the faceless members of Freud's "artificial groups," which even such a loose association as the Freikorps represents. While Kracauer insists that great criminals are "heralds of an otherwise suppressed will," volitional individuation is precisely what military formations transcend. As Freud maintains, such groups nullify the inhibitions that rule civilian life, stirring up "all the cruel, brutal and destructive instincts, which lie dormant in individuals as remnants of a primitive epoch."[21]

Bronnen's novel *O. S.* appears in 1929. On the dust jacket is a military map of Upper Silesia; depicted inside is the struggle of isolated men, who in 1921 are besieged by troops from the German republic, French occupation troops, and Polish "insurgents." Ernst Jünger welcomes the novel, claiming that *O. S.* makes it clear "that barbarism is maintained as a necessary consequence of civilization."[22] The novel depicts not only creatures such as Johann Schramm, a Tirolean roadworker from Sterzing, who had devoted himself on the Italian front to wiping out "138 sons of this only distantly human tribe," in order to get hold of their cans of tuna and ground meat. Schramm travels to Upper Silesia with the Freikorps troop Roßbach to act out his annihilating instinct against the Poles:

> Since, however, the Pole, to his disappointment, went on trembling, he smashed his skull with his rifle. That felt good. It got him going again and he went rattling up the hill with no comrade save his own shadow. . . . He surprised them one after the other . . . killing them with his rifle butt, which slowly splintered apart.[23]

The image of the werewolf from the Tirolean borderland serves to explain why the national conservatives were outraged by the novel's "shamelessness"; but it fails to convey the singular atmosphere produced by the book. For the central type of the novel emerges from the dynamism of the city.

The area of movement opened up by the novel holds the most modern of communication systems: travel by road, rail, and air; newspapers, pneumatic message delivery systems, telephones, and telegrams. The unfamiliar combination of modern media with archaic "instinct" shocked the national conservative camp and delighted a reader like Ernst Jünger. The writing of Goebbels's compatriot Bronnen in no way corresponded to the popular borderland literature of the time, which was fond of presenting images of healthy community persisting within agrarian structures.

For Bronnen's *O. S.* is a traffic novel. It begins at exactly 11:00 A.M. on 29 April 1921, when a taxi pulls up to the utility worker Krenek, who is at work on a streetlight switch box on the corner of Linden and Charlottenstraße in Berlin. The scene then shifts to the Friedrichstraße train station, where the express train D-241 has already departed. The train is missed again at the next station. New characters, whom we will meet again in Upper Silesia, appear at various stations:

> As the minute hands on all twenty clocks of the main station in Leipzig jerked forward to 11:00 A.M., shop steward Scholz made his way suspiciously from signal box no. 3 across the tracks to Platform 10, where, waiting behind white clouds of fresh steam, were the damp, black cars of the D-train from Munich to Breslau. (7 ff.)

Seventeen pages later, three more characters enter the action:

> At twelve minutes past eleven the Cologne-Breslau D-train was to arrive in Dresden; but it seemed not altogether inclined to punctuality, for at this moment it was still rolling past the gardens of Saxony. Looking worried, three young men dressed in windbreakers stood toward the front of the train, looking ahead at the baggage car. (24)

At 11:20 A.M. it seems certain that Krenek is not going to get to the D-241 on time. Without giving it much thought he decides, for 200 marks, to drive his mysterious passenger the 500 kilometers to Upper Silesia in the stolen taxi.

The reader is drawn into the narrative space of archaic struggles presented in a futurist light. The battle area is also crisscrossed by traffic networks. The narrative threads of the novel come together at the knots:

freight stations, signal boxes, loading ramps, shunting yards. The mercenaries meet at these places, then separate. Telegrams, motorized couriers, and telephone contacts make up the political nervous system. When Krenek, fleeing in panic from a Communist "lynching party," seeks refuge in a telephone booth, the scene becomes a symbol of the betrayed creature. His pursuers see him through the glass:

> Inside, leaning on the dead telephone, was Krenek; but the light didn't work, it was dark. To him, overcome by vertigo, it was even darker. His panting lungs slowly consumed the air. He trembled. (358)

The telephone is dead, the hero irretrievably cut off from the world of mediating signals. The end phase of the betrayal of the "system parties" can begin.

Bronnen's novel casts the new objectivity motto, "Instead of expression —signals, instead of substance—movement," in a strange light. Language functions in O. S. as in a comic strip; every statement moves the action forward. The way the plebeian characters speak like telegrams accelerates the action, which the labored verbal style of the authorities (when they are not letting their machine guns do the talking for them) only slows. The speeches of the heroes have the function of impelling action and setting off chain reactions. When the hero Bergerhoff is admonished not to make a decision too quickly—"Out of your mouth comes the voice of courage, but also the voice of carelessness"—he replies:

> There's nothing speaking in me, Herr Ulitza, but my vocal cords, of course with the help of my teeth. Otherwise, we can talk about anything you like, just not slowing down. (280)

What is going on here is an interlinking of psychological processes and weapons. It is tempting to think that, in Bergerhoff's short course in language, we see the linguistic theory of the avant-garde going to the dogs. The mercenary leaves no doubt: there is no time, gentlemen, for the hermeneutics of the expressive dimension, for the valuation of speech sounds, for unraveling the mysteries of articulation! The faculties of speech work in the same way that weapons talk. The voice, articulated or not, is all the signal we need, as long as it conveys aggression.

At this point, the worlds divide. The sphere of exchange and potential consensus is in enemy hands. That is what Krenek has to learn. In the opening scenes we see him meeting the nationalist slogans with the skepticism of a *Rote Fahne* reader. But then he leaves the world of Communist newspapers and opposing arguments as fast as the transport system allows, until he finds himself moving on the plane of physiological reflex. He goes to ruin; that is his ascension to the rank of the "organic construction" (Jünger) of the creature.

In Bronnen's novel a light from the borderland falls on the systemic world with which it remains entangled: the world of the railway bosses and telegraph officials. That world now becomes, in Schmitt's term, "the *intensum* of dissociation," enemy territory as such. But the mechanics of entanglement are not external to the characters. Bronnen stresses the mechanical essence of the affects in his hero Bergerhoff, the critically reflected figure among the mercenaries. Bergerhoff betrays his identity when his gaze, under the influence of "beastly feelings," gets locked on the figure of a peasant woman, in whom he senses the "breathtaking, rampant machinery of procreation" (376), of which he wants to become a part. (The "male fantasies" Theweleit identifies in the early Freikorps novels reappear here, colored by the cult of technology in the middle-phase of the republic.)

If we compare Bronnen's heroes with Jünger's cool personae, such as the storm troop commander in *Stahlgewitter,* their contours become sharper. Bronnen allows his characters no contemplative pauses (which Jünger's diarists consign to reading the classics); Bronnen's werewolves are lonely figures, but not distanced; their goal is to regress into the bonds of blood brotherhood, but there are no conventions or behavioral precepts to regulate the instincts. While Carl Schmitt defines the enemy as a conscious intensification of the "stranger," for Bronnen's heroes the enemy is never the result of a cognitive operation or anything like an analytical category. The enemy is another race that must be destroyed as soon as it shows up on native territory. Of course, this seems beneath the theoretical level of friend-enemy definition. But since Schmitt intermittently removes moral, economic, and aesthetic criteria from his definition of the enemy, their reintroduction to the empty matrix in the crude form of biologism is easy to arrange; Schmitt demonstrates just how easy it is in the forty articles he writes in the period between 1933 and 1936.

Are the rules we have identified in the conduct codes present in this biologically based novel? Bronnen's hero vaguely recalls them:

> Bergerhoff crouched down alone, letting his mind wander in the glow of the approaching fire. Scattered about in the woods, with that strange aura of dead bodies, were German soldiers. In front of him, near the pond, making with their last strength for the water like a single compacted body, lay the

group of prisoners. They had been admirably shot, with precision, like oxen in the slaughterhouse. He looked at them without feeling, without regret, without a thought for a form of justice he did not recognize; it was more a consideration of whether it was playing by the rules. But could this question be decided, here and by him? (333)

Cool persona, radar type, creature. We have become acquainted with three artificial figures, conceived by the "psychology from without" (Gehlen). What remains problematic is how to refer the figures back to sociology's ideal types and—finally—to ask whether the conceptions of the cool persona, the radar type, and the creature are not simply the physiognomic shadows of self-criticism, to which the inner-directed conscientious type rises in times of crisis. It is in any case precisely this inner-directed type, which shines in such exemplary fashion in the texts of cultural criticism, that is difficult to demonstrate empirically.[24] That is why the nineteenth-century public devoured it so eagerly in novels, in order to assimilate it as a compensatory orienting value. The numerous documents in the individual's self-stylization as inner-directed subject in the bourgeois novel do not automatically justify the conclusion that inner-direction has ever existed as an operating mode. Many documents in the cultural history of the conscience have been uncovered that call into question this self-confident assumption on the part of the bourgeoisie. It is probably most reasonable to assume that other-direction is roughly constant, although modified in particular epochs such that it appears *as if* the individual is being guided "from within." In any case, discovery of the machinelike essence of the inner world collapses the distinction between inner and outer worlds.

Afterword

In the 1930s and 1940s action theories of balance—conduct codes and handbooks to help the new objectivity individual compensate for a "basic lack of equilibrium"—were put to the severest tests. The duelist's favored slogan, *distinguo ergo sum*, was taken over by state institutions. The furor over distinguishing, one of the few manias the cool persona permitted itself, took on the form of a "purification" of all political camps. In the shadow of the dictatorship, the only possible basis for authentic decisions could be the conscience. Intellectuals in exile reacted by recasting codes of conduct that allowed them to reassert the value of humanism.

From prison in 1943 Werner Krauss reconstructs the fundamental rules of a life of balance, which he unearths in Balthasar Gracián's *Art of Worldly Wisdom*. The scholar, in the extreme situation of imprisonment, indulges a fascination for the cool persona, which gives him the courage to reestablish humanistic principle as a form of resistance.

At the end of the 1930s, Bertolt Brecht writes a chronicle of the Thirty Years' War. Here Mother Courage acts according to her understanding of the new objectivity's implicit rules, which function as survival techniques in the cool air of alienation. What Brecht teaches is that codes of conduct can indeed guarantee sheer survival, if at the cost of a joyful spirit. Courage's children get caught up and killed over just that issue. The distant prism of the seventeenth-century war refracts the new ob-

jectivity idol of men, their nomadology and praise of the refugee's existence, conceived on the ground of the republic, in a woman's form.

Mother Courage's abandonment is also the end of the new objectivity.

The fear of being abandoned is always present in a shame culture.[1] As
a sculpture of abandonment, Courage bears witness to the impossibility
of a type's existence at a moment when all is lost except attitude.

Not loneliness but abandonment, Hannah Arendt wrote, is the fundamental experience of life under totalitarianism.[2] No better fate was offered to the cool persona depicted in this book. Worse yet, the role of
the cool persona seconded the process.

What followed was the generation of air raid wardens and skeptics.
To the succeeding generation of the 1960s there seemed nothing better than a fatherless society. This generation as well took the path of
polarization, disintegrating in the 1970s into counterculture, which re-
invigorated the cult of authenticity by negation of the fathers, and marginal groupings, which lost themselves for a time in paramilitary political formations.

Here once again Gracián's conduct codes, tried and tested, serve
our turn:

> Between these two extremes of unreason is located the solid middle of pru-
> dent virtue; and it consists of a discreet audacity, often helped by luck.[3]

Notes

CHAPTER ONE

1. Manès Sperber, *Sieben Fragen zur Gewalt: Leben in dieser Zeit* (Munich, 1978), 9–10. I have commented on this case in "Blitzschnelle Metamorphosen: 7 Überlegungen zu einem Putzfleck," in *Geschichte als Literatur: Formen und Grenzen der Repräsentation von Vergangenheit,* ed. H. Eggert, U. Profitlich, and K. Scherpe (Stuttgart, 1990), 242–49.

2. See Ernst Jünger, *Der Arbeiter: Herrschaft und Gestalt* (1932), 4th ed. (Hamburg, 1941), 198.

3. Peter Hüttenberger, "Der historische Augenblick," in *Augenblick und Zeitpunkt: Studien zur Zeitstruktur und Zeitmetaphorik in Kunst und Wissenschaften,* ed. Thomsen and Holländer (Darmstadt, 1984), 222–33.

4. Ibid.

5. Carl Schmitt, *Politische Theologie: Vier Kapitel zur Lehre von der Souveränität,* 2d ed. (Munich, 1934), 49.

6. Michael Weinrich, "Macht unsere Augen hell," in *Augenblick und Zeitpunkt,* ed. Thomsen and Holländer (Darmstadt, 1984), 143–44.

7. *Reallexikon für Antike und Christentum* (Stuttgart, 1978), 10:945–1025.

8. Heinz-Dieter Kittsteiner, *Die Enstehung des modernen Gewissens* (Frankfurt am Main, 1991).

9. Norbert Elias, *Über den Prozess der Zivilisation* (Frankfurt am Main, 1976; trans. Edmund Jephcott as *The Civilizing Process: Power and Civility* [New York, 1982]).

10. See Klaus Theweleit, *Male Fantasies,* trans. Stephan Conway (Minneapolis, 1987), vol. 2.

11. Mario Erdheim, "'Heiße' Gesellschaft—'kaltes' Militär," *Kursbuch 67* (1982): 59–72.

12. See Karl Heinz Bohrer, *Die Ästhetik des Schreckens: Die pessimistische Romantik und Ernst Jüngers Frühwerk* (Munich, 1978).

13. See Helga Geyer-Ryan and Helmut Lethen, "The Rhetoric of Forgetting," in *Convention and Innovation,* ed. D'Haen, Grübel, and Lethen (Amsterdam, 1989); see also Helmut Lethen, "Kältemaschinen der Intelligenz: Attitüden der Sachlichkeit," in *Industriegebiet der Intelligenz,* ed. E. Wichner and H. Wiesner (Berlin, 1990), 118–53.

14. Karl Heinz Bohrer, ed., *Plötzlichkeit: Zum Augenblick des ästhetischen Scheins* (Frankfurt am Main, 1981).

15. Fernand Braudel, *Sozialgeschichte des 15–18 Jahrhunderts: Der Alltag,* 93.

16. Sighard Neckel, *Status und Scham: Zur symbolischen Reproduktion sozialer Ungleichheit* (Frankfurt am Main, 1991), 17, 22. The following paragraphs are guided by Neckel's sociology of shame, as well as Kittsteiner's cultural history of the conscience. But, as is evident here and in the chapter on Plessner and Serner, the conclusions I come to differ from Neckel's.

17. See Carrie Asman, "Brecht and Kafka," in *Cross-Illuminations* (Minneapolis, 1994).

18. Hans-Thies Lehmann, "Das Welttheater der Scham: Dreißig Annäherungen an den Entzug der Darstellung," *Merkur* 45, no. 10 (October 1991).

19. Léon Wurmser, *Die Maske der Scham* (Berlin, 1990), 447.

20. Neckel, *Status und Scham,* 93.

21. Helmut Berking, *Masse und Geist: Studien zur Soziologie in der Weimarer Republik* (Berlin, 1984), 65–89.

22. Karl Jaspers, *Die geistige Situation der Zeit* (Berlin, 1931), 78; cf. Berking, *Masse und Geist,* 62.

23. Jaspers, *Die geistige Situation,* 78.

24. Gustave Le Bon, *La psychologie de foules* (Paris, 1895).

25. The postwar literary landscape of the collective vexation and the armoring taken on against shaming has been depicted and analyzed in two major works. See Theweleit, *Male Fantasies;* and Peter Sloterdijk, *Kritik der zynischen Vernunft* (Frankfurt am Main, 1983).

26. Walter Serner, *Letzte Lockerung manifest dada* (1920), in *Letzte Lockerung: Ein Handbrevier für Hochstapler und solche, die es werden wollen* (1927) (Munich, 1981), 31.

27. Helmuth Plessner, *Grenzen der Gemeinschaft: Eine Kritik des sozialen Radikalismus* (1924), in vol. 5 of *Gesammelte Schriften* (Frankfurt am Main, 1982), 111.

28. *Bertolt Brecht Poems, 1913–1956,* ed. John Willett and Ralph Manheim (New York, 1976), 34–35.

29. Walter Benjamin, "Schicksal und Character," in *Zur Kritik der Gewalt und andere Aufsätze,* with an afterword by Herbert Marcuse (Frankfurt am Main, 1965), 76. The suggestion to consult Benjamin here I owe to Patrick Primavesi. See his paper, "Die Scham bei Benjamin," presented at the International Walter-Benjamin-Kongreß, Osnabrück, June 1992.

30. Ibid., 68 ff.

31. Sigmund Freud, *Reflections on War and Death* (1915).

32. Ibid.

33. See Neckel, *Status und Scham*, 41–59.

34. The most important analysis of these dichotomous concepts in our context is in Elias, *Über den Prozess der Zivilisation*. A useful overview can be found in Hans Joachim Krüger, "Aspekte der Zivilisationsanalyse von Norbert Elias," in *Kultur: Bestimmungen im 20. Jahrhundert*, ed. H. Brackert and F. Wefelmeyer (Frankfurt am Main, 1990), 317–43.

35. Krüger, "Aspekte der Zivilisationsanalyse," 322.

36. See Helmut Lethen, "Der Jargon der Neuen Sachlichkeit," *Germanica* 9 (1991).

37. Hannes Meyer, *Die neue Welt* (1926), in *Bauen und Gesellschaft: Schriften, Briefe, Prospekte* (Dresden, 1980), 27 f.

38. Alfred Döblin, "Der Geist der naturalistischen Zeitalters," *Die Neue Rundschau* (1924); reprinted in *Aufsätze zur Literatur* (Freiburg, 1963), 70.

39. Robert Musil, *Die Zeit der Tatsache* (1923), in *Tagebücher, Aphorismen, Essays und Reden*, ed. Adolf Frisé (Hamburg, 1955), 8:1384.

40. Hermann von Wedderkop, "Wandlungen des Geschmacks," *Der Querschnitt: Das Magazin der aktuellen Ewigkeitswerte*, July 1926.

41. Alfred Adler, "Körperform, Bewegung und Charakter," *Der Querschnitt*, September 1930, 342.

42. Walter Benjamin, *Einbahnstrasse* (Berlin, 1928), 63.

43. Ibid., 47 ff.

44. Bertolt Brecht, *Schriften zum Theater, 1918–1933* (Frankfurt am Main, 1963), 116 ff.

45. Neckel, *Status und Scham*, 51.

46. Bertolt Brecht, *Gesammelte Werke* (Frankfurt am Main, 1967), 18:180 ff.

47. This idea was stressed in Kittsteiner's various commentaries on cultural history.

48. Brecht, *Gesammelte Werke*, 18:117.

49. See Lethen, "Jargon der Neuen Sachlichkeit."

50. Wurmser, *Maske der Scham*, 230.

51. Ulrike Baureithel stresses this point; see "Masken der Virilität," *Die Philosophin* 8 (1993): 24–35.

52. Neckel, *Status und Scham*, 151.

CHAPTER TWO

1. Siegfried Kracauer, "Die Unterführung," in *Aufsätze 1932–1935*, *Schriften*, ed. Inka Mülder-Bach, vol. 5, bk. 3 (Frankfurt am Main, 1990), 40–42. On *Unterführung* see Inka Mülder-Bach, "Schlupflöcher: Die Diskontinuität des Kontinuierlichen im Werk Siefried Kracauer," in *Siegfried Kracauer: Neue Interpretationen*, ed. M. Kessler and T. Levin (Tübingen, 1990), 253 ff.

2. ". . . which began just at that point to present itself as a permanent feature of modern society" (René König, *Leben im Widerspruch: Versuch einer intellektuellen Autobiographie* [Frankfurt am Main, 1984], 62).

3. See Jean-Luc Evard, *Einrichtungen der Angst*, ed. K. Ratschiller and

C. Subik, *Klagenfurter Beiträge zur Philosophie* (Vienna, 1991). This chapter owes certain of its critical ideas to Evard's considerations.

4. On this point see the findings of Martin Lindner, *Leben in der Krise: Zeitromane der Neuen Sachlichkeit und die intellektuelle Mentalität der klassischen Moderne* (Stuttgart, 1994), 119–42. Lindner's research offers completely new insight into the decade of the new objectivity; its polarity-based thought seems to remain deeply immersed in vitalist philosophy. Since I became aware of this book only near the completion of my own work here, I address its findings only marginally and in regard to individual points.

5. Philipp Lersch, *Aufbau des Charakters* (1942), 100; quoted in ibid., 169.

6. Felix Weltsch as cited in Thomas Anz, *Literatur der Existenz* (1988), 66; quoted in ibid., 169.

7. Gottfried Benn, "Roman des Phänotyp: Landsberger Fragment 1944," in *Der Ptolemäer* (Stuttgart, 1988), 42 f.

8. Odo Marquard, *Transzendentaler Idealismus: Romantische Naturphilosophie, Psychoanalyse* (Cologne, 1987), 38 ff.

9. Helmuth Plessner, *Grenzen der Gemeinschaft: Eine Kritik des sozialen Radikalismus* (1924), in vol. 5 of *Gesammelte Schriften* (Frankfurt am Main, 1982), 80.

10. Ibid., 95.

11. Ezra Pound, "Definitions etc.," *Der Querschnitt: Das Magazin der aktuellen Ewigkeitswerte,* ed. Christian Ferber (reprint, Berlin, 1981), 29.

12. Ernst Jünger, *Das Abenteuerliche Herz: Figuren und Capriccios* (Stuttgart, 1979), 173.

13. Siegfried Kracauer, *Aufsätze 1927–1931, Schriften,* ed. Inka Mülder-Bach, vol. 5, bk. 1 (Frankfurt am Main, 1990), 376 ff.

14. Broder Christiansen, *Das Geschichte unserer Zeit* (Buchenbach in Baden, 1930).

15. Martin Wagner, *Das Formproblem eines Weltstadtplatzes* (1929); reprinted in *Tendenzen der Zwanziger Jahre,* 15. Europäische Kunstausstellung (Berlin, 1977), catalog 2/105.

16. Christiansen, *Das Geschichte unserer Zeit,* 40.

17. Siegfried Kracauer, "Stadterscheinungen" (*Frankfurter Zeitung,* 6 August 1932), in *Schriften,* vol. 5, bk. 3, 93.

18. Siegfried Kracauer, "Kleine Signale," in *Schriften,* vol. 5, bk. 2, 234–36.

19. Carl Schmitt, "Theodor Däublers *Nordlicht*" (1916); quoted in Norbert Bolz, *Auszug aus der entzauberten Welt: Philosophischer Extremismus zwischen den Weltkriegen* (Munich, 1989), 84.

20. Arnold Bronnen, "Moral und Verkehr," in *Sabotage der Jugend: Kleine Arbeiten, 1922–1934,* ed. F. Aspetsberger (Innsbruck, 1989), 127.

21. Bertolt Brecht, "Ten Poems from *A Reader for Those Who Live in Cities,*" in *Bertolt Brecht Poems, 1913–1956,* ed. John Willett and Ralph Manheim (New York, 1976), 137.

22. Helmuth Plessner, *Die Stufen des Organischen und der Mensch* (1928; Berlin, 1965), 320.

23. Alfred Adler, "Körperform, Bewegung und Charakter," *Der Querschnitt,* September 1930, 338.

24. Béla Balázs, *Der sichtbare Mensch oder die Kultur des Films* (Leipzig, 1924), 23.

25. Siegfried Kracauer, "Der blaue Engel," *Die Neue Rundschau* (1930); reprinted in *From Caligari to Hitler: A Psychological History of the German Film* (Princeton, 1947). There is much information on resistance to psychoanalysis in Carl Pietzcker, "Brechts Verhältnis zur Psychoanalyse," in *Psychoanalyse und Literatur*, ed. W. Schönau (Amsterdam, 1984), 275–317. On the reception of behaviorism, see Jan Knopf, *Bertolt Brecht: Ein Forschungsbericht* (Frankfurt am Main, 1974), 80–90; Hans Jürgen Rosenbauer, *Brecht und der Behaviorismus* (Bad Homburg, 1970); Heinrich Berenberg-Gossler, Hans-Harald Müller, and Joachim Stosch, "Das Lehrstück—Rekonstruktion einer Theorie oder Fortsetzung eines Lernprozesses?" in *Brechtdiskussion*, ed. J. Dyck et al. (Kronberg, 1974), 121 ff.

26. Herbert Jhering, "Die Kreatur: Bruckner in der Komödie" (11 March 1930), in *Von Reinhardt bis Brecht* (Berlin, 1961), 3:48–50.

CHAPTER THREE

1. Walter Benjamin, "Erfahrung und Armut," in *Illuminationen: Ausgewählte Schriften* (Frankfurt am Main, 1961), 314.

2. Ernst Jünger, *In Stahlgewittern* (Berlin, 1942).

3. Bertolt Brecht, *Ozeanflug* (1929), in *Gesammelte Werke* (Frankfurt am Main, 1967), 2:584.

4. Walter Serner, *Letzte Lockerung: Ein Handbrevier für Hochstapler und solche, die es werden wollen* (1927) (Munich, 1981), 69.

5. Werner Krauss, *Graciáns Lebenslehre* (Frankfurt am Main, 1947), 86. [Translator's note: in this chapter's discussion, further references to *Graciáns Lebenslehre* will be by page number.] See Werner Krauss, *Lendemains* 18, nos. 69–70 (1993).

6. Werner Krauss, "Bericht über meine Beteiligung und der Aktion Schulze-Boysen," Beglaubigte Abschrift des eigenhändigen Berichts (Werner-Krauss-Archiv, Berlin), 16. Krauss also worked during his confinement on the novel *PLN: Die Passionen der halkyonischen Seele,* which was published in 1946 by Vittorio Klostermann in Frankfurt.

7. Karlheinz Barck, "Eine unveröffentliche Korrespondenz: Erich Auerbach/Werner Krauss," *Beiträge zur Romanischen Philologie* 26, no. 2 (1987): 312.

8. Balthasar Gracián, *The Art of Worldly Wisdom,* trans. Joseph Jacobs (New York, 1943).

9. Krauss, "Bericht über meine Beteiligung," 17.

10. Hans Robert Jauss, "Ein Kronezeuge unseres Jahrhunderts: Werner Krauss in seinen nachgelassenen Tagebüchern," *Romantische Zeitschrift für Literaturgeschichte* 14, nos. 3–4 (1990): 421.

11. Ibid.

12. Bertolt Brecht, "Ten Poems from *A Reader for Those Who Live in Cities*," in *Bertolt Brecht Poems, 1913–1956,* ed. John Willett and Ralph Manheim (New York, 1976), 131.

13. Ludwig Flachskamp, rev. of *Graciáns Lebenslehre* in *Romanische Forschung* 62, nos. 2–3 (1950): 263.

14. Ibid.

15. Ibid., 264.

16. Arnold G. Reichenberger, rev. of *Graciáns Lebenslehre* in *Hispanic Review* 17 (1949): 171. The third review on file in the Krauss archive also stresses the status of the persona concept: see H. Kunz, review of *Graciáns Lebenslehre* in *Studia Philosophie* (1949): 189. But Erich Auerbach, in a letter of 13 October 1947, emphasizes the chapter about Gracián's "concept of measure" (see Barck, "Eine unveröffentliche Korrespondenz"). I go into this humanist evaluative shift below, when I discuss the conduct codes' historical context.

17. Marcel Mauss, "Eine Kategorie des menschlichen Geists . . . ," *Journal of the Royal Anthropological Institute* 68 (1938) [Huxley Memorial Lecture of 1938]; reprinted in *Soziologie und Anthropologie* (Frankfurt am Main, 1978), 2:238.

18. Ibid., 252.

19. Karl Vossler, *Geist und Kultur in der Sprache* (1925) (Munich, 1960), 16; Karl Löwith, *Das Individuum in der Rolle des Mitmenschen* (Munich, 1928). Both books were in Karl Krauss's library; they led me to the René König essay, "Freiheit und Selbstentfremdung in soziologischer Sicht" (1962), in *Studien zur Soziologie* (Frankfurt am Main, 1971).

20. Krauss, "Bericht über meine Beteiligung," 16.

21. Max Weber, "Science as a Vocation," in *From Max Weber: Essays in Sociology,* trans. H. H. Gerth and C. Wright Mills (New York, 1946).

22. Max Weber, "Politics as a Vocation," in ibid., 128.

23. See Gary L. Ulmen, *Politischer Mehrwert: Eine Studie über Max Weber und Carl Schmitt* (Weinheim, 1991), 124.

24. Karl Mannheim, *Konservativismus: Ein Beitrag zur Soziologie des Wissens,* ed. David Kettler et al. (Frankfurt am Main, 1984), 214. See Pierre Vaydat, "Neue Sachlichkeit als ethische Haltung," *Germanica* 9 (1991): 37–54.

25. Carl Schmitt, *Der Begriff des Politischen* (1927; Berlin, 1963), 53 (trans. George Schwab as *The Concept of the Political* [New Brunswick, N.J., 1976]).

26. Ursula Geitner, *Die Sprache der Verstellung: Studium zum rhetorischen und anthropologischen Wissen im 17. und 18. Jahrhundert* (Tübingen, 1992), 221.

27. Ibid., 220.

28. Helga Geyer-Ryan, "Zur Geschichte des weiblichen Vernunftverbots," in *Konstellationen der Moderne: Rationalität—Weiblichkeit—Wissenschaft,* ed. Chr. Kulke and E. Scheich (Freiburg, 1992), 7. See Helga Geyer-Ryan, *Fables of Desire: Studies in the Ethics of Art and Gender* (Cambridge, 1994).

29. See Andreas Kuhlmann, "Souverän im Ausdruck: Helmuth Plessner und die 'neue Anthropologie,'" *Merkur* 45, no. 8 (August 1991).

30. Klaus Theweleit, *Male Fantasies,* trans. Stephan Conway (Minneapolis, 1987). Michael Rohrwasser, *Saubere Mädel, starke Genossen: Proletarische Massenliteratur?* (Frankfurt am Main, 1975); see Michael Rohrwasser, *Der Weg nach oben: Johannes R. Becher, Politics of Writing* (Basel, 1980); Michael Rohrwasser, *Der Stalinismus und die Renegaten: Die Literatur der Exkommunisten*

(Stuttgart, 1991). Nicolaus Sombart, *Die deutschen Männer und ihre Feinde, Carl Schmitt: Ein deutsches Schicksal zwischen Männerbund und Matriarchatsmythos* (Munich, 1991). Carl Pietzcker, *Ich kommandiere mein Herz* (Würzburg, 1988). Peter Sloterdijk, *Kritik der zynischen Vernunft* (Frankfurt am Main, 1983).

31. Ulrike Bauereithel has made these points in several publications: most recently, in "Kollectivneurose moderner Männer: Die Neue Sachlichkeit als Symptom des männlichen Identitätsverlust—Sozialpsychologische Aspekte einer literarischen Strömung," *Germanica* 9 (1991): 123–45; see also Bauereithel, *Masken;* and Peter Gay, "The Revenge of the Father: Rise and Fall of Objectivity," in *Weimar Culture: The Outsider as Insider* (New York, 1968), 119–45. Claudia Szcesny-Friedmann, *Die kühle Gesellschaft* (Munich, 1991).

32. Sombart, *Deutschen Männer,* 80.

33. Sloterdijk, *Kritik der zynischen Vernunft,* 940. See Helmut Lethen, "Von Geheimagenten und Virtuosen: Peter Sloterdijks Schulbeispiele des Zynisimus aus der Literatur der Weimarer Republik," in *Peter Sloterdijks "Kritik der zynischen Vernunft"* (Frankfurt am Main, 1987), 324–55.

34. Bertolt Brecht, *Songs der Dreigroschenoper,* in *Gesammelte Werke* (Frankfurt am Main, 1967), 11:146.

35. Robert Musil, *Der Mann ohne Eigenschaften* (Hamburg, 1952), 780.

36. Max Scheler, *Die Stellung des Menschen im Kosmos* (1928) (Bonn, 1991), 55 ff.

37. Helmuth Plessner, *Grenzen der Gemeinschaft: Eine Kritik des sozialen Radikalismus* (1924), in vol. 5 of *Gesammelte Schriften* (Frankfurt am Main, 1982), 127. [Translator's note: in this chapter's discussion, further references to *Grenzen* will be by page number.]

38. Sigmund Freud, *Civilization and Its Discontents* (1930), trans. James Strachey (New York, 1961), 67.

39. Schmitt, *Begriff des Politischen,* 59.

40. Ernst Jünger, *Der Arbeiter: Herrschaft und Gestalt* (1932), 4th ed. (Hamburg, 1941), 18.

41. See Albert O. Hirschman, *Leidenschaften und Interessen* (Frankfurt am Main, 1980), 17–19.

42. Jacob Taubes, "Leviathan als sterblicher Gott," in *Der Fürst dieser Welt: Carl Schmitt und die Folgen,* ed. J. Taubes (Munich, 1985), 12.

43. Walter Benjamin, *Der Ursprung des deutschen Trauerspiels* (Frankfurt am Main, 1963), 56.

44. Ibid., 75.

45. On these issues I am following Heinz-Dieter Kittsteiner, *Die Enstehung des modernen Gewissens* (Frankfurt am Main, 1991), 229–44.

46. Schmitt, *Begriff des Politischen,* 28.

47. This formulation, which elaborates the paradox of Hobbes's precepts of reason, comes from an instructive introduction by Wolfgang Kersting, *Thomas Hobbes* (Hamburg, 1922), 127.

48. Geitner, *Sprache der Verstellung,* 6.

49. This characterization follows Kersting (*Hobbes,* 59–98) in the details, though I do not necessarily share his interpretations.

50. Osip Mandelstam, "Gespräch über Dante," *Gesammelte Essays 1925–35* (Reinbek, 1990), 160.

51. Kersting, *Hobbes*, 78 ff.

52. Sloterdijk, *Kritik der zynischen Vernunft*, 935.

53. Helmuth Plessner, *Macht und menschliche Natur: Ein Versuch zur Anthropologie der geschichtlichen Weltansicht* (1931), in vol. 5 of *Gesammelte Schriften* (Frankfurt am Main, 1982), 147.

54. Siegfried Kracauer, *Philosophie der Gemeinschaft*, in *Aufsätze 1927–1931, Schriften*, ed. Inka Mülder-Bach, vol. 5, bk. 1 (Frankfurt am Main, 1990), 269.

55. Ferdinand Tönnies, *Gemeinschaft und Gesellschaft: Grundbegriffe der reinen Soziologie* (Darmstadt, 1979).

56. René König, "Gemeinschaft," in *Fischer Enzyklopädie des Wissens, "Soziologie"* (Frankfurt am Main, 1958), 83–88.

57. Plessner, *Macht und menschliche Natur*, 199.

58. Helmut Lethen, "Lob der Kälte: Ein Motiv der historischen Avantgarden," in *Die unvollendete Vernunft: Moderne versus Postmoderne*, ed. D. Kamper and W. van Reijen (Frankfurt am Main, 1987).

59. Quoted in Andreas Haus, *Moholy-Nagy, Fotos und Fotogramme* (Munich, 1978), 64.

60. Richard Sennett, *The Fall of Public Man* (New York, 1976).

61. Walter Benjamin, *Gesammelte Schriften* (Frankfurt am Main, 1991 [?]), 6:62.

62. Lionel Trilling, *Das Ende der Aufrichtigkeit* (Munich, 1980; originally *Sincerity and Authenticity* [Cambridge, 1971]).

63. Freud uses this allegory from *Parerga und Paralipomena* in his *Group Psychology and the Analysis of the Ego*, trans. James Strachey (New York, 1960), 41.

64. Günther Dux, "Helmuth Plessners philosophische Anthropologie im Prospekt," afterword to *Philosophische Anthropologie*, by Helmuth Plessner (Frankfurt am Main, 1970), 275.

65. Arnold Gehlen, *Der Mensch: Seine Natur und seine Stellung in der Welt* (1940) (Wiesbaden, 1986), 80; see Karl Siegbert Rehberg, "Zurück zur Kultur? Arnold Gehlens anthropologische Grundlegung der Kulturwissenschaften," in *Kultur: Bestimmungen im 20. Jahrhundert*, ed. H. Brackert and F. Wefelmeyer (Frankfurt am Main, 1990), 276–316.

66. See Martin Lindner, *Leben in der Krise: Zeitromane der neuen Sachlichkeit und die intellektuelle Mentalität der klassischen Moderne* (Stuttgart, 1994). He offers an astounding profile of the epoch of vitalism, from 1890 to 1955, in which polarization works to structure thought.

67. Georg Simmel, "Die Krisis der Kultur," in *Expressionismus: Manifeste und Dokumente zur deutschen Literatur 1910–1920*, ed. T. Anz and M. Stark (Stuttgart, 1982), 206.

68. Joachim Fischer, "Plessner und die politische Philosophie der zwanziger Jahre," in *Politisches Denken, Jahrbuch 1992*, ed. V. Gerhardt, H. Ottmann, and M. P. Thompson (Stuttgart, 1992), 61.

69. Helmuth Plessner, *Die Stufen des Organischen und der Mensch* (1928) (Berlin, 1965), 316 f.

70. Joachim Fischer, "Spricht die Seele," *FAZ,* 37.

71. Ibid.; Dux, "Plessners philosophische Anthropologie," 308.

72. See Dux, "Plessners philosophische Anthropologie," 309.

73. Léon Wurmser, *Die Maske der Scham* (Berlin, 1990), 453.

74. Dux, "Plessners philosophische Anthropologie," 305.

75. Wurmser, *Maske der Scham,* 78.

76. Ibid., 86 ff.

77. The following quotations are from Trilling, *Ende der Aufrichtigkeit,* specifically the chapter on society and authenticity, 106–33. Carl Wege referred me to artificiality's technological dimension in a conversation on 25 November 1991.

78. Friedrich Nietzsche, *The Will to Power,* trans. Walter Kaufmann and R. J. Hollingdale (New York, 1968), 496–97.

79. Nietzsche, *Werke in drei Bände* (Munich, 1963), 2:604.

80. On this see Hans-Thies Lehmann, "Das Welttheater der Scham: Dreißig Annäherungen an den Entzug der Darstellung," *Merkur* 45, no. 10 (October 1991): 836.

81. Johann Gottfried Herder, *Abhandlung über den Ursprung der Sprache* (Stuttgart, 1962), 80 f.

82. Ibid., 26.

83. Gehlen, *Der Mensch,* 84.

84. This point, which Hans Dietrich Irmscher confirms in his afterword to the 1962 edition of Herder's *Abhandlung* (174), is all the more astonishing because Plessner's habilitations lecture was about Herder.

85. Erich Auerbach, *Mimesis: The Representation of Reality in Western Literature,* trans. Willard R. Trask (Princeton, 1968), 360. Here I follow a reference Renate Schlesier gave me.

86. Ibid.; see "The Faux Dévot," 359–95.

87. Sigrid Weigel, "Zum Verhältnis von 'Wilden' und 'Frauen' im Diskurs der Aufklärung," in *Topographien* (Hamburg, 1990), 118–42. See Geitner, *Sprache der Verstellung,* 295 ff.

88. In *Philosophie in Selbstdarstellungen,* ed. Ludwig I. Pongratz (Hamburg, 1975), 1:269–307.

89. Lehmann, "Welttheater des Schams," 827 ff.

90. Gay, *Weimar Culture.* Ulrike Baureithel reinforces the thesis in ". . . in dieser Welt von Männern erdacht" (master's thesis, Universität Karlsruhe, 1987).

91. Alfred Döblin, *Wissen und Verändern: Offene Briefe an einen jungen Menschen* (Berlin, 1931), 35 ff.

92. Ibid., 36 ff.

93. Nor did Bertolt Brecht shy away from using them. See Carl Pietzcker, "Brechts Verhältnis zur Psychoanalyse," in *Psychoanalyse und Literatur,* ed. W. Schönau (Amsterdam, 1984).

94. Arnold Gehlen, *Anthropologische Forschung: Zur Selbstbegegnung und Selbstentdeckung des Menschen* (Reinbek, 1961), 56.

95. An overview of the situation of anthropology in the twenties, which I follow extensively here, is Jürgen Habermas, "Anthropologie," in *Das Fischer Lexicon, Philosophie,* ed. A. Diener and I. Frenzel (Frankfurt am Main, 1958), 18–35.

96. Plessner, *Stufen des Organischen,* 316 ff.

97. In this context see Baureithel, "... in dieser Welt von Männern erdacht."

98. See Jürgen Habermas, *On the Logic of the Social Sciences,* trans. Shierry Weber Nicholsen and Jerry A. Stark (Cambridge, Mass., 1988), 117 ff.

99. Geitner, *Sprache der Verstellung.*

100. Scheler, *Stellung des Menschen,* 18.

101. Karl Bühler, *Ausdruckstheorie: Das System an der Geschichte aufgezeigt* (1933), 2d ed., with an introduction by Albert Wellek (Stuttgart, 1968). [Translator's note: in this chapter's discussion, further references to *Ausdruckstheorie* will be by page number.]

102. See Habermas, "Anthropologie," 29.

103. Ludwig Klages, *Ausdrucksbewegung und Gestaltungskraft,* 3d and 4th eds. (1923), 47 f.; quoted in Bühler, *Ausdruckstheorie,* 165.

104. Walter Benjamin, *Fragmente: Autobiographische Schriften, Gesammelte Schriften* (Frankfurt am Main, 1991 [?]), 6:177.

105. Helmuth Plessner, "Das Lächeln" (1950), in *Philosophische Anthropologie* (Frankfurt am Main, 1970), 176.

106. Ibid., 91.

107. Helmuth Plessner, "Die Deutung des mimischen Ausdrucks: Ein Beitrag zur Lehre vom Bewußtsein des anderen Ichs" (1925), in *Gesammelte Schriften* (Frankfurt am Main, 1982), 7:67–130.

108. Scheler, *Stellung des Menschen,* 15.

109. Ibid., 77.

110. Ibid., 69.

111. Max Scheler, *Vom Sinn des Leidens,* 64 ff.; quoted in Sloterdijk, *Kritik der zynischen Vernunft,* 828.

112. Ibid.

113. Peter Heintel and Thomas H. Macho, "Der soziale Körper: Zynismus und Organisation," in *Kritik der zynischen Vernunft* (Frankfurt am Main, 1983), 828.

114. Bertolt Brecht, "Lyrik als Ausdruck," in *Schriften zur Literatur und Kunst, 1920–1932* (Frankfurt am Main, 1967), 74 ff.

115. Rudolf Leonhard, *Alles und Nichts!* (1920); quoted in *Expressionismus: Literatur und Kunst 1910–1923,* Sonderausstellung des Schiller-Nationalmuseums, catalog no. 7 (Munich, 1960), 216.

116. Brecht, "Lyrik als Ausdruck," 75. On the theory of the gesture, see Carrie Asman, "Die Rückbindung des Zeichens an den Körper," presented at the International Walter-Benjamin-Kongreß, Osnabrück, June 1992.

117. Heinrich Berenberg-Gossler, Hans-Harald Müller, and Joachim Stosch, "Das Lehrstück—Rekonstruktion einer Theorie oder Fortsetzung eines Lernprozesses?" in *Brechtdiskussion,* ed. J. Dyck et al. (Kronberg, 1974), 121–71.

118. Benjamin, *Ursprung des deutschen Trauerspiels,* 194.

119. Rüdiger Kramme has made a detailed examination of the correspondences between the theories of Plessner and Schmitt. I am indebted to his work for many suggestions, even if I do not share his conclusions. See Rüdiger Kramme, *Helmuth Plessner und Carl Schmitt: Eine historische Fallstudie von*

Anthropologie und Politik in der deutschen Philosophie der zwanziger Jahre (Berlin, 1989).

120. Schmitt, *Begriff des Politischen,* 143.

121. Plessner, *Macht und menschliche Natur,* 143.

122. Ibid., 155, 148, 234.

123. Norbert Bolz, *Auszug aus der entzauberten Welt: Philosophischer Extremismus zwischen den Weltkriegen* (Munich, 1989), 90.

124. See Eckhard Nordhofen, "Vor der Bundeslade des Bösen," *Die Zeit,* 9 April 1993, 61.

125. Geitner, *Sprache der Verstellung,* 111.

126. Weber, "Science as a Vocation," 152.

127. Quoted in Bolz, *Auszug,* 13.

128. Ernst Jünger was also termed "Lucifer." See Heinz-Dieter Kittsteiner and Helmut Lethen, "'Jetzt zieht Leutnant Jünger seinen Mantel aus . . . ,' Überlegungen zur 'Ästhetik des Schreckens,'" *Berliner Hefte: Zeitschrift für Kultur und Politik,* no. 11 (May 1979): 20–50.

129. Schmitt, *Begriff des Politischen,* 60.

130. See Ulmen, *Politischer Mehrwert,* 42.

131. Plessner, *Macht und menschliche Natur,* 192.

132. Schmitt, *Begriff des Politischen,* 27, 33.

133. Ibid.

134. Kramme, *Helmuth Plessner und Carl Schmitt,* 7, 208.

135. Plessner, *Macht und menschliche Natur,* 192.

136. Ibid., 194.

137. Raphael Gross, "Carl Schmitts 'Nomos' und die 'Juden,'" *Merkur* (1993).

138. Plessner, *Macht und menschlicher Natur,* 126.

139. An observation by Léon Poliakow, passed on by Ulrich Raulff in "Die Libido des Polizeistaats," *Frankfurter Allgemeine Zeitung,* 10 August 1991, 25. On the fascination the figure of the Grand Inquisitor held for intellectuals of the twenties, see Sloterdijk, *Kritik der zynischen Vernunft,* 344–69.

140. Helmuth Plessner, *Die verspätete Nation* (Frankfurt am Main, 1989), 189.

141. Plessner, *Macht und menschliche Natur,* 192.

142. Norbert Elias, *Die höfische Gesellschaft* (Darmstadt, 1969; trans. Edmund Jephcott as *The Court Society* [New York, 1983]).

143. Ibid., 171.

144. Norbert Elias, *Über den Prozess der Zivilisation* (Frankfurt am Main, 1976), 390.

145. Hans Joachim Krüger, "Aspekte der Zivilisationsanalyse von Norbert Elias," in *Kultur: Bestimmungen im 20. Jahrhundert,* ed. H. Brackert and F. Wefelmeyer (Frankfurt am Main, 1990), 338.

146. I am indebted to Renate Schlesier for both the reference to Kantorowicz's book *The King's Two Bodies* and the idea of "textual space."

147. Barck, "Eine unveröffentliche Korrespondenz," 169.

148. This constellation is depicted in greater detail in Hirschmann, *Leidenschaften und Interessen,* 28–51.

149. Martin Meyer, *Ernst Jünger* (Munich, 1990), 337.
150. Ernst Jünger, *Strahlungen* (Stuttgart, 1980), 1:474 ff.

CHAPTER FOUR

1. I developed this idea in conversations with Hortense von Heppe and Heinz Wismann.

2. See Sighard Neckel, *Status und Scham: Zur symbolischen Reproduktion sozialer Ungleichheit* (Frankfurt am Main, 1991), 93.

3. Paul Tillich, *Die sozialistische Entscheidung* (Berlin, 1980), 38.

4. See Klaus Garber, "Baroque und Moderne im Werk Benjamins," *Literaturmagazin* 29 (1992).

5. My argument is guided by Samuel Weber, "Taking Exception to Decision: Walter Benjamin and Carl Schmitt," paper delivered in Utrecht, December 1991. My thanks to Weber for providing me a copy of his (then unfinished) manuscript. It has since appeared in *Enlightenments: Encounters between Critical Theory and Contemporary Thought,* ed. H. Kunnemann and H. de Vries (Kampen, 1993), 141–62.

6. The idea that the literary text can become the "crooked plane" of the programmatic idea I have taken from Carrie Asman's essay, "Brecht and Kafka," in *Cross-Illuminations* (Minneapolis, 1994).

7. My attention was drawn to the following points on difference by Sigrid Weigel, Renate Schlesier, Hans-Thies Lehmann, Patrick Primavesi, and Richard Faber, in a discussion at the 1992 international Benjamin congress in Osnabrück.

8. Walter Benjamin, "Der Surrealismus: Die letzte Momentaufnahme der europäischen Intelligenz," in *Angelus Novus,* 202.

9. Walter Benjamin, "Franz Kafka" (1934), in ibid., 261.

10. Carl Schmitt, *Glossarium: Aufzeichnungen der Jahre 1947–1951* (Berlin, 1991), 234. [Translator's note: in this chapter's discussion, further references to *Glossarium* will be by page number.]

11. Benjamin, "Franz Kafka," 250.

12. S. Weber, "Taking Exception."

13. Philipp Lersch, *Gesicht und Seele* (1932), cited in Karl Bühler, *Ausdruckstheorie: Das System an der Geschichte aufgezeigt* (1933), 2d ed., with an introduction by Albert Wellek (Stuttgart, 1968), 87 ff., 206 ff.

14. Ibid., 86.

15. Lersch cited in ibid., 87.

16. Ibid., 210.

17. Ibid., 207.

18. Bertolt Brecht, "Ten Poems from *A Reader for Those Who Live in Cities,*" in *Bertolt Brecht Poems, 1913–1956,* ed. John Willett and Ralph Manheim (New York, 1976), 138 ff.

19. Joseph Roth, "Bekenntnisse zum Gleisdreieck" (1924), reprinted in *Werke: Das journalistische Werk, 1924–1928,* ed. Klaus Westermann (Cologne, 1990), 221.

20. See Max Scheler's characterization of decadence philosophy in "Der

Mensch und die Geschichte" (1926), in *Philosophische Weltanschauung* (Bern, 1954), 82.

21. Max Scheler, "Der Mensch im Weltalter des Ausgleichs" (1927), in ibid., 101–5.

22. Franz Blei, *Talleyrand oder der Zynismus* (Munich, 1984). For this reference I am indebted to Klaus Ratschiller (Klagenfurt). [Translator's note: in this chapter's discussion, further references to *Talleyrand oder der Zynismus* will be by page number.] My commentary on Blei's novel took form subsequent to my reading of Nicolaus Sombart, *Die deutschen Männer und ihre Feinde* (Munich, 1991).

23. Sombart, *Deutschen Männer*, 286 ff.

24. Stefan Zweig, *Joseph Fouché: Bildnis eines politischen Menschen* (Frankfurt am Main, 1991), 22 f.

25. See Wolfgang Iser, *Das Fictive und das Imaginäre: Perspektiven literarische Anthropologie* (Frankfurt am Main, 1991), 226–61.

26. Theodor Lessing, "Der Maupassant der Kriminalistik" (1925); quoted in Walter Serner, *Der Abreiser: Materialien zu Leben und Werk*, ed. Thomas Milch (Munich, 1984), 81–84.

27. On Iser's version of Plessner's anthropology of enactment, see *Das Fiktive und das Imaginäre*, 148.

28. Ibid., 150.

29. See Neckel, *Status und Scham*, 240. Neckel refers to Pierre Bourdieu, *Die feinen Unterschiede* (Frankfurt am Main, 1982), 500 ff.

30. Walter Serner, *Letzte Lockerung: Ein Handbrevier für Hochstapler und solche, die es werden wollen* (1927) (Munich, 1981).

31. Ernst Fuhrmann in his 1928 review of *Letzte Lockerung;* quoted in Serner, *Der Abreiser*, 156.

32. Raoul Hausmann quoted in Hanne Bergius, "Der Da-Dandy—Ein 'Narrenspiel aus dem Nichts,'" in *Tendenzen der Zwanziger Jahre* (Berlin, 1977), 3/12–3/29.

33. See Hiltrud Gnüg, *Kult der Kälte: Der klassische Dandy im Spiegel der Weltliteratur* (Stuttgart, 1988).

34. Serner, *Der Abreiser*, 19.

35. S. Lyman and M. Scott, *Coolness in Everyday Life* (1968), quoted in Neckel, *Status und Scham*, 267.

36. Agnes Heller, *The Power of Shame* (1985), quoted in Neckel, *Status und Scham,* 53.

37. Ursula Geitner, *Die Sprache der Verstellung: Studium zum rhetorischen und anthropologischen Wissen im 17. und 18. Jahrhundert* (Tübingen, 1992), 98.

38. Werner Krauss, *Graciáns Lebenslehre* (Frankfurt am Main, 1947), 20.

39. Walter Benjamin, "Kommentar zu dem 'Lesebuch für Städtebewohner,'" in *Versuche über Brecht* (Frankfurt am Main, 1966), 68.

40. Serner, *Handbrevier für Hochstapler*, 16.

41. Ibid., 19.

42. Ibid., 17.

43. Here I am following the justification of Nietzsche's behavioral doctrines in Geitner, *Sprache der Verstellung*.

44. Ibid., 12.

45. Walter Serner, *Der Pfiff um die Ecke* (Munich, 1982), 51.

46. Walter Serner, *Der isabelle Hengst* (Munich, 1983), 7 ff.

47. Peter Sloterdijk, *Kritik der zynischen Vernunft* (Frankfurt am Main, 1983), 725–28.

48. Thomas Milch, "'Ein gewaltiger metaphysischer Rülpser': Randbemerkungen zum Stand der Serner-Forschung," in *dr. walter serner 1889–1942: Ausstellungsbuch,* ed. Herbert Wiesner (Berlin, 1989), 64.

49. Ibid., 65.

50. Ibid. All of the materials are gathered in Serner, *Der Abreiser.*

51. Lionel Trilling, *Das Ende der Aufrichtigkeit* (Munich, 1980), 144.

52. Neckel, *Status und Scham,* 115.

53. Ibid., 116.

54. Ibid.

55. Milch, "Ein gewaltiger metaphysischer Rülpser," 70.

56. Serner, *Der Abreiser,* 167.

57. Walter Benjamin, *Briefe,* ed. Gershom Scholem and Theodor Adorno (Frankfurt am Main, 1966), 2:698.

58. See Kraft Wetzel, "Lug und Trug: Zum 100. Geburtstag von Ernst Lubitsch," *Freitag,* 24 January 1992, 9.

59. See Walter Benjamin, *Gesammelte Schriften* (Frankfurt am Main, 1991 [?]), 6:187.

60. Bertolt Brecht, "Nordseekrabben," in *Gesammelte Werke: Prosa* (Frankfurt am Main, 1967), 1:135. See also Klaus-Detlef Müller, *Brecht-Kommentar zur erzählenden Prosa* (Munich, 1980), 79 ff.

61. Bruno Taut, *Die neue Wohnung: Die Frau als Schöpferin,* 5th ed. (Leipzig, 1928), 46, 60, 50.

62. Ibid., 11, 51 ff.

63. Here I follow Nancy J. Troy, *The Totally Harmonious Interior: Paradise or Prison?* (The Hague, 1985). In his critique, Brecht follows a story that Adolf Loos had told in 1900: "Von einem armen reichen Mann," in *Ins Leere gesprochen, 1897–1900* (Vienna, 1962), 201–7. I am grateful to Regina Busch for the reference.

64. Klaus Theweleit has uncovered and analyzed this image reservoir in *Male Fantasies,* trans. Stephan Conway (Minneapolis, 1987).

65. Mario Erdheim, "'Heiße' Gesellschaft—'kaltes' Militär," *Kursbuch* 67 (1982): 59–72; Helmut Lethen, "Blitzschnelle Metamorphosen: 7 Überlegungen zu einem Putzfleck," in *Geschichte als Literatur: Formen und Grenzen der Repräsentation von Vergangenheit,* ed. H. Eggert, U. Profitlich, and K. Scherpe (Stuttgart, 1990), 242–49.

66. Carl Wege, "Gleisdreieck, Tank und Motor: Figuren und Denkfiguren aus der Technosphäre der Neuen Sachlichkeit," *Deutsche Vierteljahreszeitschrift* (1994).

67. Roth, "Bekenntnis zum Gleisdreieck," 218–21.

68. Walter Benjamin, "Theorien des deutschen Faschismus: Zu der Sammelschrift *Krieg und Krieger,*" in *Das Argument* 6, no. 30 (1964): 133.

69. Brecht, "Ten Poems from *A Reader,*" 137.

70. Ibid., 131–32.

71. See Helga Geyer-Ryan and Helmut Lethen, "The Rhetoric of Forgetting," in *Convention and Innovation*, ed. D'Haen, Grübel, and Lethen (Amsterdam, 1989), 305–48.

72. Brecht, "Ten Poems from *A Reader*," 140.

73. Rudof Arnheim, in *Die Weltbühne*, 14 June 1932.

74. Béla Balázs, "Sachlichkeit und Sozialismus," *Die Weltbühne*, 18 December 1928.

75. Walter Benjamin, "Der destruktive Charakter," in *Illuminationen: Ausgewählte Schriften* (Frankfurt am Main, 1961), 310–12. Benjamin, "Erfahrung und Armut," in ibid., 313–18. For more on the reception history, see my study in *The Other Brecht: Brecht Yearbook 17*, ed. H.-T. Lehmann and R. Voris (Madison, 1992), 77–100.

76. Benjamin, *Versuche über Brecht*, 67–68. In 1944, incidentally, the poem "N.N." by Koos Schuur appeared in the context of the Dutch resistance, in the loose-leaf collection *Berijmd Verzet*; it borrows passages directly from Brecht's rules for behavior in illegal conditions. My thanks to Els Andringa for the reference.

77. Benjamin, "Der destruktive Charakter," 311.

78. Benjamin, *Gesammelte Schriften*, 6:540.

79. Bertolt Brecht, *Gedichte für Stadtbewohner*, ed. and with an introduction by Franco Buono (Frankfurt am Main, 1980), 153.

80. Edmund Licher, *Zur Lyrik Brechts: Aspekte ihrer Dialektik und Kommunikativität* (Frankfurt am Main, 1984), 168–73.

81. Friedrich Nietzsche, *The Use and Abuse of History*, trans. Adrian Collins (Indianapolis, 1957), 6.

82. Ibid., 5.

83. Licher, *Zur Lyrik Brechts*, 172 f.

84. Peter L. Oesterreich, *Fundamentalrhetorik: Untersuchung zu Person und Rede in der Öffentlichkeit* (Hamburg, 1990), 139, 137.

85. "Ten Poems from *A Reader*," 146. See Licher, *Zur Lyrik Brechts*, 172 f.

86. I am indebted for this thought to a conversation on 18 November 1991 with Rüdiger Safranski.

87. My attention was drawn to this implement at the International Brecht Symposium of 1991 in Augsburg by Hans-Thies Lehmann and Susanne Winnacker. See Hans-Thies Lehmann, "Schlaglichter auf den anderen Brecht," in *The Brecht Yearbook 17* (Madison, 1992), 1–13. I am indebted to Lehmann's observations on Brecht's early lyrics for the deepest insights.

88. "Mann ist Mann, Hauptmann-Manuskript," in *Brechts Mann ist Mann*, ed. Carl Wege (Frankfurt am Main, 1982), 282. My thanks to Carl Wege for this reference.

89. Jürgen Manthey, "Staatsdichter im Kinderland," *Die Zeit*, 6 March 1992, 77–78.

90. See the publications of Ulrike Baureithel (cited above and below).

91. Paul de Man, *Blindness and Insight: Essays in the Rhetoric of Contemporary Criticism* (London, 1983), 161.

92. Telling in this context are the later passages in which Carl Schmitt re-

flects on the dialectic of legal positivism and "devouring the fathers": *Glossarium*, 26, 148, and 234.

93. Tillich, *Die sozialistische Entscheidung*, 38.

94. Ulrike Baureithel, ". . . in dieser Welt von Männern erdacht" (master's thesis, Universität Karlsruhe, 1987), 140. See also Ulrike Baureithel, "Die letzte tolle Karte im Männerspiel," *Literatur für Leser*, 3, no. 90 (1990): 141–54.

95. Marieluise Fleißer, *Mehlreisende Frieda Geier: Roman vom Rauchen, Sporteln, Lieben und Verkaufen* (Berlin, 1931).

96. Ibid., 52.

97. Ibid., 310.

98. Ibid., 170.

99. Ibid., 311.

100. Marieluise Fleißer, *Ein Pfund Orangen und neun andere Geschichten der Marieluise Fleißer aus Ingolstadt* (1929) (Frankfurt am Main, 1984), 80.

101. Marieluise Fleißer, *Avantgarde: Erzählungen* (Munich, 1963), 11.

102. Fleißer, *Ein Pfund Orangen*, 80.

103. Fleißer, *Avantgarde*, 11. See Gisela von Wysocki, *Die Fröste der Freiheit: Aufbruchphantasien* (Frankfurt am Main, 1980). On conditions between the sexes in the Weimar Republic, see the works referenced by Ulrike Baureithel and Ursula Krechel, "Linksseitig, Kunstseidig: Dame, Girl, und Frau," in *Industriegebiet der Intelligenz*, ed. E. Wichner and H. Wiesner (Berlin, 1990), 96–117. See also Sissi Tax, *marieluise fleißer—schreiben, überleben: Ein biographischer versuch* (Frankfurt am Main, 1984).

104. Fleißer, *Ein Pfund Orangen*, 80.

105. Carl Schmitt, *Der Begriff des Politischen* (1927; Berlin, 1963), 26.

106. Fleißer, *Ein Pfund Orangen*, 83.

107. Fleißer, *Mehlreisende*, 57.

108. Fleißer, *Avantgarde*, 10.

109. Siegfried Kracauer, *Ginster: Von ihm selbst geschrieben* (Berlin, 1928). My discussion takes its lead from the commentary by Inka Mülder-Bach, *Siegfried Kracauer—Grenzgänger zwischen Theorie und Literatur* (Stuttgart, 1985), 125–45.

110. Kracauer, *Ginster*, 226 f.

111. Ibid., 334.

112. Ibid.

113. Ibid., 216.

114. Ibid., 221 f.

115. Ernst Jünger, *Der Arbeiter: Herrschaft und Gestalt* (1932), 4th ed. (Hamburg, 1941), 7. [Translator's note: in this chapter's discussion, further references to *Der Arbeiter* will be by page number.]

116. Robert Musil, "Triëdere," in *Nachlaß zu Lebzeiten* (Hamburg, 1957), 82. On the attitude of the sharp-sighted dandy, see Karl Heinz Bohrer, *Die Ästhetik des Schreckens: Die pessimistische Romantik und Ernst Jüngers Frühwerk* (Munich, 1978).

117. Ossip Mandelstam, "Gespräche über Dante," *Gesammelte Essays 1925–35* (Reinbek, 1990), 160.

118. Walter Benjamin, "Programm eines proletarischen Kindertheaters" (1928), in *Gesammelte Schriften*, vol. 2, bk. 2 (Frankfurt am Main, 1977), 766.

119. Ernst Jünger, "Über den Schmerz" (1934), in *Sämtliche Werke* (Stuttgart, 1986), 7:143–95.

120. Ernst Jünger, *Strahlungen* (Stuttgart, 1980), 2:131.

121. Benjamin, "Der Surrealismus," 210.

122. Jünger, "Über den Schmerz," 182.

123. Bertolt Brecht, *Der Dreigroschenprozeß*, in *Bertolt Brechts Dreigroschenbuch: Texte, Materialien, Dokumente*, ed. S. Unseld (Frankfurt am Main, 1960), 93.

124. Siegfried Kracauer, *Die Angestellten: Eine Schrift vom Ende der Weimarer Republik* (Allensbach, 1959), 9.

125. Robert Musil, "Ansätze zu neuer Ästhetik," in *Gesammelte Werke*, 8:1146.

126. See Helmut Lethen, "Eckfenster der Moderne: Wahrnehmungsexperimente bei Musil und E. T. A. Hoffmann," in *Musil-Studien*, ed. Josef Strutz (Munich, 1987), 15:195–229.

127. Karl Popper, *Ausgangspunkte* (Hamburg, 1979), 68 ff.

128. See Bernhard Waldenfels, "Wahrnehmung," in *Handbuch philosophischer Grundbegriffe* (Munich, 1974), 6:1669–78.

129. Wolfgang Kaempfer, *Ernst Jünger* (Stuttgart, 1981), 111.

130. Musil, "Triëdere," 82.

131. Carl Schmitt in *Glossarium*; see the following discussion.

132. Vilém Flusser, *Für eine Philosophie der Fotographie* (Göttingen, 1983), 122 ff. Carl Wege drew my attention to this text.

133. During our conversation in November 1991 Rüdiger Safranski gave me this reference.

134. Flusser, *Für eine Philosophie*, 31.

135. Ibid.

136. Ibid., 34, 26.

137. Ibid., 20.

138. Vilém Flusser, *Gesten: Versuch einer Phänomenologie* (Düsseldorf and Bensheim, 1991), 140.

139. Flusser, *Für eine Philosophie*, 26.

140. Siegfried Kracauer, "Die Photographie" (1927), in *Aufsätze 1927–1931, Schriften*, ed. Inka Mülder-Bach, vol. 5, bk. 2 (Frankfurt am Main, 1990), 83–97.

141. Ibid., 96.

142. Geitner, *Sprache der Verstellung*, 255.

143. Martin Lindner, *Leben in der Krise: Zeitromane der neuen Sachlichkeit und die intellektuelle Mentalität der klassischen Moderne* (Stuttgart, 1994). Linder cites here Heinrich Schmidt's formulation in the *Philosophisches Wörterbuch*, 9th ed. (Leipzig, 1934), 677.

144. Lindner, "'Krise' und 'Leben,'" 173.

145. Gottfried Benn, "Dorische Welt: Eine Untersuchung über die Beziehung von Kunst und Macht," in *Essays und Reden*, ed. Bruno Hillebrand (Frankfurt am Main, 1989), 305.

146. Robert Musil, *Gesammelte Schriften*, 8:1404.

147. Quoted in H. G. Vierhuff, *Die Neue Sachlichkeit: Malerei und Foto-grafie* (Cologne, 1980), 71. An instructive overview of the tendency in painting and photography to isolate types is Jost Hermand and Frank Trommler, *Die Kultur der Weimarer Republik* (Munich, 1978), 396–401.

148. Jünger, *Strahlungen*, 2:139 f.

149. Benjamin, "Der Surrealismus," 290.

150. See Marcus Paul Bullock, *The Violent Eye: Ernst Jünger's Visions and Revisions on the European Right* (Detroit, 1992), 25.

151. Jünger, "Über den Schmerz," 160.

152. Ibid., 158.

153. Ibid., 170.

154. Ibid., 160.

155. Wieland Schmied, "Die Neue Sachlichkeit: Malerei der Weimarer Zeit," *Germanica* 9 (1991): 222.

156. On this see Baureithel, "Die letzte tolle Karte," 141–54.

157. Wilhelm Reich, *Charakteranalyse* (Vienna, 1933).

158. Alfred Adler, *Studie über die Minderwertigkeit von Organen* (Munich, 1927). See Adler's summary in the chapter "Der Minderwertigkeitskomplex," in *Der Sinn des Lebens* (1933) (Frankfurt am Main, 1973), 67–79, esp. 69.

159. See the works mentioned above by Klaus Theweleit, Nicolaus Sombart, and Ulrike Baureithel.

160. Jünger, "Über den Schmerz," 175.

161. Robert Musil, "Der Riese Agoag" (1936), in *Nachlaß zu Lebzeiten* (Hamburg, 1957), 101–5.

162. Walter Benjamin, *Einbahnstraße* (Berlin, 1928), 80 ff.

163. For analysis of this issue see Martin Meyer, *Ernst Jünger* (Munich, 1990), 163–214.

164. Lindner, "'Krise' und 'Leben,'" 148.

165. Ibid., 150.

166. This example was advanced as a central argument against Ernst Bloch's theory of non-simultaneity in *Heritage of Our Times*. See Hans Günther, "Erb-schaft dieser Zeit," *Internationale Literatur* 6, no. 3 (1936): 91.

167. This example is taken from Friedrich Kittler's study, *Grammophon, Film, Typewriter* (Berlin, 1986), 154.

168. Ibid., 26. On the theory of sound, see also Helmut Lethen, "Sichtbar-keit: Kracauers Liebeslehre," in *Siegfried Kracauer: Neue Interpretationen*, ed. M. Kessler and T. Levin (Tübingen, 1990), 195–228.

169. Russell A. Berman, "Written Right across Their Faces: Ernst Jünger's Fascist Modernism," in *Modernity and the Text: Revision of German Mod-ernism*, ed. A. Huyssen and D. Bathrik (New York, 1989), 68.

170. Robert Musil, "Die Amsel," in *Nachlaß zu Lebzeiten* (Hamburg, 1957).

171. Marshall McLuhan, *Understanding Media* (New York, 1964), 83.

172. An appendix to the 1981 edition includes excerpts from letters that mention canonical names and sources, such as Goethe's theory of primeval plant life, Marx's analysis of industrialization, and Leibniz's monadology.

173. See Helmut Lethen, "Ernst Jünger, Bertolt Brecht e il concetto di 'modernizzazione' nella republica di Weimar," in *Ernst Jünger: Un convegno internazionale,* March 1983 (Naples, 1987), 55–71. See also the recent work by Uwe-K. Ketelsen, "Ernst Jüngers *Der Arbeiter*—Ein faschistisches Modernitätskonzept," in *Kultur: Bestimmungen im 20. Jahrhundert,* 219–54.

174. Lindner, "'Krise' und 'Leben,'" 185.

175. Arnold Gehlen, "Über kulturelle Kristallisation," in *Studien zur Anthropologie und Soziologie* (Neuwied, 1962).

176. Boris Groys, *Gesamtkunstwerk Stalin: Die gespaltene Kultur in der Sowjetunion* (Munich, 1988), 12.

177. Sombart, *Deutschen Männer,* 240, 245, 323.

178. See also Raphael Gross, "Carl Schmitts 'Nomos' und die 'Juden,'" *Merkur* (1993).

179. Walter Benjamin, "Zu Ignatius von Loyola," in *Fragmente: Autobiographische Schriften, Gesammelte Schriften* (Frankfurt am Main, 1991), 4:71 ff.

180. Carl Schmitt, *Ex Captivitate Salus: Erfahrungen der Zeit 1945–47* (Cologne, 1950), 79 f.

181. The verse is taken from the new biography: Paul Noack, *Carl Schmitt* (Berlin, 1993), 282. [Translator's note: a more literal rendering of the final line would signal that where Jaspers belongs is in the mirror (*Spiegel;* also the news magazine's name) and on the "telewiper"—which "wipes," presumably, according to the wishes of reigning prejudice.]

182. Schmitt, *Ex Captivitate Salus,* 76.

183. My thanks to Gerd Giesler for the information that Carl Schmitt was tormented by auditory hallucinations in his final years. Giesler mentions Ernst Hüsmert ("Die letzen Jahren von Carl Schmitt," in *Schmittiana,* ed. P. Tommissen [Brussels, 1988], 1:46), who reports Schmitt's experience: "Sound waves permeate the house from all sides. The emanations of all kinds of electrical appliances conduct voices of extreme clarity over hundreds of miles. Surveillance bugs were hidden all over the house."

184. Sombart, *Deutschen Männer.*

185. Benjamin, "Franz Kafka," 248 ff. I owe this reference to Carrie Asman, who uses the Pushkin anecdote to discuss the gestural in Kafka and Brecht: "Die Rückbindung des Zeichens an den Körper," presented at the International Walter-Benjamin-Kongreß, Osnabrück, June 1992.

186. Gross, "Carl Schmitts 'Nomos.'"

187. Carl Schmitt, *Gesetz und Urteil,* quoted in Gross, "Carl Schmitts 'Nomos.'"

188. This point is amply documented in ibid.

189. Quoted in Wolfgang Kersting, *Thomas Hobbes* (Hamburg, 1922), 75.

190. See Carl Schmitt, "Raum und Rom," *Universitas* 6, no. 1 (1951): 963–67. See also Ernst Jünger, "Lob der Vokale," in *Sämtliche Werke,* vol. 8 (Stuttgart, 1986).

191. Hugo Ball, *Die Flucht aus der Zeit* (Zurich, 1992), 100. My thanks to Mariusz Kieruij for this reference.

192. McLuhan, *Understanding Media,* 83.

193. Vilém Flusser, *Nachgeschichten,* ed. Volker Rapsch (Düsseldorf, 1990), 90 ff.

194. Max Horkheimer and Theodor W. Adorno, *Dialectik der Aufklärung* (Frankfurt am Main, 1971), 143.

195. Franz Kafka, "Betrachtungen über Sünde, Leid, Hoffnung und den wahren Weg," in *Franz Kafka* (Frankfurt am Main, 1965), 199.

196. Franz Kafka, *Das Schloß* (1926; Frankfurt am Main, 1992), 91.

197. Siegfried Kracauer, "Franz Kafka: Zu seinem nachgelassenen Schriften" (1931), in *Schriften,* vol. 5, bk. 2, 367.

CHAPTER FIVE

1. David Riesman's *Lonely Crowd* (New Haven, 1950) was published in a German edition in 1958. In the introduction to this edition, Helmut Schelsky shows how difficult it would be for German sociology to separate the "other-directed" type from the "collectivism" of the National Socialist regime, on the one hand, and the ideal type of the bourgeois, on the other: "We in Germany experience the materialism of a life devoted to enjoyment . . . as a setback over against the disappointed idealism of political engagement and as the consequence of a period of material want" (*Die einsame Masse: Eine Untersuchung des amerikanischen Charakters* [Reinbek, 1958], 13).

2. Riesman, *The Lonely Crowd,* 74.

3. Ibid., 250.

4. Siegfried Kracauer, "Der Sklarek-Prozeß," in *Aufsätze 1932–1935, Schriften,* ed. Inka Mülder-Bach, vol. 5, bk. 3 (Frankfurt am Main, 1990), 11–15.

5. Bertolt Brecht, *Gesammelte Werke,* 18:171 ff.

6. Siegfried Kracauer, "The Mass Ornament," in *The Mass Ornament: Weimar Essays,* trans. Thomas Y. Levin (Cambridge, Mass., 1995), 79.

7. Walter Benjamin, "The Work of Art in the Age of Mechanical Reproduction," in *Illuminations,* trans. Harry Zorn (New York, 1969), 238.

8. Ibid., 240.

9. Max Horkheimer and Theodor W. Adorno, *Dialectik der Aufklärung* (Frankfurt am Main, 1971), 220.

10. Ernst Jünger, *Der Arbeiter: Herrschaft und Gestalt,* 4th ed. (Hamburg, 1941), 267.

11. Quoted in Karin Hirdina, *Pathos der Sachlichkeit: Traditionen materialistischer Ästhetik* (Berlin, 1981), 49 ff.

12. Albert Sigrist [Albert Schwab], *Das Buch vom Bauen* (1930), 135; quoted in Hirdina, *Pathos der Sachlichkeit,* 50 ff.

13. Ibid.

14. Hannes Meyer, *Bauen und Gesellschaft: Schriften, Briefe, Prospekte* (Dresden, 1980), 52.

15. See the commentary on Tucholsky by Friedrich Rothe, in *Geschichte der deutschen Literatur,* ed. Saalfeldt, Kreidt, and Rothe (Munich, 1989), 576.

16. Riesman, *The Lonely Crowd,* 146.

17. See Ulrike Baureithel, "Reisende durch viele Leben: Wiederbegegnung mit Irmgard Keun," *Freitag,* 5 July 1991, 20.

18. See Heinz Dieter Kittsteiner, "Max Weber und die schöne neue Welt," in *Kultursoziologie—Symptom des Zeitgeistes?*, ed. Helmut Berking and Richard Farber (Würzburg, 1989), 116–39.

CHAPTER SIX

1. Karl Rahner and Herbert Vorgrimmler, *Kleines Theologisches Wörterbuch* (Freiburg, 1962), 215.
2. See Walter H. Sokel, *Der literarische Expressionismus* (Munich, n.d.), 73.
3. Leonhard Frank, *Die Räuberbande* (1914), 291; quoted in ibid., 84.
4. See Peter Sloterdijk, "Prothesen—vom Geist der Technik: Funktionalistische Zynismen II," in *Kritik der zynischen Vernunft* (Frankfurt am Main, 1983), 2:791–807.
5. Leonhard Frank, *Der Mensch ist gut* (Zurich, 1919), 182, 143.
6. Ibid., 153.
7. Ibid., 166.
8. Heinz-Dieter Kittsteiner and Helmut Lethen, "Ich-Losigkeit, Entbürgerlichung und Zeiterfahrung: Über die Gleichgültigkeit zur 'Geschichte' in Büchners *Woyzeck*," *Georg Büchner Jahrbuch* 3 (1983): 240–70.
9. Ludwig Turek, "Leben und Tod meines Bruders Rudolf," in *30 neue Erzähler des neuen Deutschlands,* ed. Wieland Herzfelde (Berlin, 1932), 17–28.
10. I am following here the commentary by Hans-Thies Lehmann, "Der Schrei der Hilfslosen," in *Bertolt Brechts "Hauspostille": Text und kollektives Lesen,* by Hans-Thies Lehmann and Helmut Lethen (Stuttgart, 1978), 74–99. The poem's English text comes from *Bertolt Brecht Poems, 1913–1956,* ed. John Willett and Ralph Manheim (New York, 1976), 89–92.
11. Arnold Zweig, *Der Streit um den Sergeanten Grischa* (Berlin, 1929). The commentary from Brecht is in *Gesammelte Werke,* 18:52–53.
12. See Helmut Lethen, "Zynismer der Avantgarde und Arnold Zweigs Roman *Der Streit um den Sergeanten Grischa,*" in *Arnold Zweig—Poetik, Judentum und Politik, Jahrbücher für internationale Germanistik,* ser. a, 25 (1989).
13. Walter Benjamin, *Der Ursprung des deutschen Trauerspiels* (Frankfurt am Main, 1963), 148.
14. Gert Mattenklott, "Ostjuden in Berlin," in *Reise nach Berlin* (Berlin, 1987), 210–16. Arthur Tilo Alt, "Zu Arnold Zweigs *Das ostjüdische Antlitz,* in *Arnold Zweig—Poetik, Judentum und Politik, Jahrbücher für internationale Germanistik,* ser. a, 25 (1989): 171–86.
15. Zweig, *Streit um den Sergeanten Grischa,* 527.
16. Arnold Gehlen, "Über die Geburt der Freiheit aus dem Geist der Entfremdung" (1952).
17. Zweig, *Streit um den Sergeanten Grischa,* 493.
18. Joseph Roth, "Bekenntnisse zum Gleisdreieck" (1924), reprinted in *Werke: Das journalistische Werk, 1924–1928,* ed. Klaus Westermann (Cologne, 1990), 2:218–21.
19. Siegfried Kracauer, *Aufsätze 1927–1931, Schriften,* ed. Inka Mülder-Bach, vol. 5, bk. 1 (Frankfurt am Main, 1990), 321 f.

20. Walter Benjamin, *Zur Kritik der Gewalt und andere Aufsätze* (Frankfurt am Main, 1965), 39, 56.

21. Sigmund Freud, *Group Psychology and the Analysis of the Ego,* trans. James Strachey (New York, 1960), 15.

22. Ernst Jünger, review of O. S., in *Der Scheinwerfer* 3 (1929): 29–30.

23. Arnold Bronnen, O. S. (Berlin, 1929), 311. [Translator's note: in this chapter's discussion, further references to O. S. will be by page number.]

24. I owe this thought to conversations with Heinz-Dieter Kittsteiner.

AFTERWORD

1. Léon Wurmser, *Die Maske der Scham* (1990); quoted in Hans-Thies Lehmann, "Das Welttheater der Scham: Dreißig Annäherungen an den Entzug der Darstellung," *Merkur* 45, no. 10 (October 1991): 825.

2. Hannah Arendt, *Elemente totaler Herrschaft* (Frankfurt am Main, 1958), 277.

3. Balthasar Gracián, *El Discreto,* quoted by Werner Krauss, *Graciáns Lebenslehre* (Frankfurt am Main, 1947), 149.

Index

Acoustic space, 176–78, 180, 181–83
Adler, Alfred, 162
Adorno, Theodor W., 21, 97, 163, 184, 190
Aesthetics: and anthropology, 59, 62–63; and architecture, 130; and Benjamin, 103–4; and body, 103–4; and cool persona, 107; and horror, 6; and irrationalism, 7; and Nietzsche, 62; and Plessner, 58–59, 62–63, 64, 103; and sudden transformation, 6–7
Alain (Émile-Auguste Chartier), 74
Alienation, 47, 56, 109, 215
Allegory, 87
Alter ego, 37
Anarchism, 50, 104, 198
Anders, Günther, 163
Angerstein, Fritz, 206–10
Animal behavior, 70, 71, 78, 81, 106, 109, 148, 195
Annales school, 2
Anthropology: and aesthetics, 59, 62–63, 64; and armoring, 65; and artificiality, 56, 61, 62–63, 64, 65; and conduct codes, 72, 81–82, 107; and cool persona, 72, 73, 107; and creature, 204–5; and dualism, 60; and expression, 75, 81–82; and Herder, 65; and natural drives, 48–51, 65, 70; and new objectivity, 73, 81–82; and perceptual acuity, 148; and pessimism, 63; and Plessner, 55–57, 59, 61–66, 72, 73, 88–89, 91, 92, 96, 107, 116, 158,

182, 205; and political relations, 88–89, 91, 92, 103, 111; and radar type, 73; and ridiculousness, 61–62; and Scheler, 72; and Schmitt, 172; and shame, 13, 15, 61–62; and sudden transformation, 4, 5
Anti-Semitism, 93, 171, 180, 182
Anxiety, 22, 25, 97, 103, 109, 193, 205
Apel, K. O., 51
Appearance, 40, 46, 123, 178
Architecture, 21–22, 54, 109, 128–31, 190, 191
Arendt, Hannah, 216
Armoring: and anthropology, 65; and coolness, 85, 95, 161; and cool persona, 46, 107, 161; and dignity, 59–60; and ego, 23, 36, 46, 50, 65, 122, 136, 145, 161–62, 195, 197; and fictional characters, 33, 139; and gaze, 157; and individuality, 62–63; and mobility, 30–31; and psychoanalysis, 161–62, 163; and subjectivity, 23, 107, 108, 131–32, 145, 188, 205
Arnheim, Rudolf, 135
Artificial groups, 5, 210
Artificiality, 53–67, 72, 73, 82, 83, 115, 123, 205, 214
Asman, Carrie, 87
Auerbach, Erich, 34, 65, 97, 222n16
Authenticity, 14, 37, 46, 46, 54, 57, 58, 63, 88, 115, 118, 123, 126–27, 195, 216
Authoritarianism, 50, 187, 194

Authority, 13, 15, 186
Autonomy: and cool persona, 47, 143; and ego, 39, 47, 118, 198, 206; and free will, 69; and persona, 39; and political relations, 40–41; and radar type, 187, 188, 194; and subjectivity, 156
Avant-garde: and armoring, 145; and cool persona, 145; and crystalline structure, 169, 170; and extremism, 102; and fictional characters, 33, 145; and forgetting, 141; and humanism, 97; and Lucifer, 90; and morality, 39, 147; and natural drives, 48–49, 51; and perceptual acuity, 147; and spatial relations, 8; and suddenness, 6–7; and traffic, 26, 28–29

Balázs, Béla, 16, 135
Ball, Hugo, 171, 183–84
Balzac, Honoré de, 112
Barbarism, 5, 8, 14, 17, 50, 71, 88, 97, 110, 129–30, 210
Bauereithel, Ulrike, 47
Bauhaus, 54, 109, 128–31
Beauty, 21
Bechterev, V. M., 74
Behavior: animal, 70, 71, 78, 81, 106, 109, 148, 195; civil, 14; and conduct codes, 17–18; cool, 10; and culture of shame, 16; Dionysian, 84; mass, 20; and natural drives, 71, 84; and new objectivity, 28; prebourgeois, 96; rational, 96; reflexive, 28, 51; and scientific research, 70–71, 74–75; and traffic, 27, 28–29; and visibility, 74
Behaviorism, 73, 75, 76, 87, 189, 196
Bell, Charles, 84
Benedict, Ruth, 13
Benjamin, Walter, 12, 44, 58, 73, 81, 87, 89, 90, 94, 126, 137, 148, 156, 172, 179, 190, 194, 210; and baroque tragedy, 49, 57, 103, 170, 173; and Brecht, 136, 201; and electromagnetic field, 163, 166
Benn, Gottfried, 105, 154–55, 172
Berlin, 21, 22, 28, 29, 163, 211
Birth trauma, 161
Bismarck, Otto von, 66, 104
Blei, Franz, 111–15, 133
Bloch, Ernst, 179
Bloch, Marc, 36, 139
Bloy, Léon, 174
Body: and aesthetics, 103–4; and amorphousness, 183; and artificiality, 61; and boundaries, 53, 58; and community, 53, 57–58; and coolness, 105, 164; and culture of shame, 16, 19–20;

and expression, 76, 77, 80, 83, 84, 87; and forgetting, 59, 103–4, 182; and mind-body dualism, 60, 70; and natural drives, 71; and reflexivity, 59; and typology, 154, 155
Bohrer, Karl Heinz, 7
Boundaries: and blurring, 107, 150; and body, 53, 58; and conceptual realism, 149, 155–56; and cool persona, 24–25; and ego, 59, 182; and fluidity, 101, 113, 150; and morality, 147; and new objectivity, 32; and Plessner, 53, 57–58, 59, 62, 64, 91, 93, 103; and political relations, 41; and self, 57, 103, 137, 143; and shame, 62
Bourdieu, Pierre, 16
Bourgeoisie: and conduct codes, 138–39; and cool persona, 107; and creature, 200–201, 206; and cultural gradation, 101; and inner-directed type, 188, 189, 214; and interiority, 37; and liberalism, 112; and modernity, 5, 8; and morality, 148; and public sphere, 61; and Tallyrand, 112, 113
Braudel, Fernand, 8
Brecht, Bertolt, 28, 33, 37, 47, 58, 64, 73, 85, 88, 108–9, 127–32, 145, 147, 148, 149, 158, 164, 172, 230n63; and conduct codes, 127–28, 131–32, 133–42, 215, 231n76; and coolness, 130, 131, 145; and cool persona, 131–32, 132, 145; and creature, 198–201; and new objectivity, 128, 134, 145, 215–16; poetry of, 11–12, 17, 31–32, 38, 48, 73, 108, 133–42, 198–200; and radar type, 108, 190; theater of, 15, 17, 51, 87, 131
Bronnen, Arnold, 28, 30, 64, 109, 210–14
Büchner, Georg, 103, 202
Bühler, Karl, 75–80, 86, 88, 105–6
Buono, Franco, 136
Buytendijk, F. J. J., 83

Canetti, Elias, 19–20
Capitalism, 23, 50
Catholicism, 91, 106, 174, 195
Chaos, 21–22, 50, 128, 130, 131
Chaplin, Charles, 146
Characters, fictional: and armoring, 33, 139; and cool persona, 102, 103, 106, 143, 145; and eccentricity, 74, 116; and gender, 73–74; and masking, 116; and mobility, 33, 142; new objectivity, 111, 141, 145; and psychology, 33; and radar type, 192–93; subcomplex, 33, 70
Character type. See Typology
Christianity, 38, 197

Cinema. *See* Film
Circulation: of commodities, 30; and conduct codes, 26, 32; frenzy of, 30, 32; of traffic, 26–28, 29–30
Civil behavior, 14, 15
Civilization: and anxiety, 97; and barbarism, 97, 210; and conscience, 13; distinguished from community, 52–53, 73, 110; distinguished from culture, 14; and fragmentation, 53
Classification mania, 22–23
Class struggle, 69–70, 73. *See also* Social class
Cold War, 171, 178
Comedy, 65, 65, 122–23, 125–26, 126–27, 131, 145–46
Commodity, 88, 110, 111, 175, 193
Communism, 42, 44, 73, 106, 131, 132, 136, 159
Communitarianism, 53, 54, 94, 95
Community, 46, 47, 52–53, 72–73, 82, 92, 95, 110, 141, 143, 211
Conceptual realism, 148–53, 155, 180, 181
Conduct codes: and anthropology, 72, 82, 107; and artificiality, 61, 73; and Blei, 112–13; and body, 164; and Brecht, 127–28, 132, 133–42, 215, 231n76; and Bronnen, 213; and circulation, 26, 32; and Communism, 132; and confidence man, 115; and coolness, 101, 145; and cool persona, 107, 118, 120, 157, 195, 215; courtly, 37, 40–41, 96, 97, 115, 123; and distance, 107, 113, 143, 164; and Döblin, 42; and ego, 18, 37; and gender, 82–83, 138, 142–43; and Gracián, 34–38, 40, 44, 46, 46, 67, 98–100, 112, 120, 136, 137, 173, 175, 216; and heroism, 96; and Hobbes, 50–51; and identity, 95; and Jünger, 157, 163–64; and Krauss, 34–38, 40, 44, 46, 46; and masculinity, 83; and masking, 164; and modernism, 50; and modernization, 96; and morality, 63, 136; and new objectivity, 18, 42, 44, 51, 134, 138–39, 163–64; and objectivity, 17–19; and Plessner, 54, 55–56, 61, 63, 65, 66, 67, 73, 81–82, 83, 88, 95, 96, 107, 113, 158; and power, 95, 96; and radar type, 96; and Scheler, 72; and Schmitt, 175–76; and Serner, 115, 118, 120–21, 122, 123, 125; and shame, 17–18; and subjectivity, 36–37; and Tallyrand, 112–13; and Weber, 42–44
Confidence man, 17, 115–16, 120, 122, 125, 135

Conscience, 4–5, 11–13, 15, 37, 38, 44, 113, 122, 132, 175, 214, 215
Constructivism, 54, 156
Consumerism, 132, 188, 189, 190, 193–94
Contours, 31, 101, 150, 151, 153, 159, 160, 168, 190
Contradiction, 57
Coolness: and architecture, 130; and armoring, 85, 95, 161; and authenticity, 123; and body, 105, 164; and Brecht, 130, 131, 145; and community, 53; and conduct codes, 101, 145; critique of, 46–48; and culture, 6, 131; and distinction, 46; and family relations, 73; and Fleißer, 143, 145; and gaze, 105–6, 148, 151, 158, 196; and gender, 142–43, 143–44; and Jünger, 147, 158, 164; and military, 6, 131–32; and mobility, 101; and morality, 147; and paternal law, 140; and perceptual acuity, 148; and Plessner, 53, 54, 55; and romanticism, 123; and science, 147; and Serner, 123, 124
Cool persona: and aesthetics, 107; and anthropology, 72, 73; and anxiety, 25; and armoring, 46, 107, 161; and artificiality, 214; and autonomy, 47, 143; and Blei, 115; and boundaries, 24; and Brecht, 132, 133, 145; and comedy, 65; and Communism, 132; and conduct codes, 107, 118, 120, 157, 195, 215; and confidence man, 115; and conscience, 44; and creature, 172, 195; critique of, 46–48, 107; and dandy, 117–18; and economic relations, 107; and electric media, 167–68; and fate, 20; and fathers, 102; and fictional characters, 102, 103, 106, 143, 145; and Fleißer, 143, 145; and gender, 46, 47, 142–43; and Gracián, 44, 56; and heroism, 107; and Jünger, 66, 107, 132, 145, 147, 148, 152–53, 157, 160, 163, 167–68, 213; and Lucifer, 170, 171; and Marxism, 107; and masking, 195; and military, 106, 131–32; and mobility, 44; and moderation, 100; and morality, 44; and neurosis, 47, 48; and new objectivity, 72–73, 104, 118, 142, 145; and perceptual acuity, 147, 148, 150, 157; and photography, 148, 152–53; and Plessner, 72, 107, 145, 182; and polarization, 24; and proletariat, 198; and psychoanalysis, 47, 120, 161–62; and psychology, 44, 46, 47, 214; and radar type, 188; and Rousseau, 46; and Schmitt, 115, 145, 171, 172, 173; and

Cool persona (*continued*)
  self-portraits, 104, 106; and Serner,
  115, 117, 118, 120, 145; and social
  class, 107; and sovereignty, 103, 104;
  and totalitarianism, 216; and Weber,
  43
Courtly codes, 37, 40–41, 96, 97, 115,
  123
Creativity, 57
Creature, 20, 25, 61, 64, 73, 85, 103,
  107, 108, 132; and anarchism, 198;
  and animal behavior research, 195;
  and anthropology, 204–5; and artificiality, 214; and authenticity, 195; and
  Brecht, 198–201; and Bronnen, 213;
  and cool persona, 172, 195; and disgrace, 197, 205; and expression of
  pain, 196, 197; and Kracauer, 206–
  10; and legal relations, 198, 200–201,
  206–10; and magic, 198; and masking, 195, 197, 209; and new objectivity, 196, 197, 198, 205, 206; and psychoanalysis, 195, 209; and radar type,
  195; and shame, 195; and theology,
  195–96, 198, 200–201; and Zweig,
  198, 201–3
Crowds, 10, 19, 21, 23
Crystalline structure, 169–70
Culture: and artificiality, 56; and coolness, 6, 131–32; and counterculture,
  216; and culture industry, 163, 190; of
  guilt, 8, 11–15, 17, 118, 172, 173–74;
  of shame, 8, 12–17, 18, 19–20, 67,
  103, 118, 173, 216
Curtius, E. R., 172
Cynicism, 31, 52, 111, 114, 123, 124,
  125, 188, 192

Dadaism, 11, 31, 65, 109, 117, 120,
  122, 124, 156
Dandy, 62, 117–18, 132, 142, 148, 156,
  206
Darwin, Charles, 83
Darwinism, 105
Däubler, Theodor, 93, 171
Decadence, 71, 72, 110
Decentering, 23, 145
Decisionism, 92, 94–95, 96, 103, 104,
  113, 143, 145, 154, 183
Deconstruction, 136, 183
Democracy, 66, 187
Denazification, 173
Desublimation, 110, 111
Dialectical image, 23
Dialectics, 22, 49, 111, 181
Dignity, 15, 59–60, 61
Dilthey, Wilhelm, 93

Diogenes of Sinope, 47–48, 82
Dionysian quality, 84, 130, 135
Disenchantment, 42, 109, 110, 198
Disgrace, 8–10, 65, 117, 161, 174, 197,
  205
Disillusionment, 44, 52, 79, 124
Disraeli, Benjamin, 114
Dissimulation, 51, 118, 123, 137
Distance, 47, 52, 54, 55, 56, 57–58, 58,
  62, 65, 66, 81, 96, 122; and conduct
  codes, 107, 113, 143, 164
Distinction, 37, 46, 107, 168, 215
Distraction, 190
Dix, Otto, 105
Döblin, Alfred, 42, 69–70, 71, 198
Donne, John, 67
Dostoyevsky, F. M., 93
Drives, 47, 48–49, 51, 59, 65, 70, 71,
  82, 84, 97
Dualism, 60, 70, 82, 83, 159

Eccentricity, 59, 72, 73, 74, 91, 116
Economic relations: and Blei's work, 113;
  and cool persona, 107; and free will,
  69–70; and liberalism, 91; and psychology, 70; and radar type, 189
Ego: and alter ego, 37; and armoring, 23,
  36, 46, 50, 65, 122, 136, 145, 161–
  62, 195, 197; and autonomy, 39, 47,
  118, 198, 206; and boundaries, 59,
  182; and conduct codes, 18, 37; and
  culture of guilt, 13; and illusion, 38;
  and persona, 38–40, 206; and sudden
  transformation, 6
Electric field, 70, 163, 165, 166–68
Elias, Norbert, 5, 47, 96–97
Enemy. *See* Friend-enemy relation
Engel, Johann Jakob, 76
Engels, Erich, 58
Epic theater, 15, 87
Essentialism, 53
Ethics: and relativism, 44, 112; and science, 44, 51; of Spinoza, 84; and truth,
  112
Ethnology, 13, 32, 155
Evil, 84, 90, 91, 114, 148, 156, 170,
  171, 172
Exceptional circumstances, 4
Exchange cynicism, 31
Exposure, 59–62, 63, 63
Expression, 74–88, 118–19, 158–59,
  196, 197; Bühler's theory of, 75–80,
  88, 105–6; Darwin's theory of, 83,
  105; Klages's theory of, 76–79, 83, 88;
  Plessner's theory of, 61, 63, 75, 78,
  81–85, 87, 88; Scheler's theory of, 83,
  85

Expressionism, 24, 48, 50, 54, 60, 81, 86, 122; compared to new objectivity, 4, 17, 31, 44, 46, 138–39, 140, 141, 196, 197
Exteriority, 15, 33

Family relations, 73, 121, 139–41, 206
Farce, 2, 7, 9
Fascism, 10, 94, 110, 168, 187
Fate, 20, 42, 69
Fathers, 47, 68–69, 102, 104, 139–42, 161, 176, 186, 216
Femininity, 46, 47, 66–67, 73–74, 142–45
Feminism, 46, 68, 73
Fetishism, 69, 145, 171
Film, 16, 32, 74, 75, 79, 126, 190, 192
Fleißer, Marieluise, 28, 74, 142–45
Flusser, Vilém, 152–53, 184
Force field, 24, 163, 166–67
Fordism, 26
Forgetting, 59, 103–4, 136, 139, 182
Fouché, Joseph, 114–15
Frank, Leonhard, 48, 197
Freedom, 57, 58, 63
Free will, 69
French moralists, 98–99, 112
Freud, Sigmund, 5, 13, 47, 48, 60, 66, 70, 93, 104, 162, 187, 209, 210
Friend-enemy relation, 91, 92, 93, 102, 176, 213
Fromm, Erich, 194
Functionalism, 26, 28, 48, 87–88, 128, 130
Fusion, 101–2, 107
Futurism, 6, 16, 211

Game playing, 55, 63
Gay, Peter, 68
Gaze: and armoring, 157; cool, 105–6, 148, 150, 158, 196; functionalist, 28, 87; and guilt, 11, 13; and objectivity, 63; and perceptual acuity, 147, 148, 163; public, 85, 209; and shame, 9; supervisory, 18
Gehlen, Arnold, 56, 65, 75, 170, 202–3, 214
Geiger, Theodor, 53, 132
Geitner, Ursula, 154
Gender: and conduct codes, 83, 138, 142–43; and cool persona, 46, 47, 143; and Fleißer's work, 142–45; and Gracián's work, 46, 99; and new objectivity, 73–74, 216; and Plessner's work, 66–67, 82–83; and radar type, 193
Gesture: Bühler's theory of, 75, 76, 79–80; and culture of shame, 16, 20; and

epic theater, 87; and mass psychology, 10, 79; and traffic, 27–28, 75
Giesler, Gerd, 235n183
Goebbels, Joseph, 211
Goethe, Johann Wolfgang von, 76, 234n172
Goffman, Erving, 16, 118, 125
Goodness, 48, 50, 50, 91, 97, 100, 111–12
Gracián, Balthasar, 33–41, 44–45, 113, 115, 117, 133, 138, 139, 141, 215; and concept of persona, 37–41, 46, 99, 135; and conduct codes, 34–38, 40, 44, 46, 67, 98–100, 112, 120, 136, 137, 173, 175, 216
Gross, Raphael, 93, 180
Grosz, George, 48, 105, 140
Guilt: culture of, 8, 11–15, 17, 118, 172, 173–74

Hausmann, Raoul, 117
Hedonism, 189, 192
Hegel, G. W. F., 4, 181
Heidegger, Martin, 40, 58, 89, 94–95, 135, 139, 185
Heinrich, Klaus, 31
Heller, Agnes, 118
Herder, Johann Gottfried, 65
Heroism, 16–17, 20, 41, 54, 65, 96, 107, 146, 160, 162, 163
Hirschfeld, Magnus, 65
Historicism, 93, 97
History: and anxiety, 22; and artificiality, 56; and crystalline structure, 170; and dialectics, 22; and historical moment, 3–4; philosophy of, 41, 98; and suddenness, 2–4, 7–8
Hitler, Adolf, 177, 182
Hobbes, Thomas, 50, 51, 52, 91, 111, 170, 171, 175, 180
Hofmannsthal, Hugo von, 6, 65
Horkheimer, Max, 97, 163, 184, 190
Horror literature, 6
Horváth, Ödön von, 28, 110–11
Humanism, 50, 51, 54, 72, 97–98, 158, 171, 215, 222n16
Huxley, Aldous, 64
Hygiene, 54, 54, 82, 128, 129

Id, 33, 161
Idealism, 59
Identity: and anxiety, 103; and conduct codes, 95; and persona, 37; racial, 93; and self-knowledge, 39; and visibility, 74
Immediacy, 62, 63, 69, 82, 86
Impotence, 45, 52, 58, 61, 64, 81, 109

Impressionism, 151, 156
Indifference, 117
Individuality: and armoring, 63; and
    community, 53; and decisionism, 94–
    95; and distance, 55–56; and masking,
    62–63; and mass behavior, 20; and
    modernization, 15; and morality, 39;
    and new objectivity, 23, 24, 32; and
    polarization, 24, 24; and reflexivity,
    58, 59; and social roles, 55; and sover-
    eignty, 103; and sudden transforma-
    tion, 4–5; and technical reproduction,
    23
Individuation, 37, 210
Industrial design, 130
Industrialism, 50, 54
Inferiority complex, 162
Inner-directed type, 187–89, 214
Institutions, 18, 44, 57, 62, 91, 96, 102,
    188, 202–3, 215
Interiority, 14, 37, 58, 75, 123, 124
Intersubjectivity, 26, 62, 83, 88
Intimacy, 54–55, 55, 62, 96, 154
Irony, 137, 139
Irrationalism, 7, 45
Isherwood, Christopher, 111

Jaspers, Karl, 10, 16, 79, 174, 235n181
Jesuitism, 34, 37, 38, 41, 45, 173
Jhering, Herbert, 58
Jugendstil, 110
Jünger, Ernst, 6, 48, 49, 80, 81, 94, 95,
    98, 109, 114, 132, 133, 147–70, 172,
    176, 181, 210, 211; and armoring,
    157, 161–63; and Bronnen, 210, 211,
    213; and conceptual realism, 149, 153,
    155–56; and conduct codes, 157,
    163–64; and coolness, 148, 158, 164;
    and cool persona, 65, 107, 131–32,
    145, 147, 148, 152, 157, 160, 163,
    167–68, 213; and crystalline structure,
    169–70; and electric media, 165, 166–
    69; and expression of pain, 158–59;
    and magic, 156; and masking, 161,
    164; and mobility, 155; and perceptual
    acuity, 147, 150, 157, 163; and pho-
    tography, 148, 150–53; and traffic,
    155, 165; and typology, 152, 153–56,
    158, 159

Kafka, Franz, 104, 173, 184–86
Kallai, Ernö, 54, 58
Kantorowicz, Ernst, 97
Kästner, Erich, 28, 192–93
Keaton, Buster, 117
Kessel, Martin, 192
Keun, Irmgard, 188, 193
Kierkegaard, Søren, 44, 58, 90

Kitsch, 61
Klages, Ludwig, 71, 76–79, 83, 88
Kracauer, Siegfried, 21–22, 27, 30, 52,
    58, 88, 145–47, 148, 153, 186, 206–
    10
Kramme, Rüdiger, 226n119
Krauss, Werner, 33–42, 44–45, 46, 97–
    98, 120, 215
Kretschmer, Ernst, 153–54
Krockow, Christian Graf von, 94

Lavater, Johann Kaspar, 76
Law, 44, 93, 178, 180, 181, 185–86,
    198, 200–201, 206, 210; and legal
    positivism, 104, 180, 186. See also
    Paternal law
Le Bon, Gustave, 10, 44
Lehmann, Hans-Thies, 140
Leibniz, Gottfried Wilhelm, 234n172
Lenin, V. I., 90, 172
Leninism, 132
Leonhard, Rudolf, 86
Lersch, Philipp, 80, 105–6
Lessing, Theodor, 53, 116
Liberalism, 50, 89, 91, 112, 151
Lichtenberg, Georg Christoph, 76
Lindner, Martin, 154, 220n4
Locke, John, 50
Loos, Adolf, 230n63
Löwith, Karl, 39, 40
Loyola, Ignatius of, 115
Lubitsch, Ernst, 126–27
Lucifer, 90, 170, 171
Lukács, Georg, 30, 172
Lumpen proletariat, 159–60, 197
Luther, Martin, 89
Lutheranism, 45

Machiavellianism, 94, 111, 112
Magic, 156, 198
Magnetic field, 24
Malinowski, Bronislaw, 32, 154
Mandelstam, Osip, 147
Mann, Thomas, 6, 14, 58, 72, 102
Mannheim, Karl, 43, 58
Manthey, Jürgen, 140, 177
Market relations, 8, 23, 40, 50, 88, 187
Marx, Karl, 3, 7, 44, 167, 234n172
Marxism: and cool persona, 107; and
    fetishism, 69; and Gracián's work, 38;
    and idealism, 71; and masking, 71,
    135; and modernization, 167; and
    traffic paradigm, 29
Masculinity, 46, 47, 60, 73, 74, 83, 99,
    213
Masking, 39, 45, 60, 62–63, 67, 71, 80,
    116, 117, 127, 135, 161, 164, 195,
    197, 209

Masses: amorphousness of, 159, 160;
  and culture of shame, 19–20; distrac-
  tion of, 190; and gesture, 10, 16, 20,
  79; and political relations, 10, 41; psy-
  chology of, 10, 20; and sudden trans-
  formation, 5; and theatrics of disgrace,
  9, 10
Mass society, 16, 187
Master-slave dialectic, 4, 181
Materialism, 69, 71
Maternal relations. See Mothers
Mauss, Marcel, 38–40
McLuhan, Marshall, 169, 184
Mead, George Herbert, 16, 37
Mead, Margaret, 13
Meaninglessness, 42, 168, 169
Media, 32, 63, 86, 88, 120, 121, 148,
  165–69, 184, 211; and radar type, 73,
  188, 189, 190, 191, 192, 193, 195
Mehring, Walter, 192
Melville, Herman, 186
Meyer, Hannes, 28
Middle Ages, 5
Middle class, 190
Milch, Thomas, 124, 126
Military: and Bronnen, 210; and comedy,
  65, 145; and coolness, 6, 131–32; and
  cool persona, 106, 131–32; and de-
  structive instincts, 210; and Jünger,
  159–60, 161; and militarization, 26,
  30, 40; and new objectivity, 131–32;
  and radar type, 132; and sudden transformation, 5–6, 132; and traffic, 26,
  30–31
Mind: and mind-body dualism, 60, 70,
  82; and natural drives, 72
Mobility: and Brecht, 133–34; and coolness, 101; and cool persona, 44; and
  femininity, 142; and fictional characters, 33, 142; and Gracián, 37; and
  Jünger, 155; and Krauss, 37; and military, 131–32; and new objectivity,
  131–32, 212; and persona, 37; and
  radar type, 188, 193; and reason, 51;
  and science, 51; and subjectivity, 51,
  88; and traffic, 26–31, 155
Moderation, 97–98, 99
Modernism, 50, 102, 131, 145, 163, 168
Modernity, 5, 8, 62
Modernization, 7, 15, 25, 30, 63, 70, 72,
  109, 163, 167, 169
Moholy-Nagy, László, 191
Molière, 65–66
Morality: and boundaries, 147; and
  Communism, 132; and conduct codes,
  63, 136; and coolness, 147; and cool
  persona, 44; and culture of guilt, 11,
  13; and Gracián, 34, 38; and individu-

ality, 39; and Krauss, 34, 38; and natural drives, 48–49, 50; and objectivity,
  27; and perceptual acuity, 147, 157;
  and Plessner, 63; and political relations,
  112; and radar type, 188, 193; and
  traffic, 27. See also French moralists
Moses, 104
Mothers, 67, 73–74, 102, 141, 186,
  215–16
Mülder-Bach, Inka, 23, 146, 147
Müller, Heiner, 157
Musil, Robert, 6, 48, 102, 145, 149,
  155, 162, 168, 198

Narcissism, 46, 59–60, 145
Naturalness, 66
Nazism, 34, 41–42, 46, 102, 126, 159,
  182, 193, 236n1
Neckel, Sighard, 125
Negation, 44, 49, 50, 65, 72, 91, 102,
  108, 135, 147, 190, 216
Neurosis, 47, 48, 60, 161–62
Neutrality, 55, 75, 87, 90, 136
New objectivity: and anthropology, 73,
  81–82; and architecture, 54, 191; and
  artificiality, 63, 72, 73; and boundaries, 32; and Brecht, 127–28, 134,
  145, 215–16; and Bronnen, 212; and
  capitalism, 23; and civilization, 72–
  73; and community, 58; and conduct
  codes, 18, 36, 42, 44, 51, 73, 134,
  138–39, 163–64; and cool persona,
  73, 104, 118, 143, 145; and creature,
  196, 197, 198, 205, 206; critique of,
  73–74; and dandy, 132; and decadence, 110–11; and design, 54, 128,
  191; and desublimation, 110–11; and
  disenchantment, 109–11; and disillusionment, 43; and distance, 57–58;
  and expressionism, 4, 17, 31, 44, 46,
  138–39, 140, 141, 196; and expression of pain, 85–86; and family relations, 73–74, 206; and fathers, 68–69,
  73–74; and feminism, 73; and fictional
  characters, 111, 142, 145; and Fleißer,
  74, 142, 143; and functionalism, 87–
  88; and gender, 73–74, 111, 142, 143,
  216; and goodness, 48; and guilt, 12,
  17; and individuality, 23, 25, 32; and
  Jünger, 147, 160–61, 163–64; and
  Kracauer, 145; and Krauss, 36, 39, 40;
  and military, 131–32; and mobility,
  131–32, 212; and modernization, 63,
  109, 110; and mothers, 215–16; and
  painting, 31, 140, 161; and perceptual
  acuity, 147; and Plessner, 66–67, 68,
  72, 73; and polarization, 23, 24,
  220n4; and portraiture, 31, 140; and

New objectivity (*continued*)
  psychoanalysis, 70; and radar type, 73,
  187, 189, 191, 192; and reification,
  88; and ridiculousness, 65; and
  Schmitt, 172, 175; and sentimentality,
  65; and Serner, 117, 133; and shame,
  17; and subjectivity, 88; and traffic, 28,
  29–30; and turn from culture to civilization, 14; and vitalism, 220n4; and
  Weber, 44; and women, 73–74, 111,
  138, 141–45, 216
Nietzsche, Friedrich, 7, 12, 36, 44, 85,
  90, 94, 117, 123, 139, 183, 189; and
  aesthetics, 62–63; and barbarism, 17,
  71; and Dionysian quality, 84, 135;
  and North Pole explorer, 43, 104; and
  Plessner, 56, 62–63, 82
Nihilism, 49, 152
Nuremberg trials, 173

Objectivity: and authenticity, 58; and
  conduct codes, 17–19; critique of, 47;
  and fetishism, 145; and gaze, 64; and
  Gracián, 36; and Kracauer, 206; and
  Krauss, 40; and morality, 27; and paternal law, 186; and Plessner, 56, 58;
  and Schmitt, 186; and social roles,
  206; and traffic, 26, 27, 29–30; and
  virility, 73; and Weber, 44. *See also*
  New objectivity
One-dimensionality, 187, 190
Origin, 46, 101, 102, 141
Other, 18, 37, 39, 74, 93, 120, 143, 214,
  236n1; and radar type, 25, 187–88,
  193
Otherness, 20, 58, 91, 102, 158

Pain, expression of, 85–88, 158–59, 197
Painting, 31, 140, 161, 234n147
Paradox, 108, 111, 137, 139, 141, 145
Parody, 31, 139
Paternal law, 140–41, 186
Patriarchy, 47, 59, 68, 186. *See also*
  Fathers
Paul, Saint, 4
Pavlov, Ivan, 74, 78, 79
Perceptual acuity, 147–50, 157, 163
Persona: Gracián's concept of, 37–41,
  46, 99, 135; Plessner's concept of, 59,
  61, 65–66. *See also* Cool persona
Pessimism, 64
Petit bourgeoisie, 114, 206, 207
Phenomenology, 62, 149, 150
Photograms, 80–81
Photography, 23, 86, 88, 148, 150–53,
  155–56, 234n147
Pietism, 5

Pietzcker, Carl, 47
Pleasure principle, 84
Plessner, Helmut, 11, 26, 32, 37, 40, 48,
  52–67, 71, 122, 125, 129, 133, 135,
  143, 161, 163; and anthropology, 20,
  56–57, 58–59, 61–65, 72, 73, 88–89,
  91, 92, 96, 107, 116, 158, 182; and
  boundaries, 53, 58, 59, 62, 63, 91, 93,
  103; and conduct codes, 53, 56, 61,
  63, 65, 66, 67, 73, 81–82, 83, 88, 95,
  96, 107, 113, 158; and cool persona,
  72, 107, 145, 182; and decisionism,
  92, 94–95, 96, 103, 104, 113, 143,
  145, 154, 183; and political relations,
  59, 61, 88–94, 114; and ridiculousness, 59–62, 63, 66, 81–82, 84, 107,
  121–22; and Schmitt, 88–95, 96, 103,
  104, 172, 182–83, 226n119; and sovereignty, 59, 73, 103, 104; and theory
  of expression, 61, 64, 75, 77, 78, 81–
  85, 87, 88
Poetry: of Brecht, 11–12, 31–32, 38, 48,
  73, 133–42, 198–200; of Kästner, 192
Polarization, 13–14, 22–26, 30, 46, 56–
  57, 59, 101, 102, 130, 216, 220n4
Political parties, 41, 44, 106–7
Political relations: and aestheticization,
  94; and anthropology, 88–89, 91, 92,
  103, 111; and autonomy, 40–41; and
  Blei, 111–15; and boundaries, 41; and
  Christianity, 38; and decisionism, 92,
  94–95, 96, 103, 104, 113; and free
  will, 69; and friend-enemy relation, 91,
  92, 93, 102, 143; and goodness, 50;
  and Gracián, 38, 40–41; and heroism,
  41; and Krauss, 38, 40–41; and
  masses, 10, 41; and morality, 112; and
  natural drives, 48–49; and Plessner,
  59, 61, 88–94, 114; and polarization,
  101, 102; and racial identity, 93–94;
  and radar type, 189; and romanticism,
  113, 141, 186; and Schmitt, 89–94,
  102, 111, 112, 113, 143–44, 170; and
  separation, 101–2; and typology, 155;
  and Weber, 44
Portraiture, 31, 106, 107, 140
Positivism, 70; legal, 104, 180, 186
Postmodernism, 131, 187
Potemkin, Grigory Aleksandrovich, 179,
  180
Pound, Ezra, 26
Power, and conduct codes, 95, 96
Pragmatism, 51
Prebourgeois subject, 6, 96, 131, 197
Print medium, 32
Private property, 30
Private sphere, 56, 58, 67

Progress, 26, 110
Projection, 8, 13, 15
Proletarian literature, 6, 110, 132, 198
Proletariat, 4, 73, 109, 160, 193
Protestantism, 37, 96, 173, 174, 187
Psychoanalysis: and armoring, 161–62, 163; and cool persona, 47, 120, 161–62; and creature, 195, 209; and culture of guilt, 13; and exteriority, 33; and natural drives, 70; and new objectivity, 70–71; and shame, 66; and sudden transformation, 6
Psychology: and artificiality, 57; and behavior research, 70–72, 74–75; and cool persona, 44, 46, 47, 214; and culture of guilt, 12–13; and economic relations, 70–71; and expression, 75, 76–77, 80–83, 88, 105–6; and fictional characters, 33; mass, 10, 20; and natural drives, 48–51, 70, 72; and radar type, 193, 214; subcomplex, 33, 70; and sudden transformation, 4–5; and typology, 154; and visibility, 31, 32
Public sphere, 56, 57, 58, 59, 61, 62–63, 67–68, 82, 88, 174

Quintilian, 75, 81

Racial identity, 93
Radar type: and anthropology, 72; and architecture, 191; and artificiality, 214; and autonomy, 187, 188, 194; and Brecht, 108, 190; and conduct codes, 96; and conformity, 188, 190; and consumerism, 188, 189, 190, 192–93; and cool persona, 188; and creature, 195; and cynicism, 188, 192; and economic relations, 189; and fictional characters, 192–93; and gender, 193; and hedonism, 189, 192; and media, 73, 188, 189, 190, 191, 192, 193, 195; and military, 131–32; and mobility, 188, 193; and morality, 188, 193; and new objectivity, 73, 187, 189, 191, 192, 193; and other, 25, 187–88, 193; and political relations, 189; and psychology, 193, 214; and Riesman, 25, 187–88, 193, 194; and sentimentality, 188, 193; and sociology, 187, 193–94
Räderscheidt, Anton, 140
Radicalism, 44, 52, 53, 94
Radio, 86, 184, 190
Rank, Otto, 47, 161
Rathenau, Walther, 30
Rational behavior, 96
Realism, 43, 79, 91; conceptual, 148–53, 155, 180, 181; heroic, 160, 163

Reality principle, 7
Reason: and mobility, 51; and sublimation, 84
Rebellion, 3, 4, 7
Reflexivity, 28–29, 51, 58, 59, 61, 103, 182
Reflexology, 74, 78–79, 213
Reich, Wilhelm, 161–62
Reification, 57, 88
Relativism, 43, 93, 102, 112
Richter, Hans, 124
Ridiculousness, 59–62, 63, 66, 81, 84, 107, 121–22, 127, 161
Riesman, David, 5, 16, 25–26, 97, 187–88, 193, 194, 236n1
Rohrwasser, Michael, 47
Roles. See Social roles
Romanticism, 113, 123, 141, 148, 186
Roth, Joseph, 109, 132, 164, 198
Rousseau, Jean-Jacques, 46
Russell, Bertrand, 111

Salvation, 45–46, 89, 90
Sander, August, 155
Schad, Christian, 140
Scheler, Max, 22, 40, 48, 57, 71–72, 82, 83, 85, 89, 110
Schelsky, Helmut, 236n1
Schematicism, 22–23, 30, 31, 123
Schmitt, Carl, 4, 29, 40, 45, 47, 48, 49, 50, 66, 122, 149, 171–86; and acoustic space, 176–78, 180, 181–83, 235n183; and Blei, 111–15; and conceptual realism, 180, 181; and conduct codes, 175–76; and cool persona, 115, 145, 171, 172, 173; diary of, 171–84; and friend-enemy relation, 91, 92, 93, 102, 143, 150, 176, 213; and Hobbes, 170, 171, 175–76, 180; and Jünger, 176, 181; and Kafka, 104, 173, 184–86; and Plessner, 88–95, 96, 103, 104, 172, 182–83, 226n119; and political relations, 88–94, 102, 111, 112, 113, 143–44, 170; and sovereignty, 103, 104
Schopenhauer, Arthur, 55, 90, 152
Schütz, Alfred, 150
Schuur, Koos, 231n76
Science: and behavioral research, 70–72, 74–75, 76; and coolness, 147; and ethics, 44, 51; and expression, 75, 76–77, 80–81, 83; and free will, 69; and mobility, 51; and perceptual acuity, 147; and relativism, 43
Seifert, Franz W., 156
Self: and armoring, 63; and boundaries, 57, 103, 137, 143; and conduct codes,

Self (*continued*)
18; construction of, 15; and modern-
ization, 15
Self-control, 5
Self-defense, 46
Self-direction, 5, 6, 18
Self-empowerment, 136, 138
Self-knowledge, 37, 39, 122
Self-portraits, 104, 106, 173
Self-representation, 40
Self-revelation, 55
Sennett, Richard, 55
Sentimentality, 65, 158, 188, 193
Separation, 25, 53, 101–2, 121, 134,
137, 138, 141, 143
Serner, Walter, 11, 17, 81, 95, 115–26,
133, 135, 137, 157; and cool persona,
115, 117, 118, 120, 145
Sexuality, 193
Shame: and anthropology, 61–62; and
boundaries, 62; and conduct codes,
17–18; and creature, 195; culture of,
8, 12–17, 18, 19–20, 67, 103, 118,
173, 174, 216; and dadaism, 117; and
narcissism, 59–60; and public sphere,
61, 67–69; and self-exposure, 59–62,
63; and sociology, 8–10, 16; theater
of, 8–10, 62, 67
Simmel, Georg, 54, 56–57, 194
Sincerity, 54, 55, 55
Sloterdijk, Peter, 31, 47, 52
Social change, 22–23
Social class, 5, 6, 31, 88, 107
Social Democratic party, 111, 132
Social rank, 31
Social roles, 55, 62–63, 161, 206
Society: distinguished from community,
52–53; mass, 16, 187; and neutrality,
55; and separation, 53
Sociology: and community, 52–53; and
consumerism, 132; and masking, 62–
63; and Plessner, 62; and radar type,
187, 193–94; and roles, 62–63; and
Sennett, 55; and shame, 8–10, 16; and
Simmel, 54; and typology, 187, 214,
236n1
Sombart, Nicolaus, 47, 178
Sorel, Georges, 44, 90
Sovereignty, 59, 74, 103, 104, 137
Soviet Union, 74, 78
Space: acoustic, 176–78, 180, 181–83;
and market relations, 8; multinational,
7; and perceptual acuity, 149
Spengler, Oswald, 66, 190
Sperber, Manès, 2, 3, 7, 8, 10
Spinoza, Benedict de, 84
Staël, Madame de, 113

State, 47, 49, 50, 51, 141, 155, 171, 172,
180, 215
Stirner, Max, 177
Subcomplex characters, 33, 70
Subjectivity: and armoring, 23, 107, 108,
131–32, 145, 188, 205; and auton-
omy, 156; and conduct codes, 36–37;
and conscience, 37; decentered, 23;
and masculinity, 59–60; and mobility,
51, 88; and new objectivity, 88; pre-
bourgeois, 6, 131; and unity, 150
Sublimation, 82, 84, 110
Sudden transformation, 2–8, 132
Suhrkamp, Peter, 15
Superego, 13, 187
Surrealism, 156
Szcesny-Friedmann, Claudia, 47

Tallyrand, Charles Maurice de, 111
Taut, Bruno, 129–30
Technical reproduction, 23
Technology: and acoustic space, 182; and
artificiality, 63; and community, 53;
distinguished from culture, 14; and ex-
pression, 80–81, 87; and heroic real-
ism, 160; and male fantasies, 213; and
perceptual acuity, 148
Theater, 8–10, 15, 51, 62, 65, 67, 70, 78,
79, 80, 111; Brechtian, 15, 51, 87, 131
Theology, 4, 38, 40, 41, 49, 195, 198,
200, 201
Theweleit, Klaus, 47, 213
Tillich, Paul, 58, 102, 141, 186
Tönnies, Ferdinand, 53
Totalitarianism, 216
Toulouse-Lautrec, Henri de, 131
Traffic, 26–31, 55, 63, 73, 75, 155, 211
Tragedy, 49, 54, 57, 103, 170, 173
Transcendence, 41, 49
Trilling, Lionel, 55
Truth, 40, 112
Tucholsky, Kurt, 192
Turek, Ludwig, 198
Typology, 152, 153–56, 158, 159, 187,
214, 234n147, 236n1. *See also*
Classification mania

Uexküll, Jakob von, 65, 71, 170
Uncanny, 6, 91, 93, 102, 145, 159
Unconscious, 33, 59, 67, 103, 182, 209
Unity: and community, 53; and polariza-
tion, 24; and subjectivity, 150
Utilitarianism, 145
Utopia, 22

Velde, Henri van de, 130
Verhaltenheit, 82, 85, 88, 89

Violence, 13, 14, 15, 44, 49, 53, 89, 91, 108, 210
Virility, 60, 73, 139, 143, 145
Visibility, 16, 31, 32, 74, 178; and perceptual acuity, 147–50, 157, 163
Vitalism, 22, 23–24, 30, 56, 58, 59, 167, 220n4
Vossler, Karl, 39, 40

Wagner, Martin, 28
Warmth, 25, 54, 55, 101, 130, 132, 133, 135; and community, 53, 73, 110, 141, 143
Weber, Max, 42–44, 54, 70, 72, 81, 90, 91, 109, 154, 187
Weltsch, Felix, 24
White-collar employees, 23, 132, 148, 187
Wilde, Oscar, 62

Wilhelmian period, 22, 27, 130, 161
Winnacker, Susanne, 140
Wish projection, 13, 15, 107
Wittfogel, Karl, 194
Women, 46–47, 66–67, 82–83; and cool persona, 143; and new objectivity, 73–74, 111, 138, 141–45; and radar type, 193
Working class, 25, 44, 110, 132
World War I, 5, 11, 110, 168
World War II, 98
Wundt, Wilhelm, 76
Wurmser, Léon, 10, 59, 62

Youth movement, 59, 60, 81, 83, 90, 104, 110

Zweig, Arnold, 136, 198, 201–3
Zweig, Stefan, 114

Text:	10/13 Sabon
Display:	Sabon
Composition:	G & S Typesetters, Inc.
Printing and binding:	Edwards Brothers, Inc.